Lewd women and wicked

How do men manage to maintain their power over women even though women are by no means passively compliant? Marianne Hester explains how women's experience of male sexual violence, through rape and sexual abuse, can lead to an understanding of male power over women. She demonstrates that contemporary feminist analysis of heterosexuality and male sexual violence not only holds the key to an understanding of male power over women today, but helps us to understand male power in other historical periods.

Lewd Women and Wicked Witches concentrates on the witch-hunts of early modern England and argues convincingly that they are a historically specific example of male dominance. Relying on the social construction of sexuality in terms of women's inferiority, the witch trials were part of the ongoing attempt by men to maintain their power over women. The book reviews and develops revolutionary feminist thinking to show how witches – almost exclusively women – can be seen as victims of the oppression of a male-dominated society.

Marianne Hester argues that the mechanism of male domination actually remains the same in the twentieth as in the sixteenth and seventeenth centuries. She sees men as the root of women's oppression, and gives us insights into the ways men maintain their power over women by using sexual violence and sexual constructions of women subtly as well as overtly. Stimulating and controversial, her book will appeal to anyone interested in feminist theory or the history of witchcraft, and to students of history, sociology and women's studies.

Marianne Hester is Lecturer in Social Studies and Adult Education at the University of Exeter, where she teaches a range of women's studies and other courses.

Lewd women and wicked witches

A study of the dynamics of male domination

Marianne Hester

London and New York

First published in 1992
by Routledge
11 New Fetter Lane, London EC4P 4EE

Simultaneously published in the USA and Canada
by Routledge
29 West 35th Street, New York, NY 10001

Reprinted in 1993

Typeset in Baskerville by LaserScript, Mitcham, Surrey
Printed and bound in Great Britain by
Mackays of Chatham PLC, Chatham, Kent

British Library Cataloguing in Publication Data
Hester, Marianne 1955–
  Lewd women and wicked witches.
  1. Witches. Persecution. History
  I. Title
  272

Library of Congress Cataloging in Publication Data
Hester, Marianne, 1955–
  Lewd women and wicked witches: a study of the dynamics of male
  domination/Marianne Hester.
  p. cm.
  Includes bibliographical references and index.
  1. Men – Sexual behaviour. 2. Dominance (Psychology)
  3. Sex discrimination against women. 4. Power (Social sciences)
  5. Social control. 6. Witchcraft – England – History. I. Title.
  HQ28.H47   1992
  306.7'081 – dc20   91-15068
                                                                  CIP

ISBN 0–415–07071–6
    0–415–05209–2 (pbk)

For Ruth and Tony Dahlmann,
Lynne Bell, and Elfriede Löchel,
with love

Contents

Acknowledgements

The writing of this book owes much to the advise and support of numerous friends and colleagues. I especially want to thank Al Garthwaite, Margaret Jackson, Sheila Jeffreys, Sandra McNeill, Pat Mahony, Jackie Plaster, Sheila Rowe and Jessica Wood for the many exciting and inspiring debates which we had in the Patriarchy Study Group in the early 1980s, during the initial stages of my research. I am grateful to David Coates, the supervisor for my PhD, and Jalna Hanmer for their insistence that I should develop my PhD thesis into a book. Al Garthwaite and Penny Florence have helped me to present my ideas more clearly, and their knowledge and understanding of contemporary feminist debates and ideas have been invaluable. I have also been lucky to have had the tireless support of Jane Howarth and Jill da Silva, who have typed and re-typed the manuscript; and of Helen Thompson and Stuart MacWilliam, who have helped to track down many elusive references. My Department at the University of Exeter kindly provided a small grant for the final stages of the work. My colleagues over the years have been very supportive, and I am particularly grateful to Judy Worsnop, Anne Goldthorpe and Lorraine Radford who have all been greatly inconvenienced by the writing of this book. And for Lynne Bell, who has had to endure this project more than anyone, much love.

Chapter 1

The introduction
The dynamics of male domination

In this book I set out to do two things. Firstly, to explore the specifically sexual, and dynamic, process whereby men have, and maintain, dominance over women. Secondly, in the light of this, to re-examine the early modern witch-hunts in England. I use what may be called a revolutionary feminist approach.

Men have, and maintain, power over women in many different ways and at many different levels: at work, in the home, through legislation, and so on. But the most crucial aspect of an explanation of women's oppression and male dominance is the analysis of sexuality, because it is within the constructs of male and female sexualities that we may observe the central dynamic of male domination over women. In the context of male supremacy, male and female sexualities are constructed as specifically different and unequal. This has led MacKinnon, for instance, to argue that 'male and female are created through the eroticization of submission and dominance' (1987b: 136). In other words, men's power and women's social inferiority are made 'sexy'. The process of constructing women as erotic or 'sexy' objectifies them, positioning women as subordinate and men as dominant. We can see this process especially clearly within pornography, and it is acted out within heterosexual relations: where male sexuality objectifies the female object of desire, while female sexuality is objectified by the desired male subject. But this process is more generalised than even these examples suggest, it is integral to all male–female relations within male supremacy. Moreover, it is what makes male supremacy unique and especially enduring.

Male domination over women may be appear to be natural, but this is not the case. Men have to actively maintain and perpetuate their power over women. This takes place, as in the maintenance of any social order, by pressure to consent, including force, the threat of force and ideological pressures. But the system of male domination over women is uniquely different from other systems of power because it relies on the eroticisation of inequality between men and women, and enforces control of women by the use, as well as threat, of male sexual violence against women. Feminists have documented how male sexual violence has the effect of controlling women's lives socially, and serves, furthermore, to construct men as more powerful than women.

The result is a system of male supremacy where sexuality and 'personal relations' are extremely crucial areas for acting out and maintaining male dominance, and where these unequal power relations between men and women are institutionalised in many different ways as well as reflected in social relations generally. Revolutionary feminist analysis presents the institution of heterosexuality as a linchpin of male dominance and control over women, because it is in heterosexual relations that men are able to 'do power over' women to the greatest effect (Leeds Revolutionary Feminist Group 1981). In particular, and at the present time, male sexuality is constructed so as to control women socially.

There has been a tendency amongst feminists and others to see the terms 'sex' and 'gender' as separate, sex denoting biologically-based characteristics, with gender denoting the social characteristics of men and women (Oakley 1972; Archer and Lloyd 1982; Chetwynd and Hartnett 1978; Sharpe 1976). But this is too simplistic. In male–female relations it is the social meaning attached to biology which is important, rather than actual biological features, and sex is therefore gendered. In this sense sex and gender become interchangeable, which is how I shall use them here. In addition, the commonly perceived definition of 'the sexual' or 'sexuality' is that this is based on some innate drive or instinct, where heterosexuality especially is presented as the only or main form of sexual behaviour (see Oxford English Dictionary 1975; Segal 1987; Sayers 1982). But this is incorrect. Sexual behaviour is socially constructed, and I use these terms to denote particular social constructs and social relationships.

In the context of male supremacy, men and women experience male-female relations differently, but also generally as mediated via the dominant male view. It is therefore not only vital to examine women's specific experience of male–female relations (that is sexual relations), but also to analyse women's experience in the light of the dominant male constructs. In other words, to analyse and understand male supremacy we need to study men: their behaviour, sexuality, institutions, and so on, because that is where the power lies. For instance, when we examine male violence against women we have to look at men, that is, the perpetrators, if we are to understand comprehensively why men sexually violate women, and what to do to counter this (see Scully 1990).

Revolutionary feminist theory has been criticised (alongside radical feminism) of 'ahistoricism' because of the seeming long-evity of male dominance suggested by this theoretical framework. For example, Lynne Segal in a recent book suggests that 'The revolutionary feminist ascendancy at the close of the seventies. . . [reasserted] an ahistorical image of sexuality existing outside specific social contexts and relationships (Segal 1987: 101). By applying revolutionary feminist theory to material from the six-teenth and seventeenth centuries I will show that this criticism is not justified, and that the theoretical framework does by no means impose 'ahistorical' constraints. Certain features characteristic of the male-dominated social order do seem to persist over time, but the actual expressions of these features are historically specific and subject to change. What is important is that, in terms of the material examined from both twentieth-century and early modern (sixteenth- and seventeenth-century) England, the persistent features include masculinity and femininity as sexual constructs and the use of sexual violence as a means of social control by men over women, yet the form these take differs between the two periods. Indeed, it is partly because features such as masculinity and femininity are subject to change that male dominance as a social order is so enduring: the ideological constructs and material relations change as circumstances change so as to re-establish the male status quo.

I have chosen to focus on the early modern witch-hunts because of the apparent importance of this phenomenon to male–female relations during the early modern period. The witch-hunts en-tailed the prosecution, imprisonment and execution of thousands of people, almost exclusively women, in England alone. Not only were the vast majority of the accused women, but they tended to be a particular group of women: age, marital status, kin relation to other 'witches', economic status, liaison with the Devil, and sexual 'deviance' all being important factors. Reading accounts of sixteenth- and seventeenth-century England I was struck by the enormity and importance of the witch-hunts as an obviously gendered phenomenon. I was also struck by the lack of interpretation of the witch-hunts in relation to gender, and the way writers have tended to treat these persecutions and many other contemporary social features, such as the changing economy, as entirely separate topics without making any attempts to link these (see Larner 1983; Trevor-Roper 1969). By examining some of the particularly important contextual areas which form the background to the witch-hunts, such as the period prior to the hunts, demographic, economic and ideological features of the actual witch-hunt period, and also the decline of the persecutions, we can see that sixteenth- and seventeenth-century England was a period of great change, as well as deep-rooted gender inequality.

I show that there are important links between the witch-hunts, the changing circumstances, and male–female relations. By reference to the context of the witch-hunts it may be argued that the persecutions served as a means of social control of women at a time of great social change, and when men were actively pursuing the more lucrative and influential positions within the emerging capitalist economy. Indeed the witch-hunts may be seen as an instance of sexual violence against women, relying on sexual constructs of masculinity and especially femininity, and they constituted an important part of the dynamics of male domination in sixteenth- and seventeenth-century England.

The subject matter of this book is closely associated with my own biography and development as a feminist: the problems explored have come about through my involvement with the Women's Liberation Movement, and intimate knowledge of debates among, and activities carried out by, feminists since the early 1970s. Involvement with the Women's Liberation Movement and feminist campaigns has, over a period of time, led to changes in my analysis of women's oppression. During the 1970s I saw myself as a 'socialist feminist'. In short, I thought that women's oppression was primarily in the interest of capitalist social relations, or 'economic' social relations rather than men. The late 1970s may be seen as a 'crisis point' of socialist feminist analysis for many feminists, and I was no exception (see Segal 1987; Rowbotham *et al.* 1980). 'New' feminist concerns were becoming important, in particular, racial divisions between women and male violence. But socialist and Marxist feminist theories, based largely or ultimately on analysis of capitalist production, were unable to come up with adequate answers.

The issue of male violence against women, made increasingly public by feminist campaigns about domestic violence and rape, made the problems seemingly inherent in socialist and Marxist feminist theory more pertinent (see London Rape Crisis Centre 1984; Rhodes and McNeill 1985; National Women's Aid Federation 1976). It was extremely difficult to provide an analysis of male violence against women within this framework without reliance on radical, and especially revolutionary, feminist theory (London Rape Action Group 1985; Hanmer 1978; Katyachild *et al.* 1985). Along with other feminists I found that these difficulties of applying socialist and Marxist feminist analysis were also compounded by the behaviour of men on the Far Left who were claiming to be allies of the Women's Liberation Movement (see Chester 1979; Leonard 1982; Friedman and Sarah 1982: part II). In response to feminist criticism some men were changing their behaviour; but the outcome was often a more devious and hidden means of ensuring their continuing control and power in relation to women (however unconscious), rather than an undermining of male dominance (Leonard 1982; Hester 1984; Mitchell 1971; Rowbotham 1972). Others were directly hostile to the Women's Liberation Movement, seeing feminist concerns as a 'diversion' from the 'real struggle' around economic class conflict (a situation exacerbated by the prospect of increasingly right-wing governments undermining workers' rights, as exemplified by that of Margaret Thatcher) (Segal 1987: 49–55).

I found that an analysis taking production as its starting point was inadequate for explaining these complex gender relations. Instead, a theoretical framework with a different set of priorities, that women's oppression is primarily in the interest of men and expressed by an ideology that sees men as superior to women, seemed more appropriate. Within this framework women are oppressed by men as a group, rather than by the economic system or by society. This type of perspective has, since the beginning of the present Women's Liberation Movement, been the stance of radical feminists generally (Firestone 1979; Millett 1970; Redstockings 1970; Morgan 1970). But while radical feminists in the United States were coming up with answers about male violence, in the late 1970s radical feminists were not very visible within the British Women's Liberation Movement. Revolutionary feminism developed in this apparent vacuum.

Revolutionary feminist ideas were made visible at the 1977 Women's Liberation Movement National Conference. The intention at this stage was not to create any new tendency within the Women's Liberation Movement, but rather to reassert what Jeffreys (1977) calls 'political feminism', that is, the development of a radical theory and strategy to overcome male power. However, a distinct grouping did develop as increasing numbers of women expressed their support for the general call for a 'revolutionary feminism'.

The influence of early radical (largely American) feminist writings can be seen in the revolutionary feminist papers and articles, including the ideas and discussions of Redstockings (1970), New York Radical Lesbians (1970), Shulamith Firestone (1979) and Kate Millett (1970). Also apparent in the early revolutionary feminist work is the influence of Marx and Engels's work on conflictual class relations, and their claim that the first social division was that between the sexes due to the sexual division of human reproduction.[1] Millett's work, in particular, can be seen to outline the framework of theorising women's oppression which the revolutionary feminist approach has adopted and developed further.

Radical and revolutionary feminist approaches overlap, but there are also differences. Both radical and revolutionary feminists take women's experience as the starting point of their analyses. In distinction to some radical feminists, however, revolutionary feminists in addition problematise 'men' (Leeds Revolutionary Feminist Group 1981), while radical feminists tend to emphasise women's experience and research on women, and are concerned, for example, with creating 'women's culture' and even 'women's language' (Daly 1979; Stanley and Wise 1983; Griffin 1984; Rich 1977; Chester 1979; Redstockings 1970; Henderson 1979). I think it is impossible to divorce women's experience from the social context of life in a male-dominated society, with all that may entail, such as exploitation in the home and at work and sexual violence, without ending up with an unrealistic notion of female experience. It is crucial to study 'men', their writing, behaviour, sexuality, and other constructs. Thus while women's experience forms an important basis for feminist analysis and theorising, it is not enough:

theory also needs to take the (male) context of that experience into account.

An important focus for the development of revolutionary feminist theory during the 1980s has been the Patriarchy Study Group (see Coveney *et al.* 1984b). The group met over a number of years to develop theory concerning the nature of male supremacy or 'patriarchy'. We found that there were a number of issues regarding male sexuality and women's oppression which it was especially important to answer; including why are some men apparently 'turned on' sexually by urinating in women's shoes? Or why do 'some men visit prostitutes in order to eat their excreta from teaspoons?' (ibid.: 13). Analysis of these rather horrifying and seemingly perverse activities, amongst many other issues, led us to realise that male sexuality, as it is currently constructed, is about power. We decided that male sexuality often appears to be perverse because it *is* perverse. In other words, it is about constructing men as powerful in relation to women (and about constructing some men as powerful in relation to other men), that is, about inequality rather than equality. We concluded that male sexuality is constructed so as to control women socially, acted out in heterosexual relationships as well as in rape, pornography and other forms of male sexual violence against women.

This book documents the construction of sexuality for the social control of women and the empowering of men both today and in the early modern period, examining male sexual violence and heterosexual relations in order to do so, and I begin by discussing some of the important issues raised by Marxist and socialist feminist analyses of male domination.

Chapter 2

From men partially to men primarily responsible for women's oppression

With the re-emergence of the Women's Liberation Movement in the late 1960s, Marxists were thought by some to be in a unique position to develop an analysis of women's oppression. Already the Marxist analysis of capitalist production incorporated the notion of exploitation and inequality at its centre and it was presumed that it could also be extended to analyse the specific, and oppressed, position of women. Marx had explained by his 'labour theory of value' that the central oppression under capitalism constitutes the exploitation of the working class for profit, and Marxists set out to study the subordinate position of women by linking it to this apparently central economic oppression.

The 'domestic labour debate'[1] was an early outcome of this, and centred on the extent of the contribution by women's domestic labour to the overall value of (male) labour power in the capitalist sphere (Benston 1969; Seccombe 1974; Coulson *et al.* 1975; Gardiner 1975; Harrison 1973; Smith 1978). Other approaches, focusing to a slightly greater extent on male–female relations, included the 'dual labour market thesis' (Barron and Norris 1976) and 'women as a reserve army of labour' (Beechey 1977; Bruegel 1979; Braverman 1974). Both positions argue that women's subordinate role in the domestic sphere places women in a subordinate position within the capitalist sphere, with less pay and security than men, and that this operates to the advantage of capital. An attempt was also made to overcome the economic reductionism of these approaches by theorising patriarchy at the level of ideology, that is, to see patriarchy as part of the reproduction of ideas separate from the capitalist sphere (Mitchell 1975).

By the late 1970s, however, socialist and Marxist feminist theory appeared increasingly inadequate for dealing with crucial questions of the day, questions such as racial divisions between women and male violence and, underlying these, the nature of 'patriarchy' (Kantor 1984). The Marxist work was being criticised by socialist feminists as 'sex blind' because Marxism had great difficulty explaining gender divisions specifically (Hartmann 1979; Barrett 1984). As Michele Barrett explains:

> Marxism, constituted as it is around relations of appropriation and exploitation, is grounded in concepts that do not and could not address directly the gender of the exploiters and those whose labour is appropriated.
>
> (Barrett 1984: 8)

The socialist feminist response to the problems raised by these approaches intended to link feminist analysis, that is analysis 'emphasizing precisely the relations of gender' (Barrett 1984: 8), with Marxist theory. The result has been a variety of 'dual systems' approaches.[2] 'Dual systems' usually connotes the two systems of capitalism and patriarchy, or capitalism and reproduction; and it is the way in which these systems relate, or interrelate, which has been discussed at length.[3] Attempts have been made to 'marry' the somewhat 'unhappy partners' of capitalism and patriarchy so as to develop a theory which takes into account both capitalist and gender relations. This approach is exemplified by the work of Zillah Eisenstein (1979) and Heidi Hartmann (1981); and in different ways also by Christine Delphy (1977, 1980), Cynthia Cockburn (1983) and Sylvia Walby (1986). Another direction has been to extend the work which posits patriarchy as ideology or 'discourse'. This is exemplified by the work of Chris Weedon (1987). In this chapter I will discuss the dual systems approaches of Eisenstein, Hartmann and Walby, and the post-structuralist approach of Weedon to examine the issues and problems that they raise with regard to the maintenance and perpetuation of male domination.

DUAL SYSTEMS

Both Eisenstein and Hartmann argue that it is the socially-constructed relations between men and women, or patriarchal relations, which are specificallly oppressive to women. Yet in their eagerness to 'marry' the systems of capitalism and patriarchy Eisenstein, and Hartmann to a lesser extent, obscure this crucial

oppressive relationship for women. Instead they see capitalist relations as more important than, and also separate from,
male–female relations – hence 'capitalist patriarchy' (Eisenstein)
and 'patriarchal capitalism' (Hartmann). But, if patriarchy existed
before capitalism, and continues in post-capitalist societies, as
Eisenstein and Hartmann both suggest, then patriarchy appears to
be much more persistent than any economic mode of production, also adaptable and probably dynamic. I want to examine how
Eisenstein and Hartmann, in their respective approaches, deal
with this problem.

For Eisenstein 'capitalist patriarchy' is the contemporary interrelationship between patriarchy and capitalism. Patriarchy takes
the form of a male hierarchical ordering of society, which derives
from ideological interpretations of biological differences between
men and women, in particular women's capacity to be mothers. It
provides the sexual hierarchical ordering of society while capitalism in turn feeds off this hierarchy. She suggests that the
relationship between the two systems may not be altogether
smooth, although the unequal gender relations remain in both
because of the sexual division of labour which cuts across them.

Eisenstein's analysis incorporates the notion of historical
change, and also how male dominance may be maintained over
time. She describes how, as patriarchal control in the privatised
family diminishes (as has happened historically), the same sexual
hierarchy is in turn transferred to capitalist relations such that
male dominance is maintained:

> As women increasingly enter the labour force, some of the
> control of patriarchal familial relations seems to be under-
> mined. This is compensated for such that . . . the ghettoisation
> of women within the labour force at the same time maintains a
> system of hierarchical control of women both sexually and
> economically, which leaves the sexual hierarchy of the society
> intact.
>
> (Eisenstein 1979: 28)

None the less, she argues, women's oppression may be overcome.
The stage where this will take place is the productive sphere
because the point for transformation of both capitalism and
patriarchy is the sexual hierarchy of society (as sexual division of
labour). For Eisenstein the increasing entry of women into paid
employment will thus play a major role in enabling women's

oppression to be overcome, and in this sense her approach is similar to some of the earlier Marxist feminist work.

Yet Eisenstein's analysis is also ambiguous. On the one hand she is suggesting that capitalism and patriarchy are intertwined into one system – capitalist patriarchy – while she is also suggesting that battle has to be done against both capitalism and patriarchy, that is, as two separate systems. These ambiguities are similarly reflected in her later work (1984).

Another, related, problem with the concept of 'capitalist patriarchy' is the mutuality of capitalism and patriarchy which this suggests. As Eisenstein points out: 'the mutual dependence of patriarchy and capitalism not only assumes the malleability of patriarchy to the needs of capital but assumes the malleability of capital to the needs of patriarchy' (Eisenstein 1979: 27). However, this does not take into account conflicts between men, and between men and women which are exhibited within the workplace, a criticism which may also be levelled at dual labour market theory and Marxist theory more generally. Eisenstein's analysis cannot deal with the often complex interplay between capitalist and gender relations which Cockburn (1983), for instance, has documented. Cockburn found, in her research on technological changes in the printing industry, that while male employers and male workers alike adhere to the notion of male superiority and female inferiority, this may at the same time become part of the antagonism between them. Employers have wanted to use female labour because it is cheap, while male workers have organised fierce campaigns to keep women out of printing so as not to undermine their position as men. This conflict was apparent, for example, in the Scottish printing industry in the late nineteenth century. The print workers could, of course, have organised together with the women, to make their mutual position as workers stronger. But this did not happen because of the possible threat to the male print workers' view of themselves which such solidarity entailed. 'For many of the men it was unthinkable that women should be allowed to join the all male trade society from which they drew so much of their self-respect as artisans and as men' (Cockburn 1983: 153–4). Thus the male workers in the print industry did not act in the way indicated by Eisenstein's work, where the gender-related issues would be expected to accomodate to the conflict between labour and capital rather than cutting across this.

By attempting to deal with the effect of unequal male–female relations on the organisation of the capitalist economy, Eisenstein's concept of 'capitalist patriarchy' goes much further than some of the earlier Marxist feminist analyses. Ultimately, however, she is rather ambiguous as to the nature of 'patriarchy' and the exact relationship between this concept and capitalism. Heidi Hartmann's somewhat similar work on 'patriarchal capitalism' overcomes some of these problems because she produces a more detailed account of patriarchy and patriarchal relations.

Both Eisenstein and Hartmann see patriarchy as hierarchical, but Hartmann is also more explicit about the social relations involved in the maintenance of patriarchy. She sees patriarchy as: 'a set of social relations between men, which have a material base, and which, though hierarchical, establish or create interdependence and solidarity among men that enable them to dominate women' (Hartmann 1979: 11).

By emphasising social relations between men, especially hierarchical relations between them, Hartmann goes some way towards being able to deal with the example from Cockburn, of conflict between different men, outlined above. It may be possible to extend this idea to cover racial divisions between men as well, although Hartmann does not attempt to do so. Her definition does, however, incorporate men generally as the dominant group.

In an early aspect of her work (1981) she also begins to tackle the way in which social relations between men and women operate, showing how men use a number of strategies to maintain their power over women in the labour market, the most important of which is organised male activity through trade unions. As others have shown, trade unions have been instrumental in maintaining job segregation by sex, gendered wage differentials and in excluding women entirely from certain areas of employment (Beechey 1986: 119). This aspect of Hartmann's work is a very important step beyond Eisenstein's analysis, and leads Hartmann in an unambiguous way to see that men benefit directly and materially from women through patriarchal relations.

Where Eisenstein talks about the articulation between capitalism and patriarchy as the sexual division of labour, Hartmann instead identifies the articulation point as the 'family wage'. This is a more sophisticated analysis than that provided by Eisenstein because it allows for a more conflictual and therefore dynamic conceptualisation of male dominance and its perpetuation.

Hartmann argues that with the onset of capitalism a conflict of interests developed between capitalism and patriarchy over women's labour. This conflict was resolved by the institution of the family wage, which ensured that women were paid a lower wage than men. Men became the 'breadwinners', thus perpetuating men's material advantage over women by making women dependent on men and encouraging them to choose wifery as a career. This situation still persists today, although patriarchal relations are not static and in recent years there has been an erosion of the family wage alongside women's increased entry into the labour market. The maintenance of patriarchy is consequently shifting away from the family wage, and instead 'the wage differential . . . will become increasingly necessary in perpetuating patriarchy' (ibid.: 18).

However, by focusing on the family wage and wage differentials between men and women, Hartmann is limiting the usefulness of her concept of patriarchy. For a start, the family wage, however important ideologically, has never been a generalised reality and many women (especially working-class women) have had to work in paid employment as a result (Barrett and McIntosh 1980). I use the words 'generalised reality' because some men, those in the professions, may have a 'family wage' (see ibid.). Hartmann claims that 'patriarchy' is fundamental to the oppression of women, and yet in her attempt to link capitalism and patriarchy – into 'patriarchal capitalism' – she ends up with an economic solution, with a focus on the family wage and wage differentials. This is particularly problematic for Hartmann's analysis because she recognises that women's oppression will not be transcended by changes in the mode of production alone.

Iris Young (1981) also argues that Hartmann's focus on two separate systems of patriarchal and capitalist relations is problematic. She points out that Hartmann's own suggestion, that patriarchal relations are to be found not only in the family but also in the capitalist workplace and other institutions, leads away from her conception of two systems to one: 'It seems reasonable. . . to admit that if patriarchy and capitalism are manifest in identical social and economic structures they belong to one system, not two' (Young 1981: 49). Young suggests that the one conceptual system, of capitalist patriarchy, should have the oppression of women as a core attribute.

Eisenstein and Hartmann, by their discussion of the sexual division of labour, family wage and wage differentials, do begin to look at ways in which patriarchy manages to persist and to incorporate a notion of historical change in their analyses. But the 'marriage of Marxism and feminism', should perhaps not be the most important issue here. Of greater importance are the questions concerning 'what are the *mechanisms* of the perpetuation of patriarchy?', and 'how may they lead to the different forms that patriarchy may exhibit in different historical contexts?'. It is a pity that Hartmann, who does begin to deal with these questions in her examination of male–female conflict, does not make them central to her analysis. Perhaps the problem lies, as Young suggests, with Hartmann using a 'dual systems' rather than a 'single systems' approach.

Other feminists, such as Cynthia Cockburn (1983) and Sylvia Walby (1986, 1990), also look at possible links between capitalism and patriarchy, but in addition take a more sophisticated and dynamic approach. I will now go on to examine their approaches.

MALE–FEMALE CONFLICT

Cynthia Cockburn in *Brothers* (1983) provides a fascinating account of the restructuring of compositing within the printing industry, an almost exclusively male area of work. She looks at the attempt by employers to de-skill compositors through the introduction of technology, and how, at the same time, the compositors attempt to maintain their power over women.

She is aware of patriarchal contradictions and conflicts, although ends up with a primarily economic class analysis which does not take male–female relations entirely into account. Even so, *Brothers* provides a very useful examination of the effect of male–female relations on the relations between men, which takes both economic class solidarity and economic class struggle into consideration. And Cockburn shows some important ways in which male workers maintain their general dominance over women. The book also makes the important point that the form of male domination is historically (and presumably culturally) specific, and that 'patriarchy' is thus only one such form:

> The authority of older men over younger; the economic and social dominance in the family of the male head of household; inheritance by primogeniture; individual (and often inherited) male power exercised through the ownership of the business

firm; the 'family' values of a masculine Christian church; fra-
ternal formalities within all-male societies – whether these are
the gentlemen's clubs or the craftmen's societies.

(Cockburn 1983: 197)

Cockburn argues that restructuring of the printing industry is
carried out in the context of the 'male dominated sex/gender
system' (ibid.: 7)[4] – as patriarchy. Patriarchy is also the social order
preferred by many of the compositors whom Cockburn inter-
viewed.

But, on the basis of changes which the compositors lament are
taking place around them, Cockburn argues that the sex/gender
system is now changing. Some aspects of patriarchy are becoming
less important, for example, the family with its male head is
becoming less frequent as women gain independent earnings or
other means of income, and as women bring up children on their
own. Sexual violence is also on the increase.[5] As a result she
speculates that (rather than patriarchy giving way to a sex-equal
society) the sex/gender system is changing to another format such
as andrarchy. By this she probably means the dominance of men
generally over women rather than dominance by fathers, although
the term is not explained.

In *Brothers* Cockburn attempts to link the 'class system' and the
'sex/gender system', while at the same time presenting a detailed
exploration of the resultant effect on male–female (and male–
male) relations. This allows her to examine some of the ways men
maintain power over women. Class relations are important, she
argues, for understanding the relations between print workers and
their bosses. But throughout these relations, as well as more generally, the sex/gender system cannot be ignored, although she is
ignoring the existence of race as a possible third system. Interestingly, her material also shows how the sex/gender system
shapes class relations, even if she herself is not willing to place such
emphasis on the linking of the systems. Indeed Cockburn does not
always use her own evidence to the fullest extent, a point I will
come back to later.

In her study of compositing, which can be deemed a 'male' job,
Cockburn found that the men's view of themselves and their
situation in employment is directly influenced by sex/gender
considerations. For example, at the heart of the compositors' view
of themselves as workers is the ideology of the family wage; and this

has been the case historically. The concept of the family wage has for a long time been used by print workers as part of their bargaining with employers for higher wages, and to keep women out of compositing. In the late nineteenth century, for instance, 'The question of the male breadwinner and the family wage was at the forefront of the Edinburgh Struggle' (ibid.: 181).[6] The ideology of the family wage expresses the compositors' wish to be seen as breadwinners of families where the wife should preferably be a housewife. It is this desire to live out a strict sexual division of labour which cannot, Cockburn argues, be explained by class theory, but has to take the sex/gender system into account. It is in the light of the benefits men obtain from having a wife to service them that their militancy as workers should be assessed.

Cockburn shows that in order to make the printing industry more profitable new technology started to be introduced in Britain in the 1960s. The new ways of compositing require much less brute strength than was the case with the former hot metal process, and also less mechanical knowledge and skills associated with the use of machinery. The men whose jobs have changed as a result of the new technology have learnt new skills, but still see the changes as both deskilling and as making the jobs more like 'women's work'. Crucial to the compositors' view of themselves as workers is their sense of masculinity. The hot metal process was undeniably male. But 'The comps undervalue the typing and paperhandling skills they are now being taught because they see them as female' (ibid.: 117). As a result the men are caught in a contradiction: 'they must either acknowledge themselves totally deskilled, or acknowledge that many women are as skilled as men. The dilemma accounts for much of the bitterness they feel' (Cockburn 1983: 117).

Cockburn argues that masculinity is useful to capital because it helps to fill the mass of labouring jobs. However, this may also be seen to reduce the importance of women within Cockburn's analysis, where it is not necessarily women whom men fear, but other men. In this way Cockburn tends to end up with a somewhat similar analysis to that of Hartmann. This is, of course, a very different interpretation from that of radical feminists such as Mary Daly, who argue that it is specifically women who pose a threat to men (Daly 1979). There is no doubt that the social relations between men which both Cockburn and Hartmann outline are very important considerations. But by emphasising such relations, they are making economic class relations more important than male–female relations, whereas Cockburn's evidence often points to the contrary. As she shows, maintaining masculine status is essential to the compositors in their struggle with employers, and in this instance masculine status is mainly achieved by excluding women from that area of printing.[7]

Besides the union activities already mentioned, Cockburn shows that there are other processes which are effectively used to keep women out. By recourse to biology the compositors construct a variety of arguments to explain that women cannot possibly do compositing because they are physically, intellectually and emotionally inept. In addition the men's notion of masculinity, and hence male solidarity (against the employer as well as women), is enhanced by what other feminists have called 'sexual harassment'; in other words by sexualising and objectifying women. As Cockburn explains:

> Many women who have had reason to work with compositors will confirm my experience that they make a big show of apologising for 'bad language', explaining that in the normal way, as men with men, they are accustomed to 'use language' that would offend a women's ears. By this they don't mean the odd 'damn' or 'bloody'. The social currency of the composing room is women and woman-objectifying talk, from sexual expletives and innuendo through to narrations of exploits and fantasies. The wall is graced with four colour litho 'tits and bums'. Even the computer is used to produce life-size print-outs of naked women.
>
> (Cockburn 1983: 134)

The term sexual harassment may be used to show that such behaviour is part of men 'doing power over women', and acts to exclude women from certain areas of employment. Cockburn, however, does not use the term or concept of sexual harassment and therefore largely misses the significance of this patriarchal or male supremacist process, which other studies have shown to exist, although she does see this behaviour by the compositors as a part of their oppressive relation to women, as well as to do with their masculine solidarity: 'It says something about their relationship with women. . . . But it perhaps shows as much about their relationship with each other' (Cockburn 1983: 134; see also Wise and Stanley 1987; MacKinnon 1979; Russell 1984; Hearn and Parkin 1987).

I think that Cockburn's work is important in the way she shows that 'sex/gender', or gender relations, *cut across* capitalist relations, and are a part of the struggle between labour and capital. This allows her to relate economic change to conflict between men and women, and to show that men actively maintain their power over women. Her work also begins to identify the mechanisms men use to maintain power, all of which, I suggest, serve to *belittle* women: the use of objectifying and demeaning representations of women and woman-objectifying talk – both of which may be considered part of 'sexual harassment' – as well as the presentation of men as breadwinners.

MULTIPLE SYSTEMS AND MULTIPLE STRUCTURES

Sylvia Walby (1986, 1990) sets out more explicitly than Cockburn to overcome some of the problems inherent in the particular (interrelated) dual systems approaches of Eisenstein and Hartmann. In what is an exciting and sophisticated discussion of male domination, or 'patriarchy', she adopts an approach where patriarchy may change in form depending on both time and space. This approach may be termed 'autonomous systems' because gender, class and race are separated out. Like Hartmann she separates out the different systems of gender, class, as well as race, because in this way they can all be taken fully into account. These three systems are deemed to exist at all levels of the social formation, with patriarchy being especially crucial to an understanding of gender inequality. Unlike Iris Young (1981), Walby thus argues that separation of the systems is possible, and indeed necessary, because they are distinct – patriarchy is a system in which men exploit women, while capitalism is a system in which capital expropriates wage labourers, and racism cannot be derived from either of these systems. In her earlier work, *Patriarchy at Work* (1986), Walby focuses on the link between the capitalist and patriarchal systems, while in her more recent work, *Theorising Patriarchy* (1990), she provides a detailed account of the patriarchal system.

Walby's view of patriarchy is complex, suggesting that it consists of a set of six main social structures, all relatively autonomous yet interrelated and differing in their relative importance at any time. The six structures are: 'paid work, housework, sexuality, culture, violence and the state' (Walby 1990: 16).[8]

In brief, Walby bases her *patriarchal mode of production*, or house-work, on Delphy's idea that it is the relations of production the work is performed under rather than the tasks carried out that are important. *Patriarchal relations in paid work* are crucially defined by the 'closure of access by men against women' (ibid.: 223), thereby also echoing Cockburn's analysis. She sees the *state* as reflecting the often contradictory systems of patriarchy, capitalism and racism, and argues that the state has in recent times facilitated the change in the form of patriarchal control from a private to a more public control of women. State policies confining women to the private marital sphere, such as limitations on divorce, have been reduced and instead it has become easier for women to enter the public sphere, although without any significant change in women's general position. For her understanding of *sexuality* Walby draws mainly from radical feminist work, seeing the institution of heterosexuality as a means of social control of women by men (Rich 1980), but also arguing that changes in heterosexuality have had positive outcomes for women, for instance around sexual liberalisation and birth control. She draws similarly from radical feminist work in her outline of *male violence* as a social structure, suggesting that this is only one form of men's control over women rather than the basis of other forms of control (as some radical feminists would argue (Brownmiller 1976)). Where *patriarchal culture* is concerned, Walby uses a radical feminist version of discourse theory, but tempered by consideration of interconnections with the other patriarchal structures. This leads her to see the construction of femininity and masculity as situated everywhere, and not merely in childhood or within sexuality. She argues convincingly that masculinity and femininity have changed over time, with masculinity constructed as paramount throughout.

There is no doubt that Walby's analysis of patriarchy, and her emphasis on patriarchy, capitalism and racism as separate systems provides a much more complex and sophisticated understanding of women's oppression and male dominance than any of the earlier dual systems approaches. Dividing patriarchy into a plur-ality of structures, and separating the various oppressive systems, allows for an examination of the innumerate examples of men's power over women and the conflict over that power, while moving far beyond the largely economic basis of Hartmann and Eisenstein's work. Walby's analysis shows clearly that patriarchy is a dynamic and not an ahistorical concept, as earlier dual systems theorists, and Marxist and socialist feminists in particular, have suggested (Eisenstein 1979; Hartmann 1979; Rowbotham 1982). In addition her use of a 'feminist discourse' approach is very helpful to emphasise the importance of the construction of unequal concepts of masculinity and femininity throughout patriarchal structures and institutions. But by seeing patriarchy, capitalism and racism as separate systems, Walby is also in danger of not considering all aspects of social relations as gendered, as they surely are: 'in the interest of maintaining system boundaries between patriarchy, capitalism and racism, she seems to argue that certain relations are "gender relations", while others are something else' (Acker 1989: 238).[9]

And more important, in the attempt to distinguish her own position from that of radical feminists, and Catharine MacKinnon in particular, Walby also tends to negate the importance of sexuality within gender relations. She underestimates the part the process of sexualising (or eroticising) plays within the construction and positioning of men as more important and powerful than women. She similarly underestimates the impact of male violence on the construction of men as dominant. Separating patriarchy into a plurality of structures, especially the separation of 'culture', 'sexuality' and 'male violence', serves to further obscure these general and central processes.

None the less, compared with the feminist approaches examined earlier in this chapter, Walby's analysis of 'patriarchy' goes a great deal further and shows in some detail the effect of male–female relations on capitalist relations, indicating the centrality of gender to any study of capitalism. She uses an analysis which presents men as primarily responsible for women's oppression, and takes into account that men may at times act in contradiction to one another as workers and as capitalists. Ultimately, patriarchy prevails whether male capitalists or male workers win, leaving women subordinate to and dependent on men.

Taking up the issue of historical change, Walby suggests that the household as a site of production relations is now declining as women have moved increasingly into paid work. Echoing Hartmann's analysis, it is the patriarchal relations within waged labour which are in turn increasing in significance. Walby identifies this trend as part of a general move from a private patriarchy to a more public patriarchy where women's services are appropriated collectively rather than individually. It is a shift which began with the political and social successes of 'first wave' feminism. In response to the inroads made by women into paid work, there has also been a change in the sexual control by individual husbands or fathers to a more diffuse public control of women involving, for instance, an increase in pornography. Walby concludes that the *degree* of patriarchy has changed – indeed it has been (slightly) reduced – but at the same time the *form* of patriarchy has also changed (Walby 1990: 195). One ends up with a picture where what patriarchy loses on the swings it largely regains on the roundabouts.

This analysis is very appealing, especially because it can deal with changes in women's position at different levels of society over time. But the use of separate patriarchal 'structures' as an analytical tool is also cumbersome. It allows Walby to see the process of male domination as one of conflict between men and women, but does not allow her to look more closely at this process, whereby men have managed to maintain power over women for so long.

In her earlier work (1986)[10] Walby examines both patriarchy and capitalism from the beginning of the nineteenth century to the present day. Like Cockburn she makes the important point that contemporary gender relations are the outcome of tensions between patriarchal and capitalist social relations, and vary historically. She gives the example of the nineteenth-century Factory Acts, arguing that organisation around the Acts was part of a patriarchal strategy. The Factory Acts, limiting the length of the working day, have been seen by some (for example, Marx) as a positive and victorious step for the working class. However, Walby argues instead that the legislation was actually regressive for women, if positive for men, and therefore the Acts can be 'more appropriately described as patriarchal than as reformist' (1986: 101).[11]

In general, Walby argues, women tend to be excluded from paid employment, or confined to jobs which are graded lower than those of men. Gender relations change over time in such a way that previous patterns are incorporated and built upon, resulting in a sexual division of labour which is an 'accumulation of these rounds of restructuring gender relations' (ibid.: 243). Walby's evidence clearly shows that changes take place in patriarchal relations; and how struggles over female employment lead to such changes at specific times, that is, 'at moments when there are changes in production' (ibid.: 88). As she explains:

> These changes in production may be due to technological innovations, changes in the product market, or changes in the level of activity in the economy as a whole. That is, changes in the organisation of capital often precipitate gender struggles over employment in particular occupations, since they both destabilise the old balance of gender forces and create and destroy particular forms of employment.
>
> (Walby 1986: 88)

When new terrains open up and patriarchal power is potentially threatened men resist any undermining of their power. For instance, patriarchal power may be decreased in one area, such as the family, but be largely compensated for by changes in another area such as the state.

It is in particular the economic processes affecting women's access to paid employment which Walby sees as key to the understanding of the general changes which have taken place in the patriarchal structure over the past two centuries. However, her focus on economic processes leads her to underestimate the impact of sexuality and violence against women within both household production and paid employment, and she leaves it out of her examination of the case study material on the textile industry, engineering, and clerical work (Walby 1986).[12] She argues that sexuality and male violence do not structure male–female relations within these areas, and tends to see male violence as merely an outcome of those relations.[13] By this approach she ends up trivialising women's extensive experience of violence, or the threat of violence, whether at home, at work, or anywhere else.

More crucially, she fails to understand the importance which male violence, as an example of sexualised or eroticised gender relations, plays in the process whereby women are segregated within paid employment. She does not consider how eroticising women objectifies and constructs them as inferior, justifying their lower wages, and also stopping women from going for or obtaining promotion. In this respect Cockburn's material is more illuminating, if lacking in analysis. Separating out the different patriarchal structures of 'sexuality', 'male violence' and 'culture', as Walby does in her later work, further hinders her ability to understand the importance of these features in the process of male domination across all the different structures.

While Walby considers the patriarchal relations in paid work as the most important patriarchal structure, she sees the patriarchal mode of production, or domestic work carried out by wives for husbands, as the second most important structure. Like the work of Eisenstein and Hartmann, Walby's approach thus relegates 'the domestic' to secondary importance. She argues that it is the lesser pay which women receive in employment, compared to men, which ensures that women remain housewives. This view is in distinction to other feminists who emphasise that pressures such as domestic violence also play a crucial part (Hanmer 1978).

Paid work is the most important patriarchal structure, and Walby suggests that the capitalist mode of production is primary. It is this primary mode of production which, for Walby, provides the 'motor' for change. This leads her, however, to conceptualise the patriarchal relations in the domestic sphere as static rather than dynamic:

> I do not wish to suggest that the patriarchal mode of production has any autonomous laws of development. On the contrary, I would suggest that the other mode of production with which the patriarchal mode is in articulation is particularly important in governing the nature of change.
>
> (Walby 1986: 55)

Yet Walby's evidence clearly shows that patriarchy and hence the patriarchal relations involved are dynamic, and it therefore does not make sense to see the relations specific to the domestic sphere as not dynamic. She argues that the main aspect of the patriarchal mode of production is 'the extraction of surplus', but is wrong to entirely dissociate 'laws of motion' or development (1986: 55) on the one hand from 'extraction of surplus' on the other. Both are expressions of conflictual relations. The implication is that husbands benefit by extraction of surplus from entirely compliant wives, but other studies, such as those of Homer *et al.* (1984) and Jan Pahl (1985), show that this 'extraction of surplus', or the material benefits gained by husbands from their wives' domestic labour, is a conflictual process negotiated between spouses which may at times involve violence against the women concerned. It must be stressed therefore, by contrast to Walby's approach, that patriarchal relations generally, domestic or otherwise, may be seen as conflictual relations with laws of motion geared to the perpetuation of male dominance; and we must question whether the capitalist mode of production is paramount in the way she describes.

Walby recognises that the oppressive domestic or familial relations are based on a heterosexual power relationship and argues that the patriarchal mode of production could not exist without the institutionalisation of heterosexuality. For instance, echoing some radical and revolutionary feminist writings, she draws the conclusion that: 'The experience of universal, or even widespread, institutionalized homosexuality and lesbianism would preclude the domestic relationship between the man and woman from being at the centre of the patriarchal mode of production' (Walby 1986: 66). But in her earlier work Walby restricts the importance of heterosexual power relations to the domestic sphere, without examining how these same sexual relations are to be found in the other areas of the social formation, especially paid employment, which she mentions. In her later work she does look more closely at institutional heterosexuality, arguing that 'there is an attempt to reintegrate women into patriarchal relations via sexuality, as a response to reducing patriarchal controls elsewhere' (1990: 145). But despite discussing the issue of 'sexuality' under other headings, such as the state, it is difficult to see in what way she thinks this impacts on the various patriarchal structures. For instance, she merely lists issues related to sexuality which have been taken up by the state – abortion, contraception and homosexuality – without providing any obvious analysis of state intervention.

I have wanted to stress Walby's work because it takes us much further in understanding how men maintain power over time. How, in periods of change, men shift the terrain where power is acted out so that, overall, male power over women is maintained. The idea of 'autonomous systems' of patriarchy and capitalism, with separate patriarchal structures, allows such detailed analysis to be carried out, and is in this way a useful tool; although this approach also appears to stop her from developing a thoroughly dynamic and integrated analysis where male–female conflictual power relations can be identified at all levels of society and not primarily with regard to the economic. In particular, Walby underestimates the crucial importance of sexuality and, related to this, male violence against women, to the male–female patriarchal relations which she in other respects so usefully explains. Another issue which Walby begins to discuss, but does not develop, is that of race.

In *Theorising Patriarchy* Walby states that there are three systems: patriarchy, capitalism and race. But she incorporates only a cursory look at what she calls 'ethnic relations' because she deems the relations of patriarchy and capitalism more important to an understanding of contemporary gender inequality. Her stance has been echoed by many other writers, including black feminists such as Bell Hooks (1982), who at the same time criticise most white feminist work because it does not incorporate the specific, and different, experiences of black women (Hooks 1982, 1989; Feminist Review 1984). The interrelationship of race and gender, let alone race, gender and economic class relations is complex. Depending on the particular socio-historical context, and the interests involved, black men and white men make various alliances, similarly black and white women. Black men and women, and especially white men and women, also make separate alliances. What I want to look at here, is how gender may cut across race in the way Walby (and Cockburn) shows it cuts across capitalist relations. There appear to be important similarities in the ways male–female relations affect and shape both economic class relations and racism, through conflict and the attempt by men generally to maintain power over women.

Bell Hooks, discussing the position of black women within the American women's suffrage movement, and their role within the Black Liberation Movement of the 1960s, shows the complex role of patriarchal relations within both of these movements. In 1893 'For the first time ever in American history, black women like Mary Church Terrell, Sojourner Truth, Anna Cooper, Amanda Berry Smith and others broke through the long years of silence and began to articulate their experiences'. They talked about their particular experiences as women, emphasising 'the "female" aspect of their being which caused their lot to be different from that of the black male'. Their separate 'femaleness' became especially obvious during the campaign for general suffrage when the white men supported the vote for black men but did not similarly want to enfranchise women (Hooks 1982: 3).

Alliances between black and white men against both black and white women did, however, change depending on the situation. The white women initially felt that joining with black groups would be more likely to lead to women's suffrage. But, as Hooks continues:

> when it seemed black men might get the vote while [white women] remained disenfranchised, political solidarity with black people was forgotten and they urged white men to allow racial solidarity to overshadow their plans to support black male suffrage.

(Hooks 1982: 3)

She thus shows how both white men and white women were racist towards black men and women, while the men were also sexist at the same time.[14] As a result the black women were placed in an especially difficult situation with both racism from the whites and sexism from the black men. The outcome was that the more radical black women, such as Sojourner Truth, demanded the vote for both black men and all women (black and white). Patriarchy ended up being more prominent than race as black men, but no women, obtained the vote alongside white men. Hooks shows, moreover, that the Black Liberation Movement of the 1960s, which set out to procure the liberation of all black people, men and women, actually ended up as a movement 'with its primary goal the establishment of black male patriarchy' (ibid.: 5).

Racism makes the experiences of black and white women different. It makes the experiences of black and white men different. But men, both black and white, act to ensure that male power over women is maintained.

DISCOURSES AND MEANINGS

I will now move on to quite a different set of feminist theories, which examine 'patriarchy' at the level of ideas or discourse. Juliet Mitchell's book *Psychoanalysis and Feminism* (1975) is one of the earlier feminist works to take this general approach. Mitchell was trying to overcome the problem of previous Marxist theorising which tended to reduce women's oppression to the primacy of economic class contradictions between capital and labour. But Mitchell's structuralist theory, based on the work of Althusser and Freud, has been criticised as deterministic, that is, she neglects women's ability to make choices and take action.[15]

The more recent development of feminist post-structuralism is an attempt to overcome the general economic determinism of Marxist approaches such as Mitchell's, and also to overcome what is seen as the essentialism of some radical feminist approaches (Coward 1983: 6). Feminist post-structuralists argue that sets of ideas about society – or more precisely discourses[16] – should not be theorised as a reflection of the economic, or social reality generally, but as the construction of that social reality.[17] People, whether men or women, are therefore subjects rather than objects of that reality. It is language which makes this possible, since this is a prerequisite to discourse. As Weedon explains, the founding insight of post-structuralist theory is 'that language, far from reflecting an already given social reality, constitutes social reality for us' (1987: 22).

In general the post-structuralist approach is seen by writers such as Weedon (1987) to be of general importance for developing both theory and strategy to deal with the phenomenon of women's oppression, because it is an attempt to theorise an area that has for a long time been central to feminism: the role and interpretation of 'meanings'. Both contemporary and earlier feminists have seen the social construction of women, for example as feminine, as a crucial element in the oppression of women. In different ways, 'feminist' writers such as Mary Astell (seventeenth to eighteenth century), Mary Wollstonecraft (eighteenth century) and Simone de Beauvoir (twentieth century) all talk about the importance of the social construction of the feminine and masculine to women's subordination. In other words, women's oppression is a social phenomenon relying on the construction of particular meanings which suggest women's supposed inferiority in comparison to men. Understanding the construction process, and examining the outcome, is an important part of many feminist writings. For example, Simone de Beauviour (1953) talks about the construction of women as 'other' in relation to men, who then become the subject. Examining 'meanings' has also led some writers to suggest that women's lives and experience are profoundly different to those of men (Daly 1979; Spender 1980; Smith 1987). As a result, some feminists, such as Daly, argue for the creation of an entirely women-oriented language and culture. But while also wanting to examine 'meanings', feminist post-structuralists argue for a very different approach to that of Daly and many other radical feminists.

The post-structuralist notions of competing and historically specific discourses make a useful general contribution to the understanding of individuals' construction, actions and contradictions.

But the extreme historical specificity, combined with the many possible outcomes of both deconstruction and change, also makes the development of a feminist strategy very difficult. Indeed, the outcome may be distinctly *anti*-feminist. Not only is each moment in time seen as unique, but comparison across time is difficult. As a result, the impression obtained from reading the work of post-structuralists is that of vagueness and lack of an agenda or prioritisation for feminist action. Furthermore, post-structuralism is very abstract and idealist. Although Weedon (1987), for instance, suggests otherwise, it is difficult to develop an analysis and theory of women's oppression without also taking greater account of the material interests of both men and women, as Walby's work does, for example.

Post-structuralist, or post-Althusserian, discourse theory is exemplified by the debates in the (now defunct) feminist journal *m/f*, by the work of Rosalind Coward (1983), Chris Weedon (1987) and in particular that of French feminists (see Marks and de Courtivron 1981, Duchen 1986). Here the focus will be the work of Weedon as someone who specifically sets out to link 'feminist practice and post-structuralist theory', although the post-structuralist theory will also be looked at more generally in order to do so.

Post-structuralism has largely developed within the study of linguistics, deriving in particular from semiology – the 'investigation of symbolic systems such as languages' (Cameron 1985: 17) – as well as literary criticism, psychoanalysis and anthropology.[18] The approach has, like Mitchell's work, developed from Freudian psychoanalysis. But where Mitchell attempts to resurrect an apparently biologically-based Freudian approach,[19] post-structuralism refers to the specifically social interpretation of Freud by the French psychoanalyst Jacques Lacan (see Nye 1988).

For Lacan the creation of masculinity and femininity is through a structuring and destructuring of identity where symbolic meanings are extremely important. This can be seen in his particular interpretation of the Oedipal-related castration complex. As Andrea Nye outlines:

> Here, in his account of the castration complex, Lacan showed how far he had come from biology. The castration complex for girls or for boys is not based on any physical organ or any anatomical fact: instead, it derives from a myth – that is to say from a meaning-bearing symbolic construction.
>
> (Nye 1988: 139)

According to Lacan this state of affairs is irredeemably located in language, and as a result women are destined to be inferior even before they are born. For some feminists Lacan was therefore describing things as they really perceived them to be, and the result, especially for French feminists, was to question the symbolic construction of society. Women's struggle was situated 'in a new dimension that transcended particular political or economic systems' (ibid : 141). This basic conception was in particular developed into an analysis of language.

It is argued, that at any moment social reality may be constructed in any number of ways, rather than being tied specifically to the economy, other institutions or structures. Thus, rather than taking a traditional Marxist approach, where the (economic) structure tends to constrain the development of knowledge, Weedon suggests that the post-structuralist theory allows for infinite variation:

> For example, the meanings of femininity and masculinity vary from culture to culture and language to language. They even vary between discourses within a particular language, between different feminist discourses, for instance, and are subject to historical change, from Victorian values to the suffrage movement, for example.
>
> (Weedon 1987: 22)

Chris Weedon's recent work, *Feminist Practice and Poststructuralist Theory* (1987), is an interesting attempt at developing a specifically feminist post-structuralism. Her approach (while relying on the general approach already outlined) is drawn from a number of sources, of which Foucault is the most important. This is because his work, such as *The History of Sexuality* (1979), takes into account 'competing discourses', historical specificity and power. All these are crucial to a specifically feminist post-structuralism – even though Foucault did not actually address the question of *gender* and power (see Walby 1990: 88).

> It is in the work of Michel Foucault that the poststructuralist principles of the plurality and constant deferral of meaning and the precarious, discursive structure of subjectivity have been integrated into a theory of language and social power which pays detailed attention to the institutional effects of discourse and its role in the constitution and government of individual subjects.
>
> (Weedon 1987: 107)

According to Foucault 'power is a relation' so that discourses construct differing degrees of power, and power places individual subjects in different relations within or across discourses. This gives rise to contradictions and conflict between discourses and individuals' positions within them, and may in turn lead to reaction against discourses that are perceived as oppressive and will lead to the construction of alternative discourses. In this sense the development of feminist discourses may be seen as the creation of alternative and challenging discourses. Exactly what form power will take at any time cannot, however, be predicted, because it is historically specific. This is very different therefore from conventional Marxism where power is always related to the means of production and hence is attributed to the ruling class.

The emphasis of post-structuralist theory on the coexistence of different 'meanings' (discourses), and hence the possibility of change, is useful. Human existence generally, including those aspects often perceived as biological or natural and unchanging such as sexuality, are instead a product or construct of the moment. Women, perhaps constructed as relatively passive and powerless at one time, may, as subjects, construct themselves as active and powerful; and this overcomes the idea that women are passive victims of patriarchal structures, which other theories suggest. Weedon provides an example of women's position in the nineteenth century to illustrate these ideas:

> in the nineteenth century the law defined married women as the property of their husbands, denying them the benefits of legally constituted, autonomous subjectivity. This meant that, in order to be heard, married women were forced to produce alternative forms of power and resistance. Their strategies included the assumption of male pseudonyms and manipulation from 'behind the throne', but both these strategies denied them any voice of their own. Many frustrated women, trapped within unhappy marriages, turned to negative protests, such as illness. . . [while yet others]. . . escaped the modes of government of their subjectivity extended to their married sisters [by remaining single].

(Weedon 1987: 114)

This shows how, in Weedon's terms, women act against their relatively powerless situation by constructing alternative discourses and therefore subjectivities. In this particular example women appeared to be using mainly negative strategies, including denial of their voice or self-defined illness – as one might expect in a context of male power. And the one positive strategy entailed freedom from male possession in marriage.

But this kind of interpretation is by no means confined to post-structuralist theory. For example, Wise and Stanley, in a much more detailed study of women's strategies of resistance against male power, show the many different strategies used: women may 'react against', 'join in', 'let it pass', and 'avoid' (Wise and Stanley 1987: 164).

Weedon's example also implies the existence, and importance, of profoundly 'material' features of women's lives such as the experience of illness, and the institutionalisation of oppressive male–female relationships within marriage. But her analysis hardly allows for such materiality because of the way social reality in general is theorised as determined by language, or discourse.[20] In these important ways it is actually difficult for Weedon to answer fully the questions of 'how?' and 'why?' women are oppressed. This problem is further compounded by the use of 'deconstruction' as the 'technique' of post-structuralism.

Deconstruction, a notion largely developed from literary criticism, is the reading of texts to tease out the discursive contradictions involved. Through deconstruction it is possible to examine the constantly changing construction of meanings, and the plurality of meanings, involved in any discursive field. But it is not possible, indeed according to some post-structuralists such as Derrida (1987) it would be wrong, to assume that men and women have different experiences of the text *as* men and women. Nor that the sex of the author is of importance, something other writers have claimed (Spender 1980). This is because, according to post-structuralist theory, the construction of femininity, or masculinity in any individual is only fixed temporarily.

This development has led some writers within the post-structuralist tradition to argue that it is only by deconstructing, or doing away with, categories such as masculinity and femininity that women's oppression will be transcended (see Jardine and Smith 1987). On the surface this seems fair enough, but the problem is that eradicating these categories is seen in terms of the present time. Therefore, instead of being 'liberating', this process merely becomes one of obscuring exactly those power relations which it is intended to overcome. That is, an anti-feminist analysis, which obscures the nature of male power, is the result.

Weedon's particular approach does perhaps overcome these problems, if not very clearly. As she points out 'we are far from achieving a society in which gender, race or class are non-issues' (Weedon 1987: 173). Pointing out how women and men are constructed within a context of gendered power, she explains further that: 'If language and meanings are not naturally gender specific, as they cannot be from a poststructuralist perspective, nevertheless the enquiring subject is always already constructed emotionally and psychically by gendered patriarchal discourses' (ibid.: 173). In terms of women's resistance against patriarchy, this leads Weedon to argue that women should take control of discourse because 'power is invested in her who speaks', while at the same time men should 'work to deconstruct masculinity and its part in the exercising of patriarchal power' (ibid.: 173). But with regard to women, this is not a significantly different position to, nor does it move beyond, those of other feminists who do not use a post-structuralist approach, such as Smith (1987). It does not suggest why a specifically post-structuralist approach should be necessary to an analysis of women's oppression. Furthermore, where men and male power are concerned Weedon's position is rather idealist, and possibly naïve. Men are unlikely to take as their project 'the deconstruction of masculinity'.

Chapter 3

Men as primarily responsible for women's oppression

It is men who are primarily responsible for women's oppression, and it is men, rather than 'capitalism' or 'society', who benefit from the system of male–female social relations where women as a group are kept subordinate to men. This argument is common to both radical and revolutionary feminism, but it is radical feminism with which I am mainly concerned in this chapter. The socialist and Marxist feminist theories which I examined in Chapter 2 analyse women's oppression by focusing to varying degrees on (public) 'production', and (public and/or private) 'reproduction', putting forward the possibility of transcending that oppression at the same time as the oppression arising from economic class inequality. By contrast, the approaches discussed in this and the following chapters focus on what may be considered to be the (private) 'personal' areas of sexuality and reproduction, and emphasise the process of consciousness-raising. Within these latter approaches the issues of human reproduction and sexuality is usually considered to be a product of social processes, and also increasingly related to the issue of violence against women (see Edwards 1987). While Marxist and socialist feminist theories criticise the male-orientation of Marxism generally, they still tend to work from within the Marxist framework to develop a more gender-comprehensive approach (see Mitchell 1971; Rowbotham 1972; Morgan 1970). Radical feminism, while developing from a similar place, has moved further beyond Marxism, although still employing the concept of conflictual class relations, as sex class as well as economic class.

The 'Redstocking Manifesto' (1970), is an influential radical feminist documents from the early part of the contemporary Women's Liberation Movement. The Redstockings were a

New-York-based women's group and their manifesto outlines the argument that men are primarily responsible for women's oppression, an oppression that has lasted for centuries. The manifesto provides a brief documentation of this oppression, and also the process involved in attaining women's liberation. By using a conflictual model of male–female social relations it is argued that 'women are an oppressed class', and that personal relations between men and women are 'class relationships', enforced by threat of physical violence (ibid.: 533). Men are the oppressor class, to be disempowered through the collective activity of women. The oppression of women by men is not only the oldest but also the most fundamental form of domination, from which other forms of exploitation and oppression such as 'racism, capitalism, imperialism etc'. are derived, such that 'Men dominate women, a few men dominate the rest' (ibid.: 534).

Women are often blamed for their own oppression, but this view is rejected by the Redstockings, who argue instead that it is precisely the ongoing subordination which women are subject to that undermines their position, while at the same time benefiting men. Indeed, this is part of the reason why there is a need for feminist analysis and practice to focus specifically on women's situation, to be explicitly 'woman-oriented'. As the manifesto states: 'We identify with all women. . .[and]. . . In our fight for our liberation we will always take the side of women against their oppressors' (ibid.: 535). The woman-oriented approach has also led to an emphasis on experience as the basis for examining and analysing women's oppression. It is the commonality of women's experience which is especially important, and it was the process of sharing experiences which first made women identify 'the problem with no name', as Betty Friedan (1972) has called the specific experience of being oppressed as women in a male dominated society. The manifesto points out that women's experiences of living in a male supremacist society are not only obscured and individualised, but also distorted, through ideological processes, in the interests of male supremacy. As a result, women's personal experience must form the basis for any understanding or theory of women's oppression. It is in this sense that the important slogan 'the personal is political', common to almost all feminist theories, is to be understood.

The method by which the common oppression of women can be uncovered is by consciousness-raising, with women meeting in small groups to share their experiences, and through the process of change undergone by each woman doing this, to bring about awareness of sex class. Consciousness-raising is in this way a crucial part of the process of women's liberation; it is neither therapy nor merely confidence-building but part of a political process. Therapy, for instance, merely 'implies the existence of individual solutions and falsely assumes that the male–female relationship is purely personal' (Redstockings 1970: 535).[1] Consciousness-raising on the other hand provides a collective understanding of, and the possibility of, a collective solution for women's oppression. MacKinnon, in a more recent discussion, explains that the fundamental importance of consciousness-raising is to give women an alternative to male-defined truth, a knowlededge of women's real position in society. In short, consciousness-raising pursues a 'feminist epistemology' (1989: 98).

Since the Redstocking Manifesto there has been an emphasis amongst radical feminists on the 'pro-woman' approach in both analysis and practice. This has included a stress on the autonomous organisation of women, both in general and also within specific male-dominated organisations (see *Feminist Practice* 1979; Segal 1987). In the attempt to integrate theory and practice, there has been a general tendency within radical feminism to focus on, and validate, women's experience. It is argued that, in the context of male supremacy, men's and women's life experiences are not only constructed differently, they are also given different emphases so that women's particular experiences become virtually invisible. As a result, writings about history, for example, tend primarily to contain the history of men, often presented erroneously as the history of 'people' (Spender 1982; Lewis 1981; Rowbotham 1974). Similarly in other disciplines, theorising has tended to analyse men's positions and roles in the world, omitting those of women (see Smith 1987). While feminists generally criticise these problems, only those arguing that men are primarily responsible for women's oppression tend to conclude that women's particular experience within male supremacy must be validated separately (D. Spender 1980; L. Spender 1983; Du Bois 1983). The post-structuralist approach examined in the previous chapter attempts to analyse difference in terms of 'discourses' at a very abstract level, and ends up with rather disparate sets of discourses from which only individualised strategies for change seem possible. By contrast, by basing analysis on women's experience, however seemingly disparate, it is possible to compare, and combine and convert that experience into theory, strategy and practice.

The emphasis on women's personal experience as the basis of feminist analysis has developed in a number of directions, including the so-called 'cultural'[2] approach exemplified by Mary Daly (1979), and the ethnomethodological work of Liz Stanley and Sue Wise (Stanley and Wise 1983; Wise and Stanley 1987). I will discuss these approaches below. It has also led to the development of qualitative research methods where women are the subjects rather than merely the objects of research (see Stanley and Wise 1983; Harding 1987; Duelli Klein 1983; Eichler 1988).

However, before examining the work of Daly, and Stanley and Wise, I want first to discuss the early contemporary Women's Liberation Movement texts of Shulamith Firestone and Kate Millett. Firestone, in *The Dialectic of Sex* (1979)[3], sets out to examine and explain the universality of male dominance by the critical use of theory from Marx and Engels, and Freud, while Millett, in *Sexual Politics* (1970), examines male dominance by a process of questioning male–female sexual relations in literature written by men.

FIRESTONE: THE UNIVERSALITY OF MALE DOMINANCE

Firestone argues that feminists need an analysis of the 'sex war', that is male–female relations, analogous to the analysis developed by Marx and Engels to explain economic class antagonism. While Marx and Engels's model is useful to some extent, the feminist analysis needs to be much more comprehensive because the problem of women's oppression is larger than that of economic class oppression. Marx and Engels's work established 'historical materialism' as an important analytical method. But, Firestone argues, while this is important, they provided only a very partial analysis because they omitted the whole 'sexual substratum', and this could not be remedied even by focusing on reproduction (as opposed to production) as some Marxists have done, for instance in the Domestic Labour Debate (see Chapter 2). Instead, Firestone decides to develop 'a materialist view of history based on sex' (1979: 15), and this is the 'Dialectic of Sex'.

By 'sex' she means the unequal and biological division between men and women based on procreative differences, and institutionalised in the family. She is therefore using the terms sex and gender as separate notions, where 'sex' is biological and 'gender' is social. As will be recalled, I take a different approach: that both sex and gender are social concepts, and interchangeable, because we cannot divorce 'biology' and the social meanings we attach to apparently biological characteristics. Firestone's interpretation leads her to see the task of feminism as being to overcome the procreational distinction between the sexes, to transcend biology and thereby inequality. This, she suggests, will be done by using technology to free women from child-bearing and by the development of alternatives (including homosexual relationships among both sexes) to the nuclear family with its existing oppressive gender roles. By interpreting differences between men and women in this way, Firestone ends up with a biologically determinist analysis. She recognises, however, that turning women's reproductive functions over to technological alternatives is inconceivable within a patriarchal social order, stating that to envision technological developments such as artificial reproduction, birth control and cybernetics in a male-dominated society 'is to envision a nightmare' (ibid.: 190). Thus she perceives that the social context is important, but still ends up stressing that it is women's biology as such which is oppressive to women, and not the meaning attached to it (see MacKinnon 1987a).

In the attempt to apply a Marxist framework, Firestone focuses on material factors largely to the exclusion of crucial ideological considerations (see Rose and Hanmer 1976; Hanmer and Allen 1980), even though in other areas of the book she does take ideological factors into account. For instance, in a chapter on 'The Culture of Romance' she examines how particular ideas about love, such as the construct of romance, perpetuates women's oppression. In particular, the idea of romance plays an important part in the social construction of women as sexual objects to be used by men rather than as subjects in their own right (1979: 139–47). In this way she begins to examine the role of sexuality in the oppression of women by men, an issue which feminists have focused on to a much greater extent since *The Dialectic of Sex*.

Firestone's argument that biological reproduction is central to women's oppression has become an important notion within much feminist theory, because it is potential for motherhood which is the only definite biological distinction between men and women; it is at the heart of the dominant gender ideology, and contributes to making women's subordination appear 'natural'.

Feminists have encountered this important issue in a number of ways. The early Marxist feminist work relies on the idea that men and women are separated into breadwinners and housewives, supposedly resulting from the latters' motherhood role; and the contributors do not always question these biological assumptions (see Benston 1969). From a different perspective, it has been argued that before men realised their own function in reproduction and set about controlling the whole process, women's role as reproducers was greatly esteemed and provided women with high status (Al-Hibra 1983; O'Brien 1981). While this latter view of the historical development of women's oppression may be difficult to prove, there is no doubt that in our society (both past and present) there is generalised control of women's reproductive capacities and women's bodies by men, through the male-dominated institutions of heterosexual marriage and medicine (Ehrenreich and English 1976; Easlea 1980; McLaren 1984; Oakley 1985; Rich 1977; Smart 1984). This has led to the many campaigns around women's abortion rights and the right of women to control their own bodies (see Greenwood and Young 1976; McLaren 1984; Francombe 1984). Combined with the resultant gender ideology, motherhood is generally presented as a woman's ultimate fulfilment and the proof that she is a 'real' woman. Consequently, while not a necessity for women's well-being, the need for women to be mothers is merely a socially constructed myth (Badinter 1981; Rich 1977). Biological reproduction is obviously a necessity for the human race to continue, but it is not necessary for every woman to reproduce, nor does this have to be women's main or only role (MacIntyre 1976).

Firestone's attempt to overcome the difficulty of motherhood is novel, if problematic as I have explained above. Indeed, since the early 1970s, when Firestone's work was published, techniques which for her were only just developing are now actually being used, for example *in vitro* fertilisation (IVF) and attempts to develop an artificial womb (Corea 1985a, 1985b; Duelli Klein 1985; Oakley 1985; Rowland 1984). But using a much more distinctly social approach, where male control over women is seen as the outcome of social constructions regarding motherhood, other feminists have criticised rather than applauded such developments. It has been argued that instead of overcoming women's oppression, the use of the new reproductive technologies is proving to be yet another means of maintaining and perpetuating the unequal power relations between men and women. Instead of freeing women from what Firestone perceives as the constraints of reproduction, it may be argued that these technologies are enabling men to take over women's role as mothers. In short, some feminists fear that women will be seen as redundant once they are no longer needed for what is, in the present male-dominated context, their only really important function (Arditti *et al.* 1984; Corea *et al.* 1985a).

Regarding Firestone's work, while Marx and Engels provide the background to her *Dialectic of Sex*, she bases other parts of her work on Freud. She argues that Freud's work is useful to an analysis of women's oppression because he realised that the 'crucial problem of modern life' (1979: 48) is sexuality, and his approach allows for the possibility of change in sexual relationships. As she explains: 'Both Freudianism and feminism came as reactions to one of the smuggest periods in Western civilisation, the Victorian era, characterised by its family-centredness, and thus its exaggerated sexual oppression and repression' (ibid.: 49). According to Firestone, Freud 'rediscovered' sexuality, which for him was the prime life force. His analysis is based on the patriarchal nuclear family (that is, where patriarchy = power of the father) and the cornerstone of this is the 'Oedipus Complex'. The Oedipus Complex expresses Freud's view of the development of the male child, which is a sexualised perspective based on gendered assumptions. Ultimately, for Freud, the male child wishes to sexually possess his mother in the way he sees his father doing, in order to join the ranks of adult men. As a result he also wishes to kill his father who is in this role already, leading to fear on behalf of the child that the father will castrate him in attempting to repress this wish.

While Freud's theory is not directly useful to an analysis of women's oppression, (after all, that is not what Freud sets out to achieve), Firestone argues that the concept of an Oedipus Complex can be made useful if it is reinterpreted in terms of power. The theory then becomes that the male child prefers his mother above his father because 'He has a bond with her in oppression: while he is oppressed by both parents, she, at least, is oppressed by one. The father, as far as the child can see, is in total control' (ibid.: 53). This preference does not continue into adulthood because at that point the male is himself able to be in a position of power. As Firestone further explains:

What finally convinces him is the offer of the world when he grows up. He is asked to make a transition from the state of potentially powerful, son (ego extension) of his father. Most children aren't fools. They don't plan to be stuck with the lousy limited lives of women.

(ibid.: 55)

The result is that 'They "repress" their deep emotional attachment to their mothers, "repress" their desire to kill their father, and emerge into the honourable state of manhood' (ibid.: 55). Firestone concludes, therefore, that the power hierarchies which exist within the patriarchal nuclear family are maintained by sexual repression.

Firestone's use of Freudian concept gives her an interesting insight into the sexual division of power within the family, as well as sexual relations more generally. Importantly, she also shows that both male and female sexuality is acted out in a powered context, and is a crucial element of the unequal male–female social relations in our society. However, her reliance on Freud is limiting to her perspective because it uses the rather biologistic, and therefore problematic, notion of 'repressed sexuality'. This suggests some biological and determinate 'unrepressed' sexuality is waiting to be discovered. She also uses both social and seemingly biologistic interpretations of Freud without clarifying her stance. If she used a more consistently social approach she might instead interpret women's sexuality not as 'repressed', but instead as controlled socially in the interests of men. These issues concerning sexuality are very important, as will become clearer in the discussion of Millett's work, and they will also be discussed at greater length in the following chapters.

The problem of Firestone using a Freudian analysis is also compounded by her resultant definition of patriarchy as 'power of the father'. Not only does this merely relate to culturally and historically specific types of the family (and what about single-parent families where the father is absent?), but it also makes the patriarchal system operate on a somewhat individualistic level. Women are not merely dominated by their fathers, but by men generally.

Firestone also applies her reinterpretation of Freud to the issue of racism. Focusing, as does Bell Hooks (1982), on the black liberation movement in 1960s America (see Chapter 2), Firestone argues that racism is an extension of sexism. Power relations between men and women provide the context in which physiological differences of race also become important. Following on from this link between racism and sexism, Firestone argues that race relations (in America) are a reflection of the unequal relationships within the nuclear family such that:

> the white man is father, the white woman wife-and-mother, her status dependent on his; the blacks, like children, are his property, their physical differentiation branding them the subservient class, in the same way that children form so easily distinguishable servile class *vis-à-vis* adults. This power hierarchy creates the psychology of racism, just as, in the nuclear family, it creates the psychology of sexism.
>
> (ibid.: 106)

Thus white men have most power: they have power over white women and black people generally. The white woman might, because of her husband, have power over both black men and women. But the white woman's power is very tenuous because of its dependence on the white man who is at the same time the white woman's oppressor. The black man meanwhile has power over the black woman. Firestone draws the same conclusion as Hooks, that black men were more or less given this power during the period of the Black Liberation Movement, when black women supported and shored up black men's machismo in order to empower them, unfortunately to the detriment of the black women who took a subordinate role in the struggle (ibid.: 112–20).

Firestone thus examines the relations based on race in the same way as she does with those based on sex, by reference to Freud's Oedipus Complex and Elektra Complex. In Firestone's terms therefore, the black man is faced with the same choice as that of the male child in the Oedipus Complex scenario: he must transfer his identification with the powerless mother (white woman) to that of the powerful father (white man). In other words he must become a 'man' on white men's terms, which includes becoming the oppressor of all women, white and black. The black man as a result has three choices:

(1) He can give in to the white man on the white man's terms, and be paid off by the white man (Uncle Tomism).
(2) He can refuse such an identification altogether, at which he

often surrenders to homosexuality. Or he may continue desper-
ately to try to prove that if not a 'man' in the eyes of white
society, at least he is not a woman (the Pimp Complex). By
treating 'the bitches' with open contempt, he demonstrates to
all the world that he is in the superior sex class.

(3) He may attempt to overthrow the Father's power. Such an
attempt could, but will not necessarily, encompass a wish to
become the Father.

(ibid.: 108–9)

She similarly applies the Elektra Complex to the situation of the
black woman. In this instance the black woman is the Daughter of
the white American family. Initially she, like the Son (the black
man) sympathises with the Mother (white woman) against the
Father (white man). But her relationship with the Father is
complex and she also wishes to identify with him, rejecting the
female in herself, when she discovers that it is the Father who owns
the 'world of travel and adventure' (ibid.: 109). In rejecting the
womanly element in herself, she also develops contempt for the
Mother. The black woman, as the Daughter, is faced with two
options regarding her powerlessness: 'She may attempt to gain
power directly by imitating white men', or 'she may attempt to gain
power indirectly by seducing the Father (voila the black sexpot)'
which also places her in competition with white women and leads
her to hate and be jealous of them (ibid.: 109).[4]

Firestone's discussion of black oppression tends to be specific to
a historical period and hampered by her emphasis on Freudian
theory; although she does none the less bring to light some of the
tensions involved in the intersection between race and sex, and
illustrates how sexism lurks underneath racism. She ends up by
showing that the Black Liberation Movement of the 1960s was not
about black *people's* liberation, but aimed to establish black men in
power. Thus black men attempted to carry out option (3), of the
options outlined earlier, whereby the creation of the powerful and
masculine black man was concomitant to the creation of the
passive black woman. Meanwhile white women and black women
were divided against each other, unable to see that they were
actually in the same boat.

White feminists generally, and radical feminists and revolutionary feminists in particular, have often in recent years been
criticised for failing to tackle the issues of racial and ethnic

inequality (Parmar 1986; Hooks 1985; Amos and Parmar 1984; Anthias and Yuval-Davis 1983). But Firestone and other early radical feminists, such as the Redstockings, were clearly influenced by the black struggles in America during the 1960s. More recently, issues regarding race and ethnicity have also been discussed from this approach.[5] It may be argued, however, that it is not that these issues are being entirely ignored which is the real criticism, but rather the emphasis by radical feminist (and revolutionary feminist) analysis on women's oppression as underlying racial oppression. This latter perspective is also the one presented by Firestone. In fact in recent years various women have written about race and ethnicity using radical feminist approaches. Work such as that by Linda Bellos (1985), Frankenburgh and Martens (1985), Gothoskat (1986), and Kishwar and Vanita (1984) discusses the specific experience of different groups of black or Asian women, white women's racism, and also the important links which can be made between all women especially in relation to sexual violence.

In critiques of Firestone's *The Dialectic of Sex*, the potential biologism of her work is usually the focus (see Sayers 1982). But as I have shown, Firestone's work deals with many other important issues besides the biological origins of sexual divisions, and she uses an approach which does take social factors into consideration, if not consistently so.

MILLETT: THE UNIVERSALITY OF MALE DOMINANCE

While Shulamith Firestone's *The Dialectic of Sex* (1979) is usually one of the major works mentioned in critiques of radical feminist approaches, her analysis is unrepresentative of much recent radical or revolutionary feminist work (see Hester 1988). Kate Millett's book *Sexual Politics* (1970) is much more important. Unfortunately this is not discussed as often as Firestone's work, and is at times dismissed as merely 'descriptive' because it mainly includes detailed description of instances of power inequality in male–female sexual relations, as presented in the literature of Norman Mailer and Jean Genet (Walby 1986; Barrett 1984). But Millett's work is much more than this. It is analytical, and in her development of a 'Theory of Sexual Politics' (the title of Chapter 2), she provides an extremely useful introduction to the understanding of power in relations between men and women (and between men), focusing on the mechanisms by which such power relations are both constructed and maintained. She shows how these power relations are acted out explicitly in the sex act.

Millett's work may be seen to form the basis of radical and revolutionary feminist approaches which seek to theorise the social construction of men's and women's sexualities, the role that such constructs play in the social control of women, and, directly related to these points, the issue of violence against women. These are issues which have taken an increasingly prominent position in more recent feminist literature (Dworkin 1981; Hanmer 1978; Hanmer and Saunders 1984; MacKinnon 1982; Coveney et al. 1984b; Edwards 1987). In particular, Millett's work underlies the framework of theorising women's oppression which revolutionary feminists have adopted and developed further.

Millett begins her analysis, what she calls her 'notes toward a theory of patriarchy', by defining the relationship between the sexes as political. It is political because it is a power relationship, and involves the notion of 'power over others' (Millett 1970: 24). For Millett, men are the group who have power over women by virtue of their birthright as male, a situation that is virtually unique in comparison to other inequalities such as economic class and race, and also extremely durable. Yet male power is ideologically constructed rather than biological or 'natural'. This is important because, while male dominance might appear to rest on the physical strength of the male, it actually rests on a particular value system: the political creed of male supremacy where men have power over women by virtue of being perceived as superior – biologically or otherwise. As Millett explains:

> Superior physical strength is not a factor in political relations – vide those of race and class. Civilisation has always been able to substitute other methods (technic, weaponry, knowledge) for those of physical strength, and contemporary civilisation has no further need of it. At present, as in the past, physical exertion is very generally a class factor, those at the bottom performing the most strenuous tasks, whether they be strong or not.
>
> (Millett 1970: 27)

As a political system, male supremacy has to be upheld either through consent or by force and also partly through ideological pressures. Consent for the system is obtained by socialisation of men and women into particular 'temperament, role and status' (ibid.: 26). Following on from these categories are the corresponding sex roles which place women in the domestic setting tied to her biological experience. Flowing from temperament and role is status which in turn reinforces the others.

Sexuality, both male and female, is important to Millett's analysis, and male–female power relations are acted out in the heterosex act. Referring to anthropological material, she shows how men's and women's sexualities are perceived very differently. Women's sexual functions are generally seen as 'impure' and negative and to be controlled. Men's sexuality on the other hand, is usually portrayed as positive, and specifically as genital in terms of the penis: 'The penis, badge of the male's superior status in both preliterate and civilised patriarchies, is given the most crucial significance, the subject both of endless boasting and endless anxiety' (ibid.: 47). Compared to other systems of dominance male dominance uniquely involves 'interior colonization' (by which she presumably means penile penetration). This is an important notion which has resurfaced in recent feminist literature, including that of revolutionary feminists (see Johnston 1973; Barry 1981; Leeds Revolutionary Feminist Group 1981). The idea of interior colonisation also links to a related aspect of male sexuality – the idea of the penis as a weapon. To use the penis, which is probably the most vulnerable part of a man's anatomy, as a weapon seems ridiculous. But in rape that is precisely what men are doing. Millett does not say so directly, but using the penis as a weapon is possible precisely because it invades the woman's body, making her feel degraded, humiliated and powerless (see Chapter 4). To illustrate the connection between male power and male sexuality, and also the link between male power, male sexuality and violence, Millett uses the example of the men's houses which exist in certain cultures such as Melanesia:

> The tone and ethos of men's house culture is sadistic, power-oriented, and latently homosexual, frequently narcissistic in its energy and motives. The men's house inference that the penis is a weapon, endlessly equated with other weapons, is also clear.
> (Millett 1970: 50)

Furthermore, sexuality in the context of patriarchy is specifically heterosexual, even if acted out between men. This is because only heterosexual sexuality is constructed as specifically unequal. Continuing to talk about the example of men's houses Millett explains that:

The negative and militaristic coloring of such men's house homosexuality as does exist, is of course by no means the whole character of homosexual sensibility. Indeed the warrior caste of mind with its ultravirility, is more incipiently homosexual, in its exclusively male orientation, than it is overtly homosexual. (The Nazi experience is an extreme case in point here.) And the heterosexual role-playing indulged in, and still more persuasively, the contempt in which the younger, softer, or more 'feminine' members are held, is proof that the actual ethos is mysogynist, or perversely rather than positively heterosexual. The true inspiration of men's house association therefore comes from the patriarchal situation rather than from any circumstances inherent in the homo-amorous relationship.

(ibid.: 50)

Her saying that 'the actual ethos is mysogynist, or perversely rather than positively heterosexual' is particularly interesting because it suggests that the unequal power relations of contemporary hetero-sexual relations are 'perverse', rather than 'normal' (that is, equal) and yet considered alright. This is an issue which later feminist writings have also taken up (Coveney *et al.* 1984b; Leeds Revolutionary Feminist Group 1981).

As mentioned earlier, Millett argues that male supremacy has to be upheld either through consent or by force. While the 'consent' is obtained in many sexually-related ways, force is also related to sexual constructions and 'Patriarchal force also relies on a form of violence particularly sexual in character and realized most completely in the act of rape' (ibid.: 44). Indeed Millett sees the link between sexuality and violence, or 'cruelty', as an intrinsic part of patriarchal societies:

Patriarchal societies typically link feelings of cruelty with sexuality, the latter often equated both with evil and with power. This is apparent both in the sexual fantasy reported by psycho-analysis and that reported by pornography. The rule here associates sadism with the male ('the masculine role') and victimization with the female ('the feminine role').

(ibid.: 44)

Thus she presents a framework in which male–female power

relations are explicitly sexual and her work is groundbreaking in the way it situates 'sexuality' as the crucial battleground between the sexes. For Millett the personal is explicitly political.

It is interesting to note that, as a result of her analysis, Millett sees the slackening of censorship as an important factor in the increased use of sexual hostility against women (ibid.: 45). This issue has more recently become the focus of debate and feminist activity, exemplified by the attempt by Andrea Dworkin and Catharine MacKinnon to use American Civil Rights legislation against pornography (see MacKinnon 1987a: 3–4).

Millett also extends her analysis to social relations generally. By reference to both economic class relations and racial divisions she argues that sexual relations are the more fundamental, but also the least obvious. Race, gender and economic class intersect, but in such a way that even if a woman is middle class and therefore seemingly has more status and power relative to a working-class man, it is actually the man who has a higher status because of his attachment to the 'superior' group, men; and ultimately he may use force to assert this 'superiority': 'a truck driver or butcher has always his "manhood" to fall back upon. Should this final vanity be offended, he may contemplate more violent methods' (Millett 1970: 36). Sexual factors similarly play an intrinsic part in hier-archical relations between men, both in terms of economic class hierarchy and racial hierarchy. The lower the status of a particular male, the greater his assertion of masculinity. Cockburn's data, outlined in the previous chapter, is of direct relevance here. It supports Millett's suggestion that low-status males use masculinity as a means of showing that they are not the lowest since that is the place allotted to women. Concomitantly, high-status males place less emphasis on masculinity. Millett expresses these complex relations as follows:

> The function of class or ethnic mores in patriarchy is largely a matter of how overtly displayed or how loudly enunciated the general ethic of masculine supremacy allows itself to become. Here one is confronted by what appears to be a paradox: while in the lower social strata, the male is more likely to claim authority on the strength of his sex rank alone, he is actually obliged more often to share power with the women of his class who are economically productive; whereas in the middle and

upper classes, there is less tendency to assert a blunt patriarchal dominance, as men who enjoy such status have more power in any case.

(ibid.: 36)

There are also, of course, differences between women in terms of economic class status, but Millett argues that these are less important than those between men because, not only may a woman be dependent on a man for class status, which is a precarious situation, but left to her own devices she is unlikely to rise above working-class status and prestige. Studies done since the early 1970s on income distribution within marriage, women leaving violent partners, and the general 'feminisation of poverty' provide recent evidence to support this aspect of Millett's analysis (see Pahl 1980; Homer *et al.* 1984; Scott 1984).

In addition to the social construction of male and female behaviour, including sexuality, and the use or threat of force, male supremacy according to Millett is also shored up by differential access to education and employment for men and women. This results in a general lack of knowledge by women compared to men, and also in economic dependency by women on men, which is important because knowledge and power are interlinked. Women are placed in a secondary position within paid employment, their social status determining the status of their work (see also Phillips and Taylor 1980).

Finally, Millett argues that 'Patriarchy's chief institution is the family' (ibid.: 33). Unfortunately she largely bases her discussion of this on William Goode's work, *The Family* (1964), and therefore ends up arguing in a somewhat functionalist way that the main contribution of the family is the socialisation of the young to fit the aspects of 'temperament', 'role' and 'status' mentioned earlier. Thus in her discussion of the family she loses sight of her important analysis of male–female relations in terms of sexuality and power, and therefore does not examine the social control mechanisms acting on women in the family through the heterosexual power relations, which she otherwise considers important. But despite the weakness of her analysis of the family, Millett's discussion of sexuality, and in particular the role of male sexuality in maintaining power over women, as well as between men, is an extremely important analysis of the personal as political. She suggests that these relations are more generalised than purely personal behaviour and thereby outlines a theoretical framework which analyses more comprehensively women's oppression through male–female relations than any of the frameworks which I examined in Chapter 2. She overcomes Walby's weak spot – the emphasis on a 'dominant mode of production', substituting this instead with a more generalised and fundamental notion of male–female power relations. It is also possible to apply Millett's framework to the 'economic' examples of both Walby and Cockburn. Millett's analysis is in addition explicitly social, taking into account the importance of material interests, ideological factors, and the possibility of change.

DALY: A WOMEN'S CULTURE

In *Gyn/Ecology* (1979) Mary Daly argues that men, over centuries of domination, have covered up and hidden the particular strength, knowledge and experience of women who have managed to be liberated. It is therefore necessary to uncover, or 'dis-cover' this experience, or the female 'Self' as she terms it. This process of dis-covering is the focus of her book and an important part of this process involves 'naming', that is making obvious misogynyst facts such as 'it is men who rape, who sap women's energy, who deny women economic and political power'; also overcoming the obstacles constructed by anti-female society's 'male agents and token female instruments' (ibid.: 29). Like French feminists such as Kristeva and Cixous, Daly sees the transformation of language, from male-oriented to female-defined, as a crucial part of this process; but in a more radical way, proceeds to create a new language because, in Daly's terms, women will 'spin' their way to a new woman-defined future. Her work conveys excitement and creativity, but is also often difficult to read because of her particular use of language.

Central to Daly's work is the argument that men, if not stopped, will carry male supremacy to its extreme and thus completely crush and kill women off. In other words, that men will commit 'gynocide' (ibid.: 90). This process has already begun, and Daly identifies it in a wide variety of misogynist literature and practices, carried out as what she calls the 'Sado-Ritual Syndrome', which is in effect male violence against women. Daly is presenting one of the earlier examples of contemporary feminist work to argue that male violence acts as a means of controlling women socially, and like Millett (1970), she sees sexuality as a crucial aspect of this. A large part of the book is taken up with the examination of such 'Sado-Ritual' examples of gynocide, including Indian suttee, Chinese footbinding, female genital mutilation, and the European witchburnings. Her examination of the European witchburnings constitutes one of the few feminist analyses of the early modern witch-hunts, and I will discuss this aspect of her work later (see Chapter 6).

There are, however, a number of problems with Daly's work. Most important, Daly's approach has been criticised as essentialist because of the way she assumes that there is one female 'self'. It is a self which male-defined social processes have overlain and thus obscured with all manner of behaviours, feelings, and thoughts, which do not belong to this self (Barrett 1984; Segal 1987; Weedon 1987). Daly obviously wants this focus on the female self to be empowering for women, and to suggest that women could be free if male supremacy is eradicated. But whether she intends it or not, this also gives the impression that there is only really one version of 'woman', which is the liberated version, and the rest are fakes. Like the Freudian notion of repression of desire, Daly's work can there-fore be said to suggest that there is a fundamentally similar basis to behaviour, of being, for all women. Moreover, that this is funda-mentally different to the 'essence' of maleness. Unfortunately in this way her perspective ends up with a similar outcome to biological determinism – that there is a natural femaleness which we should aspire to uncover. Daly's particular attempt to liberate women through the use of language may also be a problem. As Andrea Nye points out, the problem of language in an unequal society is not with individual words, but with the relationship between words. Therefore changing the language might not funda-mentally change anything because the new words take on meanings which reflect unequal male–female relations. As she explains:

> If the very structure of meaning depends on sexual difference, then a simple expulsion or reinstatement of meanings may not have the desired effect. If the structure of the language demands hierarchialised gender, then no matter what new words are invented or rediscovered, the same assymetrical relations will eventually reconstitute themselves, as other words shift in meaning to accommodate the addition or deletion.
>
> (Nye 1988: 179)

None the less Daly's use of language does have an effect on the reader, focusing as it does on the powered and gendered meanings of the English/American language – but only for those with access to this.

The intention of Daly's work is to validate women's experience and empower women generally by constructing an alternative women's language and culture, but she may be in danger of doing almost the opposite by validating only that experience or behaviour which she deems to be the liberationary essential female. Yet Daly is presenting an important approach, arguing also that male violence is used as a crucial means of controlling women socially (see Chapter 5).

STANLEY AND WISE: INTERACTIONISM

Stanley and Wise continue with the theme of experience, but move entirely away from essentialism and from any notion that male or female behaviour in whatever form is natural. Naturalness is merely a perception. Rejecting what they see as the determinism of structural approaches, whereby people's actions and lives are shaped by social forces outside of themselves, they argue instead that feminist analysis should take as its starting point women's personal experience:

> We believe that a feminist social science should begin with the recognition that 'the personal', direct experience, underlies all behaviours and actions. We need to find out what it is that we know and what it is that we experience.
>
> (Stanley and Wise 1983: 165)

The most useful approach, they suggest, derives from interactionism, and in particular, ethnomethodology[6] because, instead of behaviour being seen as predetermined, as in the structural approaches, it is instead constructed through interaction between individuals. Even so, social structures must be taken into account, and they argue that such structures are created in everyday interactions: '"structures" don't exist as some mechano-like thing hovering in the sky, but are to be found within everyday behaviours and events' (Stanley and Wise 1983: 137). This leaves Stanley and Wise with a problem, however, because it is unclear why particular structures (such as those giving overall power to men) are created.

Where the ethnomethodological approach is especially useful is in its concern with the personal, and everyday events both as research topics and resource. Using an ethnomethodological approach also allows for change, because it is possible to construct realities which are in contradiction to those of others, and also possible to see these alternative realities precisely *as* alternatives. This is when 'interpretive assymetry' becomes 'reality disjuncture'. As they explain:

> sometimes we find ourselves constructing events differently from other people, and 'differently' in such a way that it becomes apparent that these differences are potentially unreconcilable. When this happens, then, to use an ethnomethodological concept to describe it, an 'interpretive assymetry' will exist.
>
> (Stanley and Wise 1983: 142)

Furthermore:

> Interpretive assymetries are potential 'reality disjunctures' which are defused or dissolved. Reality disjunctures themselves are situations in which participants become fully aware that the very existence of phenomenon claimed by one is denied by the others.
>
> (Stanley and Wise 1983: 142)

This is the situation that arises when feminists present different interpretations of the facts from those of most people. But more than this, because women are constituted as 'the other' within male-dominated society, women's very existence provides a 'reality disjuncture' even though it is only through feminism and feminist consciousness that this is conceptualised. What is very important about this, according to Stanley and Wise, is the way ethnomethodology suggests that we are involved in both our own oppression and our own liberation:

> In other words, by locating 'the political' and the construction of reality within the everyday, ethnomethodology implies that we are all involved in our own oppressions and, conversely, can be equally involved in our own liberations. Individually we can effect many small changes. Together we can revolutionise all interactions, all constructions of 'reality, for all practical purposes'.
>
> (Stanley and Wise 1983: 147–8)

Thus, like the post-structuralist approach of Weedon (1987) discussed earlier, the ethnomethodological approach of Stanley and Wise provides an analysis in which all women are always actively involved in constructing alternative meanings to those which may be oppressive, rather than being the passive victims within some determining 'system' or 'structure' of male dominance. Also, Stanley and Wise's approach allows for the construction of many different meanings. Where it is more useful than the post-structuralist approach, however, is by situating the analysis at the level of experience, rather than merely idealist abstraction, so that the material conditions of women's oppression may be examined. The ethnomethodological approach 'looks to the processes involved in our construction of an objectively defined social reality as the scene in which oppression daily occurs' and this is useful because 'as feminists this is something which we are ever aware of – the rapes, insults, sexist assumptions and actions, all of the everyday experiences of sexism as an ongoing and continual oppression of women' (Stanley and Wise 1983: 148).

In *Georgie Porgie* Wise and Stanley apply this framework to an analysis of male power. They call women's oppression by men 'sexual harassment' because the oppression of women in all respects involves the social control (or harassment) of women by men:

> We don't know 'why' women are oppressed by men, its original or underlying cause, but 'how' it happens is through processes of social control enacted by men over women in which the totality of our lives are available to being policed by them.
>
> (Wise and Stanley 1987: 15)

Significantly, in this way, Wise and Stanley are arguing that all male-female interactions involve experience of the control which other feminists have identified as male violence against women (Brownmiller 1976; Dworkin 1981; MacKinnon 1979; Rhodes and McNeill 1985). Although, because the process of control is interactional rather than structural, the potential outcome of any male-female encounter is very unpredictable. Power may be experienced by women as institutional and hierachical forms or, more important to Wise and Stanley, as 'interactional power' – however, the relative effects of the two types of power are not discussed. The interactional system of power interests Wise and Stanley most, because within this power is the outcome of negotiation and interaction such that men's power is not guaranteed.

In relation to men, power isn't something they somehow have by virtue of being men (tucked away in their jeans perhaps?): rather it's something we permit them to use or they take and then use. In the system of 'interactional power' between the sexes there is no rigid hierarchy – it really is a matter for wheeling and dealing, interaction and, of particular concern to us, manipulation.

(Wise and Stanley 1987: 146)

It is therefore in the context of interactional power that women may be empowered, or take power for themselves. Many examples are given of how women may 'fight back' in situations of sexual harassment, that is, where men are attempting to do power over women. Women may use a number of strategies: reacting against; joining in; letting it pass; and avoiding it. Usually, they argue, only 'reacting against' is considered as fight back by feminists, but the other strategies may also empower women. I will look at each in turn.

– 'Reacting against' is exemplified in the case of Inez Garcia in America who was attacked by two men, and raped by one of them while the other held her down. In retaliation she shot and killed one of them, and as a result was imprisoned for murder, although released later on appeal. Wise and Stanley explain that during the attack, Inez Garcia 'had been totally objectified and made quite powerless' (Wise and Stanley 1987: 164). It was out of this power-lessness that she became empowered, driven by anger resulting from her humiliation 'in a sense it was the actual experience of sexual harassment that empowered her to "react against" it' (ibid.: 165).

– By 'joining in' Wise and Stanley mean using similar tactics to those of the harasser. In one of the examples they quote, women used lewd remarks and sexual innuendo to empower themselves against a man who had used the same against them. Besides direct physical violence, there does not actually seem to be much differ-ence between this and the previous category.

– 'Letting it pass' is a strategy that women use frequently:

We all frequently 'pass', even the most committed of feminists amongst us, because we're frightened, or because we're just too weary to bother, or because we know that the ensuing fuss and accusations of 'man hating' and 'castrating bitches' of 'kill joy' and 'ungrateful' simply aren't worth the hassle.

(Wise and Stanley 1987: 169)

What is important, is that it is an active decision based on interpretation of the relevant situation, although others might see it as 'ostrich-like ineffectuality' (ibid.: 169).

– In the same way as 'joining in', 'avoiding it' may also be an actively decided strategy even if some would argue that it is the outcome of constraint. As Wise and Stanley explain:

Avoiding sexual harassment – like not going into pubs on your own or not going to particular places at night by yourself – is also often seen as the complete antithesis of fighting back. But, as we are arguing here as well as earlier in our discussion of power, even though avoidance is constraint of a kind, it is also the rational weighing up of pros and cons to enable sensible decisions to be made.

(Wise and Stanley 1987: 171)

There is no doubt that women use a great variety and seemingly contradictory ways to fight back against male sexual harassment, and this is a strength of the work. The studies of Stanley and Wise themselves as well as others would support this (Kissling and Kramarae 1985; Bart and O'Brien 1985; Hanmer and Saunders 1984). But because of their general approach, Stanley and Wise end up arguing that any act carried out by a woman, in the context of 'interactional power', may be interpreted as fightback, and that may be problematic. I do not deny that women are actively and consistently opposing male power. On the contrary, there is much evidence to suggest that this is the case, and moreover, as Stanley and Wise state: 'If women weren't so powerful "oppression" would be much more oppressive than it is' (Stanley and Wise 1983: 195). What is important here is the overriding impression of a sex struggle, a conflict between men and women over power. But this process of women's (and men's) empowerment in Stanley and Wise's work is both very individualised, and also seemingly arbitrary. As was the case with Weedon's post-structuralist approach, connections and comparisons between different situations become difficult to make in practice; although Stanley and Wise's approach overcomes the general idealism of Weedon's work. In the final analysis Stanley and Wise's work suggests that anything women do may be construed as liberatory – to themselves as individuals even if not to women as a group. This clearly negates the collective strategy of the earlier radical feminists such as the Redstockings. The problem is that Stanley and Wise focus largely on women's *experience*, but not women's *collectivised and politicised experience.* The women they describe do not necessarily have 'conscious' knowledge of women's social position and male power, and may therefore not be acting in women's general interest.

Andrea Dworkin (1983) discussing the topic of why many women choose to be 'right-wing', shows this problem in Stanley and Wise's interactionist approach very clearly. Discussing women's survival, where Stanley and Wise talk about empowerment, Dworkin explains that just any solution will not do, and may indeed result in mysogynist anti-feminism. Thus one outcome of attempting to survive – Stanley and Wise's 'joining-in' – may at times be the exact opposite of liberatory: furthering oppression. Dworkin points out how:

> Like the chameleon, the woman must blend into her environment, never calling attention to the qualities that distinguish her, because to do so would be to attract the predator's deadly attention. She is, in fact, hunted meat – all the male auteurs, scientists, and homespun philosophers on street corners will say so proudly. Attempting to strike a bargain, the woman says: I come to you on your own terms. Her hope is that his murderous attention will focus on a female who conforms less artfully, less willingly. In effect, she ransoms the remains of a life – what is left over after she has renounced wilful individuality – by promising indifference to the fate of other women. This sexual, sociological, and spiritual adaptation, which is, in fact, the maiming of all moral capacity, is the primary imperative of survival for women who live under male-supremacist rule.
>
> (Dworkin 1983: 19)

As a result it is feminists who seek to destroy male power while 'right-wing women' who actively live in the same oppressive circumstances, accommodate themselves to male power. Women's experience of living in male supremacist society is probably the same, but the strategies of surviving in such a context may have entirely contradictory effects. While Stanley and Wise's analysis provides an extremely important means of analysing male–female relations at an individual level, their analysis also needs to critically assess these contradictory, individualised, outcomes.

Radical feminist analyses focus on the 'personal as political'; and show that the 'personal' areas of reproduction, sexuality and also violence against women are by no means merely personal or individual representations. Instead, these issues stand at the heart of the generalised system of power that is male supremacy, an understanding that has been made possible by sharing women's experiences through consciousness-raising. In the following chapters I will more fully discuss the importance of the issues of sexuality and violence to the construction and perpetuation of male domination over women.

Chapter 4

Towards a revolutionary feminist approach
Male sexual violence against women[1]

Throughout the 1970s growing feminist, and also public, awareness about the issue of male violence against women, violence specifically directed at women by men, prompted the need for explanation of this phenomenon. Domestic violence and rape were some of the earliest concerns. Evidence from women made it obvious that these experiences were very widespread (Katyachild *et al.* 1985; Jeffreys 1976; Hanmer 1978; London Rape Action Group 1985). 'First wave' feminists had also taken up the issue of male violence, as did women in even earlier periods, but their knowledge and experience of this had largely been lost.[2] The rediscovery of the issue of male violence against women brought to the fore some very important questions about male–female relations, including the role of male violence and, more recently, sexuality, in the social control of women (Edwards 1987; Kelly 1988; Jeffreys 1990).

Socialist and Marxist feminists have been unable to deal with the issue of male violence (Segal 1987). Their class-based analysis suggests that it is certain socio-economic conditions, such as unemployment, which leads men to be violent against women (Wilson 1983). But this is much too limited, and does not cover the extensive evidence of violence to women, which suggests instead that women from all classes experience violence from men from any class (Russell 1982; Hanmer and Saunders 1984). A class-based analysis also lets the main perpetrators, that is, men, off the hook, as exemplified in some recent literature by anti-sexist men who avoid challenging the reality of men's violence against women. Tim Carrigan *et al.*, for instance, while recognising that violence 'helps to make all kinds of masculinity' (1987: 89), places the blame for violence largely on the (intangible and nebulous) state.

And Andy Moye (1985) has argued that pornography is probably more damaging to men than it is to women (see Chapter 5).

Others, including revolutionary feminists, have argued that male violence against women in whatever form – harassment, rape, battering etc.[3] – is a crucial mechanism by which male dominance and control is maintained over women, where, by some men using violence against some women, all women at the same time live with the threat of violence from potentially any man, and all men benefit from the actions of some men (London Rape Crisis Centre 1984; Hanmer and Saunders 1984; Stanko 1985; Russell 1975; Brownmiller 1976; Hanmer 1978). Betsy Stanko points out the resultant effect on women's lives:

> To be a woman – in most societies, in most eras – is to experience physical and/or sexual terrorism at the hands of men. Our everyday behaviour reflects our precautions, the measures we take to protect ourselves. We are wary of going out at night, even in our own neighbourhoods. We are warned by men and other women not to trust strangers. But somehow they forget to warn us about the men we know: our fathers, our acquaintances, our co-workers, our lovers, our teachers. Many men familiar to us also terrorise our everyday lives in our homes, our schools, our workplaces.
>
> (Stanko 1985: 9)

Feminists working in rape crisis centres and refuges have uncovered a phenomenal amount of male sexual violence against women, and it has become obvious that most women have probably experienced some form of sexual abuse during their lives (London Rape Crisis Centre 1984; Kelly 1988).

It is important to realise that the work done by feminists concerning male violence against women has laid the basis for understanding the crucial part played by sexuality (particularly the social construction of male sexuality) in the oppression of women by men. The issue of male violence against women will therefore be examined in this chapter before I go on to develop the concept of male sexuality as social control of women more fully. It must be recognised, however, that it is exceedingly difficult to separate these two areas because, as Millett's work indicates, at a conceptual level the phenomenon of male violence against women and the issue of sexuality are closely linked (Millett 1970; Jeffreys 1976; Barry 1981; Dworkin 1981; Katyachild *et al.* 1985; MacKinnon 1987a).

Male violence against women covers a very wide area and I have chosen in this chapter to examine material which presents some particularly important questions. I will concentrate on the issues of rape and pornography as these show clearly the nature of male violence against women and the role this plays in the oppression of women. In particular it can be seen that rape is about sex as opposed to merely violence, and pornography exemplifies how sadism and masochism are part and parcel of heterosexual behaviour.

RAPE

Rape was *the* feminist issue in America during the 1970s. Women's widespread experience of rape was being uncovered through consciousness raising and the sharing of those experiences, as well as through research built on women's experience (Brownmiller 1976: 8–9; Griffin 1971; Russell 1973, 1975). Kate Millett (1970) briefly outlines the use of rape as force in the context of male–female power relations. At around the same time as Millett's work, Susan Griffin (1971) carried out a detailed study on rape, 'Rape: the All-American Crime', laying the basis for later feminist work and also showing that rape is about the politics of male dominance.

Feminists have shown that rape is widely experienced by women. Indeed, we may consider it to be 'normal'. Diana Russell (1982), for instance, in a survey of 930 women in the United States, found that 44 per cent had experienced one or more attempted or actual rapes during their lives, and that 1 in 7 women had been raped by their husbands.[4] Moreover, it has been shown that rapists are not 'abnormal' men. On the contrary, they are no different from other men:

> It is difficult to believe that such widespread violence is the responsibility of a small lunatic fringe of psychopathic men. That sexual violence is so pervasive supports the view that the focus of violence against women rests squarely in the middle of what our culture defines as 'normal' interaction between men and women.
>
> (Allen Griswold Johnson in Stanko 1985: 38)

A major question arising from the feminist work on rape concerns whether rape is about violence or whether it is about sex. Feminists generally agree that rape involves social control of women by men, but some argue that rape is violence (Brownmiller 1976), while others argue that rape is to do with sexuality (MacKinnon 1979, 1987c; Jeffreys 1990). In agreement with the latter, I will argue here that rape is to do with the construct of male sexuality because, in the contemporary male supremacist context, male sexuality is about male power.

The way rape is dealt with in legal terms and also practically by the state illustrates some of the conceptual problems involved in the development of a feminist analysis of rape. The law defines rape as forced or unwanted sexual intercourse from a man to a woman. In other words, rape is seen as non-consensual sex between a man and a woman (Sexual Offences Act 1976).[5] There is an immediate problem within this definition, which is that women's experience of rape is much wider than merely 'sexual intercourse'. Brownmiller outlines this experience:

> Sexual assault in our day and age is hardly restricted to forced genital copulation,. . . but the invasion may occur through the mouth and rectum as well. And while the penis may remain the rapist's favourite weapon, his prime instrument of vengeance, his triumphant display of power, it is not in fact his only tool. Sticks, bottles, and even fingers are often substituted for the 'natural' thing.
>
> (Brownmiller 1976: 378)

Women may also be urinated or defecated upon, or be exposed to other horrendous activities, as part of the rape act. For the women who experience these acts, whether or not the experience includes penile penetration, the physiological and psychological effects are similarly traumatic and damaging (London Rape Crisis Centre 1984).

In practice, the legal apparatus also takes acts other than penile penetration into account, but in a contradictory manner. The law states that rape is specifically sexual intercourse (or penile penetration of a woman) where the woman does not consent. But in practice it is virtually impossible for a woman to prove that she has been raped without additional physical evidence, such as extensive evidence of violence (bruising, cuts, etc.) (London Rape Crisis Centre 1984; Stanko 1985). Thus the rape legislation presents rape as an act of sex, although not as 'normal' sex, while in practice the law also recognises, indeed places more emphasis on, rape as an act of violence. As MacKinnon pertinently points out, 'Rape is a sex crime that is not a crime when it looks like sex' (MacKinnon 1987a: 143). This is also part of the reason why, even though rape is apparently condemned in our society, in practice rapists are seldom convicted. Violence and sex are both important notions in understanding rape, but not in the way suggested by the law, although the law and state practice provide important pointers to an explanation of rape. I want to argue that rape is actually an act of *sexual* violence that can only exist in a context where sexuality generally is constructed as, and acted out as, a power relation, that is as dominance and submission.

In terms of the law on rape an even greater problem is the notion of consent. Some feminists, such as Brownmiller, argue that women may consent to heterosexual intercourse, while recognising that there is also a general expectation that women should have, or should submit to, intercourse within a male-dominant context. This expectation has, for example, been instituted in marriage, which is why the rape legislation has historically exempted the marriage relationship. This has only recently, as a result of feminist pressure, begun to be changed (L. Kelly 1987). Others, critical of the notion of 'consent', argue that consent cannot be a question of free choice for any individual woman within a male supremacist context – consent is merely a construct which appears as free choice (MacKinnon 1987a; London Rape Action Group 1985; Jeffreys 1990). I want to examine these distinctions further, focusing in particular on the difference between male violence as 'violence' and male violence as 'sex'.

The argument that male violence is violence is exemplified by Susan Brownmiller's work. Brownmiller defines rape as primarily heterosexual intercourse where the woman concerned has not agreed to, or chosen, the act:

> A female definition of rape can be contained in a single sentence. If a woman chooses not to have intercourse with a specific man and the man chooses to proceed against her will, that is a criminal act of rape.

> (Brownmiller 1976: 18)

It can be seen that she distinguishes between heterosexual intercourse which is seemingly consensual, and which she therefore deems to be alright, and heterosexual intercourse which is non-consensual and therefore oppressive to women. The implication is that there is an acceptable (normal) heterosexuality as well as an unacceptable (abnormal) heterosexuality. This unfortunately bears a resemblance to the legal definition of rape. Unfortunate, because it suggests the existence of precisely the type of 'normal biological sexuality' which Brownmiller is attempting to criticise.

It is because of Brownmiller's attempts to thus separate 'normal' and 'abnormal' heterosexuality, that she ends up defining rape specifically as an act of violence. She places rape alongside murder, assault and robbery, all of which (including rape) she terms 'criminal violence' (Brownmiller 1976: 181). Her examples emphasise this notion of rape as violence. She looks at rape in war, in riots and revolutions, in the context of racism, in prison, and as sexual abuse of children. These are all presented as common, but extreme and extraordinary events. It is not 'rape in normal circumstances, in everyday life, in ordinary relationships, by men as men' (MacKinnon 1987a: 141) which feminist studies have shown rape, and male violence against women generally, to be. None the less, her documentation of rape presents some interesting points regarding rape and power, as well as criticising some of the myths about rape.

There are a number of general implications from Brownmiller's work which need to be addressed. Firstly, it appears from her example of rape in war, amongst others, that rape is a product of some form of 'extreme' masculinity. Such apparent division of masculinity into 'extreme' and 'non-extreme' is similar to her division of heterosexuality into apparently 'normal' and 'abnormal' forms and obscures the widespread nature of male violence against women.

Secondly, she suggests that it is in situations of extreme power discrepancy between men and women that rape takes place. This point, although correctly showing that rape is a product of a male-dominated or male supremacist society, at the same time appears to limit rape to specific 'extreme' situations rather than presenting it as a more generalised event. This point is also in contradiction with Brownmiller's main thesis where it is argued that rape leads to 'all men keeping all women in a state of fear' (Brownmiller 1976: 15). In other words, Brownmiller's data in this instance provides a different impression than she is apparently intending. An example serves to underline this problem, and shows how in reality Brownmiller limits the term 'rapist' to cover only certain groups.

Applauding the work of Menachim Amir (1971), Brownmiller points out that Amir's most important contribution was 'to place the rapist squarely within the subculture of violence' (Brownmiller 1976: 181). As a result she presents the rapist as prevalent in only particular socio-economic and racial groups: the rapist is highly likely to be working-class and black. This conclusion is both classist and racist but also sits uneasily with her emphasis on all men keeping all women in a state of fear. If Amir's analysis is correct, which it is not, then women only need to fear black working-class men.

Thirdly, the implication from Brownmiller's examples is that male violence against women is primarily carried out by men not known to the woman concerned, which is patently untrue. Even Amir's study showed that rapes are predominantly carried out by men known to the women who are raped. These points begin to expose the problems related to an analysis where rape is seen as violence. Of course, it must be recognised that the notion of rape as violence has had an important part to play in the development of a feminist analysis of rape. In particular, seeing rape as violence has come about as a result of focus on women's experience of rape rather than the act as perceived by the rapist. Women who have been raped experience this as a violent act, rather than an act of sex which may be defined in other, more pleasant emotional terms. Rape is experienced as an act of terror whereby 'a woman endures an invasion of self, the intrusion of inner space, a violation of her sexual and physical autonomy' (Stanko 1985: 9).

There is no doubt that for women, rape is a violently traumatic act. In saying this it may appear that I am beginning to contradict myself. But the important lesson to be learned from the documentation of women's experiences of rape, is that this material shows us the *effect* of rape and the *extent* of rape. But it does not necessarily tell us *why men rape*. The reason why requires further analysis, and in this respect Brownmiller's work has limitations. We are again faced with the problem that women's experience is not necessarily the same as an understanding or conscious knowledge about women's position *vis-à-vis* men (see Chapter 3).

A number of feminists have taken women's experience as the starting point of their analysis, but also moved beyond this to incorporate the specific, gendered, context of that experience (see MacKinnon 1987a; Russell 1975; Medea and Thompson 1974; Clark and Lewis 1977; Griffin 1971; Millett 1970). By reference to some of this material, I want to consider why rape should be seen as sex rather than merely as violence.

It was suggested earlier that the legal definition and state practice concerning rape presents rape as sex, but requires evidence of violence in order to acknowledge that rape has taken place. This is because rape is seen as an abnormal sex act between a man and a woman. It is the evidence of explicit violence which proves to the police or judge that an 'abnormal' rather than a 'normal' act has taken place. But it is important to stress that this is the male view, arising out of a context where men dominate and where it is men's experience which predominates. As MacKinnon succinctly explains:

> I propose that the state is male in the feminist sense. The law sees and treats women the way men see and treat women. The liberal state coercively and authoritatively constitutes the social order in the interests of men as a gender, through its legitimizing morals, relation to society, and substantive policies.
>
> (MacKinnon 1987a: 140)

Thus it is men's experience which is constructed as more important, and taken as the 'correct' version of events. This is also illustrated by the following example which is a compilation of women's experiences. It is a male–female scenario leading, for the man, to an obvious and acceptable situation which includes sex:

> He asks her to dance. She accepts. (She wants to or she doesn't want to but she's afraid of hurting his feelings, she's afraid of making him angry, she wants a man to dance with.) He asks her out, she accepts. (She wants to, or she doesn't want to, but all her friends have got blokes, she's afraid of making him angry, he might feel hurt, she can't go out if she's on her own.) He kisses her. He puts his hand on her leg, her breast, her cunt. He wants to see how far he can go. She let's him. (She wants to or she doesn't want to but he's taken her out after all, and spent money on her, she needs a lift home, she doesn't want to seem a prude, he might be angry.) He asks her to sleep with him. She accepts. (She wants to, or she doesn't want to but she thinks she might as well, she can't back off now, it might be O.K., she's flattered that he wants her, he might be angry.)
> Or she refuses. He tries to persuade her. He tells her he loves her. He says she doesn't love him. He calls her a prude,

immature, frigid. He says he 'needs' sex, so if she won't come across, he'll have to find a girl who will. Each time they meet he carries on a bit further, a bit further. (Why not go all the way?) He buys durex to demonstrate his sense of responsibility. Each time she finally tells him to stop, breaks away, he gets angry, he rages, he sulks; he tells her how bad it is for men to be left 'excited'. (Prick-teaser!) He teaches her to suck him off. He works towards his goal, which is her vagina. He means to have, to possess this woman.

(London Rape Action Group 1985: 27–8)

I am not claiming that this scenario provides the actual totality of male–female encounters; but it typifies the process involved in many such encounters. The scenario illustrates the way the different experiences of men and women are constructed through interactions within the unequal power context of male–female relations in a male supremacist society. Within this scenario both the man and the woman are active participants, but the 'script' being acted out is geared towards the man.[6] For the man the scenario represents a normal sexual encounter while for the woman it is an intrusive and violent encounter. As anyone who works in a Rape Crisis Centre will attest, this is a common rape experience, and one that leaves women very confused because they are not quite sure whether their own feelings – that they have been violated – are correct, or whether the man's version – that it is what should have happened – is the right one. The example helps us to understand in greater detail how an encounter between a man and a woman can be construed and perceived as 'normal sex' by the man even though for the woman it is sexual violence.

In other words, in practice, for men, 'sex' and 'violence' may not actually be separate since violence towards women is an integral part of normal sex – rape turns men on. What women experience as violence, then (in accordance with the dominant male definition and construction of the term), is actually normal heterosexual sex: not only do rape and normal heterosexual relations have common characteristics, but they are part and parcel of the same act of sexual activities. Rape is therefore *sexual* violence. That is also why women who have experienced rape may find it difficult to separate their experience of heterosexual sex generally from that of rape. As MacKinnon explains:

A common experience of rape victims is to be unable to feel good about anything heterosexual thereafter – or anything sexual at all, or men at all. . . . That, to me, is sexual. When a woman has been raped, and it is sex that she cannot then experience, without connecting it to that, it was her sexuality that was violated.

(MacKinnon, 1987a: 87–88)

This brings us back to the notion of 'consent', and the legal definition of rape.

The judges would consider the example given earlier of male–female relations (from the London Rape Action Group 1985) as a consensual situation, that is, in their terms, not rape but sex. But as indicated earlier, although the legal definition apparently sees rape as sex, in practice only evidence of violence actually renders a particular act 'rape'. This is because men's construction and experience of normal heterosexuality *includes* violence, and it is in the interests of the male-defined state to present rape as other than such violent normal heterosexuality. In the practice of the state rape therefore becomes *purely violence* and not 'sex'. This is very important because it is this discrepancy between the male interpretation of rape and women's experience of rape which also makes women reluctant to report rape to the police. These women know that the state is unlikely to prosecute in most instances of (women-defined or women-perceived) rape:

in all these situations, there was not enough violence against them to take it beyond the category of 'sex'; they were not coerced enough. Maybe they were forced-fucked for years and put up with it, maybe they tried to get it over with, maybe they were coerced by something other than battery, something like economics, maybe even something like love.

(MacKinnon 1987a: 88)

MacKinnon goes on to make the crucial point that within the context of male supremacy, dominance is 'eroticized'. This is similar to the 'sexualization of male–female power relations', which Kate Millett (1970) outlines as a central aspect of 'sexual politics'. For MacKinnon it is this eroticisation of dominance which lies at the core of male supremacy, reconstructing and thereby maintaining and perpetuating the male supremacist social order. In this way sexuality is not only central to the existence of male supremacy, but rape is an instance of *sexual* violence.

> the molding, direction, and expression of sexuality organises society into two sexes – women and men – which division under-lies the totality of social relations. Sexuality is that social process which creates, organizes, expresses, and directs desire, creating the social beings we know as women and men, as their relations create society.
>
> (MacKinnon 1982: 2)

Thus it is, as a part of normal heterosexuality, that rape is an important feature of the maintenance and perpetuation of male dominance. In short, rape, as an integral part of heterosexual relations, may also be seen as integral to the dynamics of male domination.

Rape is both an expression of the male sexual construct and constructing of women's behaviour: rape and the threat of rape profoundly affect women's lives, placing constraints on women's activities at all levels. The effect of rape is to control women socially, and it is men who benefit. This links in with the discussion of Cockburn's and Walby's work in Chapter 2, where it was made apparent how sexual violence, including rape and the threat of rape, enables men to restrict women's economic activity, in turn making women more dependent (and thus subordinate) to men.

PORNOGRAPHY

Robin Morgan has argued that 'Pornography is the theory, and rape the practice' (Morgan 1982: 131), by which she means that pornography provides the legitimation for rape through the visual representation of male sexual violence against women. This issue has led to much debate regarding whether or not pornography leads to or even increases rape of women by men.[7] For example, in 1970 the United States Presidential Commission, which was set up to examine 'Obscenity and Pornography', suggested that there is no link between pornography and rape (what they termed 'criminal sexual behaviour'). At the time, President Nixon disagreed with the Commission's conclusion arguing that:

> The Commission contends that the proliferation of filthy books and plays has no lasting effects on a man's character. If that

were true, it must also be true that great books, great paintings and great plays have no ennobling effects on a man's conduct. Centuries of civilization and ten minutes of common sense tell us otherwise.

(Katyachild *et al.* 1985: 16)

One of the authors of the original Report, Martin Wolfgang, now appears to have entirely changed his mind and argues instead that portrayal of violence *does* tend to encourage use of violence by those exposed to it (Wolfgang 1979: 64). Recent research also backs up this view (Everywoman 1988: 13–22).

In 1983 public hearings on pornography were held in Minneapolis for a Bill, championed by Catharine MacKinnon and Andrea Dworkin, which would define pornography as a violation of the Civil Rights of Women.[8] The hearings provided evidence from women and men who had experienced the link between pornography and violence, from workers with survivors of such violence, and from researchers. At the hearings women and men told of how pornography is used by men both as a direct turn-on and also to provide them with ideas for doing violence to women, to children and sometimes to other men. One woman told how she and other women working as prostitutes were constantly expected to act out scenes from pornograpic magazines or films. Another woman told of facing racist abuse as part of sexual abuse. Yet another how her boyfriend (who later became her husband) expected her to act out degrading and humiliating, as well as dangerous, poses from pornographic magazines for him to photograph:

> we went to the perfect site, it was an abandoned bus in an overgrown field. When we got there he asked me, he told me to take off my clothes and to pose in various positions where I acted as if I was running towards the door. And then he asked me to put my body in contorted different positions, draped down the stairs of the bus, and they were quite jagged, and at that moment I realized that we were depicting a murder. I became very terrified and scared and was really cold. . . .
>
> While we were doing this. . .I wasn't achieving the right facial expressions for the picture so he started telling me stories that depicted pursuits during rape so that I would have the right expressions on my face like the women in the magazines.

(Everywoman 1988: 66)

For feminists, especially in the United States, and also since the late 1970s in Britain, analysing pornography has been an important aspect of developing an understanding of male dominance and specifically the role of male sexual violence and sexuality within this. Analysing pornography has helped us understand the social construction of male and female behaviour within a male supremacist context, and particularly the notions of objectification and fetishisation as applied to women. Analysing pornography has also led feminists to further examine the link between brutality and sexual pleasure in the construction of heterosexuality which Millett also outlined.[9]

Despite the powerful evidence that pornography acts against women's interests, some (socialist and libertarian) feminists are at present arguing against the censorship of pornography, and even for the use of pornography by women in sexual relationships (with men or with women) (Sellen and Young 1987; Segal 1987; *Feminist Review* 1990). The lobby against censorship argues that extending censorship to pornography would more easily allow the state to increase censorship in other areas, and that instead we should be arguing for a general freedom with regard to publication (see Burstyn 1985). But this argument is peculiarly liberal, not radical as it purports to be. 'Freedom' in the present context does not mean the possibility of actual equality. Instead 'freedom' allows freedom only for those who already have greater power, that is white middle-class and heterosexual men. Lack of censorship against pornography is therefore highly unlikely to lead to lack of censorship against other areas of publication. Instead, it is the publication of oppressive material, such as pornography, which is likely to increase. The focus on censorship as the major issue in the debate about pornography is, in any case, a red herring which merely obscures the real issue, that is, male power.

Those who argue in favour of the use of pornography by women in sexual relationships suggest that the use of pornography and the acting out of pornographic scenarios is sexually 'liberating'; that it overcomes the male dominance and female submission inherent in pornography because the women who use pornography in this way are chosing and consenting to do so (see Callifia *et al.* 1986; Hunt 1990). I strongly disagree. It is not possible to overcome oppression by acting out oppressive relationships, as such behaviour merely serves to reinforce existing power divisions. This becomes very clear if we examine the nature of pornography more closely. So what is pornography? According to Helen Longino (1982), pornography is:

> Verbal or pictorial explicit representations of sexual behaviour that have as a distinguishing characteristic 'the degrading and demeaning portrayal of the role and status of the human female as a mere sexual object to be exploited and manipulated sexually'.
>
> (Longino 1982: 28)[10]

The London Rape Action Group extend this definition to highlight the degradation of women as being in the specific interests of men. As they explain:

> Pornography includes all forms of visual and verbal humiliation of women for the sexual titillation of men from Page 3 in the *Sun* (newspaper) to striptease and flagellation movies, plus the exploitation and humiliation of women for economic gain, e.g. advertising, entertainment, etc.
>
> (Katyachild *et al.* 1985: 13)

Thus, pornography not only presents women as subordinate and inferior to men, but it is a specifically sexual subordination – with black women as the most exploited due to the added effect of racism (see Walker 1982: 84-93). In pornography, therefore, as in rape, we see the sexualisation or eroticisation of male–female power relations. Furthermore, pornography presents male–female sexual relations not only as unequal, but as violently so. To recall what Millett argues:

> Patriarchal societies typically link feelings of cruelty with sexuality, the latter often equated both with evil and with power. This is apparent both in the sexual fantasy reported by psychoanalysis and that reported by pornography. The rule here associates sadism with the male ('the masculine role') and victimisation with the female ('the feminine role').
>
> (Millett 1970: 44)

Andrea Dworkin, in one of the most comprehensive studies of pornography, sets out specifically to examine and analyse 'the power of men in pornography' (1981: 9), arguing that the central concern of pornography, its direction, is men and the empowering of men. Women are the means to such empowerment. Dworkin's work, like that of many other feminists, is suggesting that men inhabit a different and primary 'world' to that of women, and where the women's 'world' is defined on male terms. She ends up concluding that 'The first tenet of male-supremacist ideology is that men have this self and that women must, by definition, lack it' (Dworkin 1981: 13).[11] Pornography serves to construct men as powerful and dominant. The central feature of this is the creation or construction of the male self as different and distinct from those who are not men, and this involves seeing women (and children) as objects, external to the male self. It is this process of objectification which feminists generally have recognised as a part of the 'sexism' expressed in many forms, from advertisements to what might be considered more specifically as pornography (see Coward 1982). Dworkin argues that the process of turning women into objects is actually 'cruel', although (as was also seen in the case of rape) objectification of women is usually seen as normal. The cruel objectification by man (sadism) as well as the objectified woman (the masochist) is presented as natural. Thus women are constructed as (eroticised) objects in order that men, by comparison, can be constructed as powerful and dominant subjects.

But more than this, pornography shows that this object/subject dichotomy, or masochism and sadism, has been constructed as a part of normal heterosexual relations. It was suggested in the discussion about rape, that sexual violence appears to be integral to what are, within a male supremacist context, defined as normal male–female sexual relations. Analysing pornography presents a similar picture: that the humiliation and degradation of women found in pornography is a generalised, normal phenomenon.

Lal Coveney *et al.* (1984a) in their article on *Forum* magazine provide numerous examples of how male sadism and female masochism are indeed integral to normal male and female sexual constructs. They also show how such constructs become internalised and thereby part of individual behaviour. *Forum* is a widely available magazine that is not usually considered 'pornographic' in the sense of being about 'exploitative sex', and even *The Times* newspaper has praised *Forum* for being a 'social service' (ibid.: 88). However, Coveney *et al.*'s own research found that the material in *Forum* was explicitly pornographic, that it presented women's role in heterosexual relations as degrading and humiliating, and that *Forum* showed clearly how the distinction between 'normal' heterosexual sex on the one hand and pornography as 'abnormal' or 'perverse' on the other hand, is false. They conclude that:

the sexual relationships which *Forum* illustrates and reinforces
are the dominance and submission relations characteristic of
'normal' heterosexuality from which in the last instance only
men gain; that the sexual attitudes and practices it promotes
normalize sexual practices based on the further humiliation of
women, and that the 'new norms' it establishes (as the magazine of 'sexual liberation') demand not only willing participation of women in their own degradation but, in addition,
their active initiation in it.

(Coveney *et al.* 1984a: 88)

We must not forget that when we talk about sexuality and sexual
practice we are talking about sexual arousal and the central tenet
of Dworkin's discussion of pornography is that the depiction of
women in porn not only shows them in a degraded, humiliated
and thus inferior position to men, but that this is specifically
geared to sexually arouse men: 'Objectification – that fixed
response to the form of another that has as its inevitable consequence erection – is really a value system that has ejaculation as its
inexorable, if momentary, denouement' (Dworkin 1981: 113).
The point is that, within the context of male supremacy, crucial to
the construction and perpetuation of this unequal social order is
the link between male sexual pleasure and male dominance on the
one hand, and the sexual objectification and subordination of
women on the other. In this way, for men, inflicting pain can be
directly linked to feelings of pleasure.

Objectification, as revealed by pornography (but also generally
apparent in male–female relations) presents a number of resultant
paradoxes. Creating woman as a sexual object is meant to ensure
that women become powerless relative to men, but women may
not always accept this situation. Moreover, constructing women as
sexual objects in turn necessitates the construction of male desire
for such objects; although objects are by definition lesser beings to
be despised, and may thus taint the desirer. Yet, Dworkin argues,
pornography helps men to gloss over these problems:

In pornography, men express the tenets of their unchanging
faith, what they must believe is true of women and of themselves
to sustain themselves as they are, to ward off recognition that a
constituent to masculinity is a double-edged commitment to
both suicide and genocide. In life the objects are fighting back,
rebelling, demanding that every breath be reckoned with as the

breath of a living person, not a viper trapped under a rock, but an authentic, willful, living being. In pornography, the object is a slut, sticking daggers up her vagina and smiling.

(Dworkin 1981: 68)

Fetishisation of different parts of women's bodies for the purpose of male sexual arousal is another important aspect or extension of objectification. This may include male sexual arousal from dismembered female bodies; the ultimate example of this being the Snuff movies where women are actually murdered during the production of the film (see ibid.: 71). Importantly, the fetish is valued, not for itself, but 'because it constantly enables penile erection' (ibid.: 127) and thus masculinity is assured. Anything may be fetishised, whether 'bodily part or piece of apparel or substance' (126), although ultimately it is the woman who is constructed as the fetish. To reiterate, pornography is primarily about men and the empowerment of men. Women are the means to such male empowerment, and women as fetish especially so. This eroticisation of inequality is, of course, duplicated by men in relation to other socially inferior groups, children especially and, to some extent also, other men (see Ward 1984). But it is male–female relations which provides the template.

Sexual desire is another important, and related, aspect which we must consider here. Desire is a socially constructed, and powered, concept which is constructed in the interests of men. Paradoxically, it is constructed as a part of the eroticisation of women's subordination, and also makes women accept their subordinate position. As MacKinnon points out

sexual desire in women, at least in this culture, is socially constructed as that by which we come to want our self-annihilation. That is, our subordination is eroticized in and as female; in fact we get off on it to a degree, if nowhere near as much as men do. This is our stake in the system that is killing us.

(MacKinnon 1987c: 57)

Furthermore, femininity, which is the objectified and also eroticised or sexualised construct of women, is specifically heterosexual. Women learn to want to be objects because they are rewarded with the illusion of power, that is, male approval – although this actually negates their possibility of becoming subjects in their own right. Also, women learn to desire men as (dominant) subjects, which only further entrenches their subordi-nate position as objects. Within the context of male supremacy, therefore, women are constructed to be masochists. Justine Jones (1981) discusses this process, drawing on her own experience, and I will briefly refer to her work.

Jones outlines how as a child she played games which linked notions of brutality with notions of the erotic. Later in her life she realised how the associations had become internalised and a part of her sexual make-up, such that images of degradation became a 'turn-on'. In particular she had learnt to find masochism – both image and in practice – as sexually exciting. As she explains:

> In 1969, aged 22, I read 'Story of O' and my horror and disgust was deepened by the then unspoken-for-many-years, ultra-guilty realisation that reading of O's total degradation was to me – a turn-on. Passages from the book came unbidden to my mind when my boyfriend penetrated me and however fast I banished them they worked – I did enjoy it more.
>
> (Jones 1981: 21)

Even so, Justine Jones argues that it is possible to change one's sexuality, including those associations which are apparently erotic, and to create a self-defined female sexuality not based on power but on equality; although this is by no means an easy task, and is probably impossible to complete within the context of male supre-macy: 'until we have ended male supremacy, we won't have a truly self-defined sexuality, full control over our bodies and our lives. It's fighting for this that will end male supremacy' (ibid.: 22).

Jones's analysis of her experience together with the rest of the discussion of pornography presented here, allows us to contem-plate the question of women's rape fantasies. Brownmiller, for instance, points out that women at times fantasise about rape, thus perceiving rape as sexually arousing to themselves. Considering that women are constructed and construct themselves within the context of male supremacy not only to be sexual objects, but to perceive male subjects as sexually desirable, it is not surprising that some women fantasise about rape in the manner indicated by Brownmiller. The fantasy, as well as the sexual desire, are the social products of a male supremacist context. This is also why it is counterproductive for women to endorse, let alone use, porn-ography within sexual relationships. Pornography can in no way be either liberating or empowering for women, as some claim.

Finally, the discussion of male sexual violence, and pornography in particular, allows us to re-evaluate the important point which Sylvia Walby (1990) makes – that pornography is being used as an attempt at maintaining patriarchal power in response to women's encroachment on 'male areas' such as employment. It will be recalled that Walby does not give a detailed analysis of pornography (nor other aspects of male violence), and also that she argues vehemently against MacKinnon's approach in particular. Yet if we apply the analysis presented here, that the eroticisation of male–female relationships, as exemplified by pornography, is fundamental to male domination over women, it also becomes clear that an increase in male sexual violence would be an obvious backlash against female encroachment on male power. The particular focus on pornography, which Walby documents, is not only a product of the specific socio-historical context, but also serves to further increase other sexual violence by men against women, and thereby further degrades and constructs women as inferior.

This brief discussion of rape and pornography has indicated the crucial importance of sexuality within any analysis of male–female power relations, because sexualisation or eroticisation is fundamental to the construction of unequal male–female relations. The discussion within this particular chapter does, however, leave us with a question regarding the link between sexuality and violence. By focusing on issues such as rape and pornography, the resultant impression is that oppressive male–female sexual relations perhaps always exhibit a high degree of violence. This poses the question whether social control of women is necessarily acted out through sexual violence *per se*. The importance of the heterosexual construct to the maintenance and perpetuation of male power has been pointed out in this chapter, but a detailed discussion of what may be described as 'pleasurable heterosexual experience' has not been presented. The following chapter takes this issue further, and thereby also questions the more generalised role of male sexuality in the social control of women.

Chapter 5

A revolutionary feminist approach
Male sexuality as social control of women

INTRODUCTION

Heterosexuality must be recognised as a political institution whereby male sexuality, constructed as the primary (and usually penetrative) sexuality, serves as social control of women in the interests of men. This is the social process which Rich has termed 'compulsory heterosexuality' (1980: 631), and it is a social process where heterosexual intercourse, or coitus, is the primary sexual act (see also Leeds Revolutionary Feminist Group 1981; MacKinnon 1979, 1982; Dworkin 1987). By recourse to analysis of male sexual violence towards women it can be shown that not only does 'normal' heterosexuality, as constructed contemporarily, include sexual violence (the main argument of Chapter 4), but the resultant ideology and also practice of heterosexuality coerces women into acceptance of these oppressive social relations. The outcome, for men, involves a range of benefits including power and status, economic advantage, as well as emotional and domestic servicing (see Hanmer 1978; Rich 1980; Mahony 1985). MacKinnon, in her well-documented study of *Sexual Harassment of Working Women* (1979) shows how this applies within the specific sphere of paid work.

MacKinnon demonstrates how the eroticisation of women, in compliance with the heterosexual 'norm' within male supremacy, is an intrinsic part of women's working conditions. Concomitant to this construct is the expectation, and resultant requirement, that women will 'market sexual attractiveness to men, who tend to hold the economic power and position to enforce their predilections' (1979: 174). In other words, men enforce a heterosexuality which appears to be normal and natural, but which in actual fact acts as coercive harassment towards the women concerned. The result is, in this particular instance, the convergence of the two forces of 'men's control over women's sexuality and capital's control over employee's work lives' (ibid.), but where it is the former which is more important in determining women's subordinate place in paid work. This point is, of course, relevant to the discussion of both Cockburn's and Walby's work (see Chapter 2). But it also has a particular relevance here because of the more generalised process of male domination which this point regarding paid work exemplifies. Women, MacKinnon suggests, learn to endure sexual harassment in order to keep their jobs and at the same time learn to respond in a complaisantly heterosexual way. Sexual harassment becomes normalised and the part this eroticisation of women plays in the generalised oppression of women within male supremacy becomes obscured.

Taking this argument a step further, Rich argues that the issue of how women are maintained in a position of subordination to men is inseparable from the issue of enforced or 'compulsory' heterosexuality. As she concludes:

> when we look hard and clearly at the extent and elaboration of measures designed to keep women within a male sexual parlieu, it becomes an inescapable question whether the issue we have to address as feminists is, not simple 'gender inequality', nor the domination of culture by males, nor mere 'taboos against homosexuality', but the enforcement of heterosexuality for women as a means of assuring male right of physical, economical and emotional access.
>
> (Rich 1980: 647)

It is against this analytical background that the material in this chapter will be examined. Within this context it is also important to reiterate the point made by both Redstockings (1970) and Millett (1970) that male–female relations are conflictual power relations, and that consequently the construction of male and female sexuality in the specific interests of men can by no means be interpreted as 'conspiratorial', or based on a 'conspiracy theory' (Jackson 1987: 75). Instead, the constructs of male and female sexualities are the outcome of the unequal struggle between men and women.[1]

It was suggested earlier, through the examination of feminist analyses concerning rape and pornography, that sexual violence by men against women relies on particular dominant notions about male sexuality. Within such dominant gender ideology, male sexuality appears to be a biologically-based drive, leading men to experience 'uncontrollable sexual urges' which have to be acted out because 'repression' may be harmful (indeed may result in rape). It has been argued that it is men rather than women who rape because female sexuality does not involve such uncontrollable urges or desires. Furthermore, male sexuality is perceived as aggressive while female sexuality is perceived as passive. It is this biologically-based view, variously described as a 'natural model' and a 'hydraulic model' which underlies the legal, or state, interpretation of rape (see Jackson 1984b; Hanmer 1978; MacKinnon 1987a; Stanko 1985). It is argued by Margaret Jackson (1984a, 1984b, 1987) and Sheila Jeffreys (1984, 1985a) that this biologically-based view of sexuality has become the dominant view of sexuality in our society, particularly through the work of the sex researchers, or sexologists, such as Havelock Ellis, Alfred Kinsey, and William Masters and Virginia Johnson. The more recent work of socio-biologists such as Corinne Hutt, Robert Trivers and Edward O. Wilson can be seen to further emphasise the biological basis of human sexual behaviour (Sayers 1982, Bland 1981). The result is a 'scientific' model of sexual behaviour which presents male sexuality, and men generally, as naturally (and thereby inevitably) dominant over women.[2] Despite criticisms of the socio-biological work in particular, this general 'model' may, none the less, be seen to be part of the general taken-for-granted view of sexuality.

Feminists now, as well as in the past, have been at pains to point out the inherent misogynism of 'scientific' or biologistic models of human behaviour generally (see Sayers 1982). None the less, there is still disagreement regarding the extent to which sexual practice may be seen as in some way based on biological desires or drives, rather than as the result of socially-constructed sexual desires. Some feminists suggest, for instance, that there is a female sexuality which it is desirable to 'reclaim' from male influence (see Hamblin 1974; Oakley 1974a; Whiting 1972; Segal 1987). While these contributions generally recognise the influence of social or cultural factors on the expression of female sexuality, the resultant impression is one of a basic and true female sexuality waiting to be discovered. This view was especially prevalent in the debates about sexuality in the early 1970s, but more recently the problem has again become apparent in the work of feminists and others who suggest that sado-masochistic practices (as in pornography) should be considered an acceptable part of both heterosexual, as well as gay male or lesbian sexual practice. They are actually basing their view on an essentialist or 'natural' model of sexuality which suggests that there is a sado-masochistic sexuality in all of us merely waiting to be expressed – although they purport to be criticising this (English *et al.* 1982; Weeks 1982; Vance *et al.* 1984). This has led Jackson to point out how:

> the claim, made by Samois (1979), that such [sado-masochistic] fantasies exist in all of us and should therefore be accepted and expressed, seems to be based on the essentialist position that sexual desires and impulses are given rather than socially constructed, and that it is harmful to repress them.
>
> (Jackson 1984b: 83)[5]

So as to make clear my own, specifically social constructionist, approach there is a brief section in this chapter examining one of the more obviously 'biological' viewpoints: the socio-biological work of, for instance, psychologist Corinne Hutt. Also a brief examination of the work of the sexologists identified earlier, who can be seen as having had (to various degrees throughout this century) a profound influence on the construction of sexuality within western society. In short, it will be shown that both the sexologists and the socio-biologists are, in the guise of 'science', actually expressing particular ideologies concerning gender. The expressly male-oriented approach of these works merely serve to legitimate the sexual constructs at the heart of male supremacy (see Jackson 1984b).

Another concern of this chapter will be to examine how the (male) dominant gender ideology is acted out in practice. In order to do this, writings by men regarding their own experience will be examined, in particular the work of (self-defined) 'anti-sexist' men who have presented critical appraisal of the male sexual construct (Metcalf 1985; Snodgrass 1977; Litewka 1977; Pearson 1984). It is useful to examine the work of 'anti-sexist' men because they themselves suggest that they are critically examining both existing dominant gender constructs, as well as attempting to construct alternative sexual behaviour (Brod 1987a; Hodson 1984; Tolson 1977; Metcalf 1985). Finally, I will briefly examine the feminist response to, and resistance against, male supremacy as exemplified by the notion of 'political lesbianism' (Leeds Revolutionary Feminist Group 1981)

THE SOCIO-BIOLOGICAL CONSTRUCTION OF SEXUALITY[4]

Of major concern to socio-biologists is the effect of evolution on male and female sexual behaviour, and consequently on reproduction (see Hutt 1972; Wilson 1978; Trivers 1972).[5] Because female ova are larger than male sperm, women are deemed by the socio-biologists to have a greater 'parental investment' in both the developing embryo and the eventual child. But survival of male genetic material is not best served by women focusing their energies on a few children bearing a limited amount of genetic material. Instead, male genetic material has a better chance of survival if a man makes numerous women pregnant, that is, if men are promiscuous. It is important to recognise that the implication of this argument is the acceptance of sexual behaviour such as rape and sexual assault by men towards women as the 'natural' result of the male promiscuity and aggression necessary for survival of the species.

The entire framework of the socio-biological work is problematic, and it is instead to social factors that we should look in order to explain male dominance and related effects such as sexual violence. Even on its own terms there are problems with the socio-biological approach: male polygamy is not necessarily advantageous because in Darwinian terms 'Selection favours those individuals who succeed in producing, not the maximum possible number of offspring, but simply more offspring relative to others of their species' (Sayers 1982: 52). Cross-cultural and transhistorical studies suggest in addition that human behaviour is much more varied than that allowed for by the socio-biological view. Socio-biologists such as Hutt consider women's lives and work to be dictated by reproduction. However, while reproduction has probably always been an important part of women's lives, in practice it has more likely been the other activities which women are involved in, such as food production, that actually define what 'motherhood' involves. Flandrin's (1979) study on childhood, for example, shows that the concept of motherhood has changed over time. Women spent less time on the rearing of each child during the feudal period, and it was not even necessarily the biological mother who cared for her children.

Hormonal activity is another sex-specific feature which socio-biologists argue is the result of evolution. Hutt suggests that girls and boys are different physiologically and behaviourally from birth due to the effects of their different sex hormones. The different female and male hormones affect the reproductive system and produce the secondary sex characteristics at puberty. They also have other effects such as determining brain organisation, and Hutt argues that it is the male hormone which plays an active and critical role. 'Male' hormones are also deemed to cause aggressive behaviour. Using studies of rats and monkeys, Hutt argues that aggression is greater in males since the male hormone causes a propensity in the male brain for such behaviour, and males are apparently more aggressive from birth. Studies of school children, showing that boys are more (twice as) aggressive than girls, are used as further evidence for her argument (Hutt 1972: 110–17). 'Ambition' and 'drive' are forms of behaviour also deemed closely related to aggression. Hutt claims that ambition and drive are mainly exhibited by men, and again the behaviour is biologically induced by the presence of male hormones (specifically testosterone in this case).

However, many criticisms may be made of the argument about biological aggression predominating in males or men. Not only can rat studies be deemed irrelevant to human behaviour, but the evidence concerning the impact of 'male' hormone on human behaviour is not at all conclusive (Archer 1978). Furthermore, such comparisons are highly selective and the range of animal behaviour is far wider than they suggest. Rats are more amenable to laboratory experiments, and why should it be assumed that the human male should be compared to them rather than, say, lions or a praying mantis? Instead, the aggressive behaviour Hutt found to be prevalent in boys, rather than in girls, had probably been learned rather than inborn. It is a social expectation that boys should be more aggressive than girls and they are therefore encouraged to be so (Sharpe 1976; Mahony 1985). Females do indeed exhibit aggression, but studies on aggression have tended to be male biased. Moreover, recent work on the link between hormones and behaviour suggests that hormonal levels are likely to be influenced by external social considerations (Birke 1986).

THE SEXOLOGICAL CONSTRUCTION OF SEXUALITY

The work of the early sexologist, Havelock Ellis, was profoundly influenced by, and constituted a response to, the threat to male supremacy posed by the feminist campaigns at the turn of the twentieth century (Jackson 1987; Jeffreys 1982, 1985a). Feminists at the time, realising (in a similar way to feminists of today (see Barry 1981; Jeffreys 1982, 1985a)) that child sexual abuse and prostitution resulted from a particular dominant social view of male sexuality as aggressively dominant, argued that men should control their sexuality. At the height of the militant suffrage campaign this was expressed by the slogan 'Votes for Women, *Chastity for Men*' (Jackson 1984a: 50, my emphasis).

Ellis's work can be seen as providing a new ideological construct regarding sexuality and gender resulting from the material threat of reduction in male sexual power posed by feminists. Importantly, he presented a form of sexuality (specifically heterosexual) where the man is primary, and where the woman should learn to fit with her husband's sexual expression. His analysis suggests that male behaviour such as rape and other sexual violence towards women is both normal and natural. Ironically Ellis himself claimed to be pro-feminist although he was extremely hostile to militant feminism and particularly to the Women's Social and Political Union, led by the Pankhursts (Jackson 1984a: 49).

Ellis was writing at a time when Freud had already begun to theorise about the nature of male and female sexuality, and Ellis built on this work. According to Freud there exists some form of innate sexual drive which, during the socialisation process, is moulded, modified or repressed by the operation of social forces, that is, learning involves the curbing of instinctual urges. Within the context of such Freudian analysis, by early this century the supposedly passive sexuality of Victorian women was considered to be an extreme form of repression of natural sexual urges, an analysis that has given Victorian women the label of 'prudes'. This label was not correct, and many of these women can instead be considered to be resisters against male supremacy (Jeffreys 1985a). Ellis wanted to overcome this supposed 'prudery', and in this way he has been seen as a champion of sexual pleasure, including female sexual pleasure. His work, and the work of the other early-twentieth-century sexologists has thus been regarded as leading everyone out of the 'darkness' of Victorian prudery and sexual repression into the 'light' of twentieth-century existence. But as Jackson argues, while Ellis's view of sexuality was actually a positive step for men, it was not so for women (Jackson 1984a).

So what exactly does Ellis's view of sexuality involve? Central, as outlined in his six-volume *Studies in the Psychology of Sex* (1913), is the existence of biological sexual impulses in both men and women similar to those which he believed could be found in animals. These impulses are seen as distinctly different in the two sexes. In men the instinct is to pursue and conquer the female who, in turn, starts out by acting 'modestly' and appears to reject the man's sexual advances, while actually (if unconsciously) desiring heterosexual coitus. This pursuit and sexual conquest by the man of an apparently unwilling woman is extremely important according to Ellis, since it is specifically the 'modesty' of the woman which arouses male passion. Women who do not exhibit such modesty or 'fear', as he also terms it, are not attractive to men: 'the woman who is lacking in this kind of fear is lacking also, in sexual attractiveness to the normal and average man' (Ellis 1913, vol 1: 1). This also puts women who are powerful outside the bounds of the normal.

What emerges, then, is a picture of a natural and heterosexual sexuality where it is essential that men are dominant, and women submissive. One of the major themes throughout Ellis's work is indeed that of power: 'The notion that normal heterosexual sex is based on a power relation which is biologically determined; masculine domination and female submission are therefore not only inevitable but essential to sexual pleasure' (Jackson 1984a: 53).

If a woman does not want to go through with a particular sex act then in Ellis's terms she is merely being 'modest'. Ultimately her unconscious, if not her conscious, wants the act to take place. In this way it is virtually impossible for any heterosexual act to be seen as rape or assault because the woman always 'asks for it'. If a woman resists male sexual advances, she is in actual fact, according to Ellis, positively wanting coitus. In other words, the more a woman says 'no' to sex with a man, the more she really means 'yes'; and therefore women cannot be believed at face value. But this is only the basis of his thesis. The other major theme, expressed in particular through Ellis's discussion of female 'modesty', or fear, shows that Ellis takes these notions of inequality much further. Indeed he presents all forms of sex, both 'normal' and 'abnormal', as extensions of each other and therefore as normal: '. . . all forms of abnormal sex are merely extensions of the normal; even the most violent and dangerous forms of sexual perversion are ultimately rooted in "innocent and instinctive impulses", and thus, it is implied, harmless and acceptable' (ibid.: 53). This is, of course, in direct contradiction to when Millett, for instance, says that heterosexual constructs are perverse because unequal and therefore *not* alright.

Not only is forced heterosexual intercourse seen by Ellis as inevitable, he also argues that women are highly likely to experience pain as a result. Indeed, he explains that women actually enjoy this resultant pain, just as men find sexual gratification in its infliction. As he states:

> While in men it is possible to trace a tendency to inflict pain, or the simulacrum of pain, on the women they love, it is still easier to trace in women a delight in experiencing physical pain when inflicted by a lover, and an eagerness to subjection to his will. Such a tendency is certainly normal.
>
> (Ellis 1913, vol 1: 68–9)

Thus, the male sadist and female masochist identified by Dworkin (1981) as a central feature of contemporary pornography is presented by Ellis as a biologically-based, and therefore natural, phenomenon. According to Ellis, it is especially women who link pain and pleasure.

Ellis's view of male and female sexuality outlined here is also reflected in the more recent work of Kinsey, and Masters and Johnson, as well as in popular sex manuals and literature, as will be shown below. There remains, however, another important aspect to his view, again reflected more widely, and this is the 'art of love' (Ellis 1913, vol. 3).

As indicated earlier, Ellis was compiling his analysis at a time when the dominant, Victorian, view suggested that on the one hand female sexuality was passive and on the other hand women were virtually without a sexual drive or any sexual desire. Thus women were seen by the Victorians to be congenitally sexually anaesthetic, although this applied only to 'good' women and not 'fallen' women (see Jackson 1984a: 6). Ellis was, of course, arguing contrary to this that women do have strong sexual desires or impulses (which is why he's been seen as 'liberating' female sexuality), although these had become repressed. The reasons for this repression according to Ellis, was partly because husbands failed sexually to arouse their wives and partly as a result of women's failure to merge the sensations of pain and pleasure within coitus. Ellis saw these problems as resulting from basic differences between men and women: women are often slow to arouse while men are often brutal and clumsy. Yet, as Ellis stressed, female sexual repression, or 'frigidity', must be overcome because coitus is essential to marriage, an institution of which Ellis was highly in favour.[6] The answer lay in 'training' for marriage, the aim of which was to teach women to actively participate in, and also to enjoy, coitus. And it was the husband who should be the teacher. As Jackson points out, this may at first seem surprising, considering that Ellis sees husbands as clumsy and brutal. But in respect to his general thesis Ellis was being quite consistent. He suggests, using a musical image from Balzac, who compared the husband to an orang-utan playing the violin, that the husband should play the wife to produce 'sweet and harmonious melodies': 'She [the wife] is, on the wife physical side, inevitably the instrument in love; it must be his [the husband's] hand and his bow which evoke the music' (Ellis 1913, vol 6: 539). Of course, the 'music' would be the particular form of coitus, which Ellis saw as natural. In other words, women were being trained through the 'art of love' to accept a form of heterosexual relations specifically involving female submission and pain, as well as male domination. Jackson suggests, as a result, that the 'art of love' should be more accurately termed the 'art of possession and control' (Jackson 1984a: 65).

Overall Ellis's account of male and female sexuality presents a view which women were arguing against, and creating alternative practice to, at the time. His view denied the feminist critique of male sexual power, as well as any notion of female sexual autonomy, including lesbianism:

> The morbidification of love between women and the orchestration of female sexual pleasure combined to undermine female sexual and emotional autonomy; and, together with scientific legitimation of the idea that sex and power are inseparable, they constituted a powerful ideology, conscripting women into heterosexuality, and thus re-establishing men's right of access to their bodies.
>
> (ibid.)[7]

This 'powerful ideology' was profoundly to influence sexual practice by forming the basis of the highly popular sex manuals, including those of Van de Velde, Marie Stopes and Helena Wright, which have remained popular to the present day (Dworkin 1987; Robinson 1976). In particular, Ellis's 'art of love' has become part of the emphasis in contemporary sex manuals and also sex therapy on 'foreplay' (see Comfort 1975; Masters and Johnson 1966), and is still presented as either an optional extra or substitute for the 'real thing', that is, heterosexual coitus. (It has therefore been suggested that 'foreplay' may more aptly be termed 'conquest by manipulation' (Jackson 1984a: 65.))

In the work of Alfred Kinsey, and William Masters and Virginia Johnson, it may be seen that the important features remain the same as those identified in Ellis's work.[8] These features include: sexual desire as a basic biological drive, which must be satisfied; that the male sexual drive will find satisfaction in illegitimate outlets (for example, rape) if denied legitimate outlets; or if repressed will lead to physical or mental illness (including 'neurosis' in women); that sex is a basic need like food; and that this basic sexual need is based on coitus (see Jackson 1987).

The picture of sexuality which emerges from Kinsey's work, and that of his close colleagues, is of a rather unequal mainly 'natural' heterosexual practice where women should accommodate themselves to the acting out of the more important male sexuality. There is a negation of women's experiences of rape and other sexual assault – experiences which are incorporated within Kinsey's view of normal male sexual practice. For example, even instances of unwanted pregnancy, venereal disease, and physical damage are not seen as especially deleterious effects of heterosexual sex:

> The disturbances which may sometimes follow coitus *rarely depend on the nature of the activity itself*, or upon its physical outcome. An occasional unwanted pregnancy, a rare instance of venereal disease, or a very rare instance of physical damage are about the only undesirable physical after-effects.
>
> (Kinsey *et al.* 1953: 320, my emphasis)

These 'disturbances', according to Kinsey, are more a consequence of women's attitudes than of the way heterosexual sex (a natural act after all) is experienced.

We see, then, in Kinsey's account of sexuality an extension of the concepts used by Ellis and also a marked similarity to the view of rape expressed by the police and legal authorities today regarding women's claims of rape (see J. Radford 1987; L. Radford 1987; Stanko 1985). What is clear is that for Kinsey, as well as for Ellis, the notions of male dominance and female submission, power and violence, are integral to their 'scientific' presentation of sexuality, as is the idea of sexuality as universally male oriented, and they thereby deny the possibility of any autonomous female sexuality.

Kinsey claimed to quantify sexual behaviour, and thus accurately ('objectively' and 'scientifically') to describe this. His material was largely based on interviews, which, as has later become apparent from his biography by his colleague Wardell Pomeroy (1972), were rather unreliable. For example, he obtained data on the sexual behaviour of a large number of children purely through interviewing a man who claimed to have had sexual relations (homosexual and heterosexual) with them and there was no attempt to follow up these claims.

Kinsey sees both male and female sexual response as physiological, although psychological responses are also important and these differ in male and female. There is an ambiguity, however, regarding the extent to which sexual responses are either instinctual or conditioned (Jackson 1984b: 75). In particular, female attitudes towards sex are deemed to have a biological basis, whereas men are easily conditioned and therefore easily aroused sexually by the, what he considered to be, 'ever present' erotic 'stimuli' around him, in particular, women (Dworkin 1981: 182). According to Kinsey, men have a higher sex drive than women, but due to restrictions placed on men by women, men's sexuality is not acted out to its fullest extent. Considering animal sexual activity as the norm which human behaviour should be expected to mimic, he concludes that for men: 'average frequencies of sexual outlet are distinctly below those which are normal among some other anthropoids and which would probably be normal in the human animal if there were no restrictions upon his sexual activity' (Kinsey *et al.* 1948: 468). He also considers that, if 'unrestricted', the human male would be promiscuous.

Kinsey states that it is women, partly because of their low sex drive, who restrict men's natural sexual activity, sometimes, apparently, even with the support of the state. For instance, women may be granted divorce due to 'the coital frequencies which the husband had demanded' (Kinsey *et al.* 1953: 369). But, despite her low sex drive, Kinsey reckons that it is quite possible for a woman to enjoy heterosexual intercourse (which is why his work has been hailed as 'liberatory' for women), and especially to enjoy providing her husband with pleasure. Kinsey is suggesting, then, that fulfilment of male sexuality is the more important, and that women should orientate themselves specifically to male sexual pleasure. In this way the wife and the prostitute are also seen by Kinsey as being similar (ibid.: 595). Any attempt by women to assert some form of female sexual autonomy is consequently rejected as an attempt by women to restrict men (see Dworkin 1981: 184).

Since for Kinsey the 'problem area' of sexuality is specifically women's reactions and actions, rather than those of men, he also concludes that rape is usually a false claim made by women against an otherwise harmless act carried out by a man. It is interesting to note that Kinsey did not find evidence of either marital rape or wife battery; while he did find 'several instances of wives who half murdered their husbands because they insisted on mouth–genital contacts' (Kinsey *et al.* 1948: 578). Thus it is the accused rapist whom he presents as the unfortunate victim, for example:

> Many small girls reflect the public hysteria over the prospect of 'being touched' by a strange person [sic]; and many a child, who has no idea at all of the mechanics of intercourse, interprets affection and simple caressing from anyone except her own parents, as attempts at rape. In consequence, not a few older men serve time in penal institutions for attempting to engage in a sexual act which at their age would not interest most of them, and of which many of them are undoubtedly incapable.
>
> (ibid.: 238)

Another important point made by Kinsey (and also made implicitly by Ellis) is that there is no such thing as 'abnormal' male (or female) sexuality. Instead, he argues that all male sexual behaviour is merely an extension of the norm. For Kinsey there are no sexual perversions.[9] If one does not accept inequality between men and women as biologically determined, and accepts social equality as the aim of the Women's Liberation Movement (as I do), then a male sexual construct allowing exploitation of women by men must be seen as a perversion.

While both Ellis and Kinsey presented men's sexual potential as greater than that of women, William Masters and Virginia Johnson,[10] in their laboratory-based research, argue that women actually have a much greater orgasmic potential than men. The earlier sex research located female sexual pleasure largely in the vagina, and penile penetration of this, but Masters and Johnson argue that women's multi-orgasmic potential is specifically related to clitoral rather than vaginal stimulation:

> The clitoris is a unique organ in the total of human anatomy. Its express purpose is to serve both as a receptor and transformer of sexual stimuli. Thus the female has an organ system which is totally limited in physiologic functioning to initiating or elevating levels of sexual tension. No such organ exists within the anatomic structure of the human male.
>
> (Masters and Johnson 1966: 45)

In this sense, the female clitoris is uniquely pleasure-oriented, rather than playing any role in human reproduction as is the case with the vagina. Not only do women have a sexual organ not related to reproduction, but according to Masters and Johnson, the clitoral orgasm is most likely to be achieved through (self) manipulation rather than through coitus. Therefore, by comparison to Ellis and Kinsey, Masters and Johnson initially appear to be presenting an entirely different account of sexuality, emphasising a greater sexual potential in women than in men, and also suggesting that female sexual expression without coitus is much more sexually fulfilling for women. As Patricia Miller and Martha Fowlkes point out, Masters and Johnson appear to be providing 'the ultimate testimony to the autonomy of female sexuality' (Miller and Fowlkes 1980: 788). It is this aspect of Masters and Johnson's work which feminists have hailed as liberatory for women, and have used to validate their own experience of female sexual pleasure, whereby it is clitoral stimulation and not penile penetration which is important (see Hamblin 1974; Whiting 1972; Koedt 1970).

However, despite their 'scientific' findings, Masters and Johnson ultimately reject the prime importance of clitoral orgasm in women, and instead argue that it is the vagina and, in particular, penile penetration of the vagina, which constitutes the ultimate sexual act. This they relate to the essentially reproductive function of the vagina, and argue that the function of clitoral stimulation is merely to prepare the vagina for penetration, a preparation which at the same time serves for the male as the 'psychologic demand to mount' (Masters and Johnson 1966: 69). They suggest that it is ultimately the role of the man to provide both his own and the woman's orgasm through penile penetration: 'The functional role of the penis is that of providing an orgasmic means for physiologic and psychologic increment and release of both male and female sexual tensions' (ibid.: 188). Thus clitoral stimulation may be seen as merely another form of 'foreplay' or 'art of love'. Masters and Johnson's work, therefore, although apparently suggesting that male sexual pleasure does not rely on penile penetration, let alone heterosexuality, actually stresses that women are after all intrinsically heterosexual and reliant on penile penetration for sexual pleasure, including orgasm.

While their work is seemingly very different from that of Ellis and Kinsey, Masters and Johnson similarly stress the inherent naturalness of heterosexuality, a naturalness based on their collective view of sex as ultimately reproductive (Jackson 1984b: 73). Yet even in terms of Masters and Johnson's own 'scientific' methodology, they can easily be accused of falsifying their laboratory data. Indeed, it may be argued that their evidence gives us greater insight into the way people actually 'do sex' at the present time, rather than what sexual relationships involve. The context and quality of the relationship, that is, the social factors, are likely to be more important to sexual fulfilment than merely technique. As a result, Miller and Fowlkes stress that Masters and Johnson's view is not about biological sexual functioning but about control of women, so that 'Women's sexuality has again been reined in to conform to traditional heterosexual expectations' (Miller and Fowlkes 1980: 788).

Overall, the different sexological work, while based on somewhat spurious methodologies, presents a view of male and female sexuality which is specifically heterosexual and unequal, focusing on coitus, with male sexuality primary. This is despite the fact that even Masters and Johnson have found that women obtain greater sexual pleasure from autonomous clitoral stimulation. There have obviously been some changes in the sexologists' approaches over time, notably the change between Ellis and Kinsey on the one hand, and Masters and Johnson on the other regarding the frequency as well as extent of female sexual expression. None the less, all the theories examined here present women as essentially reliant on men for sexual pleasure, particularly orgasm.[11] While the sex research is presented as 'scientific', it actually rests on normative assumptions regarding a 'natural' and male-dominant heterosexuality. The constructions of sexuality, as presented by the sexologists, may more accurately be viewed in the context of compulsory heterosexuality and the control of women:

> the sexologists have constructed a model of sexuality which both reflects and reproduces the interests of male supremacy; in other words, that the particular form of male sexuality that exists under male supremacy has been 'neutralized' and 'universalised'.
>
> (Coveney *et al.* 1984b: 11)

I now want to turn to the male anti-sexist literature, to show how they respond to the dominant sexual and gender constructs already outlined, and how these are acted out in practice.

ANTI-SEXIST MEN AND THE SOCIAL CONSTRUCTION OF SEXUALITY

Since the early 1970s in Britain there has been an ongoing, if not regular, debate amongst a number of men regarding men and sexism.[12] This debate has come about largely as a direct result of feminist critique of male behaviour and assertion that the 'personal is political'. I do not wish to discuss the composition or nature of the so-called 'men's movement' here, but focus on attempts by anti-sexist men to analyse male oppressive behaviour including their experience of male sexuality.

From the earlier male anti-sexist literature, one point stands out particularly strongly – the centrality of male sexuality to men's perception of themselves as masculine (a point also borne out more generally by *The Hite Report on Male Sexuality*, Hite 1981). Male sexuality, as discussed in the literature, is specifically and explicitly concerned with penile erection and penile penetration. Some of the male anti-sexist writers identify this sexual focus as a phenomenon which they have learnt as a result of, and in the context of, male supremacy, and argue as a result that male sexuality must be critically examined and changed. These are the concerns, for example, of John Stoltenberg's article 'Refusing to be a Man' (1977) and Jack Litewka's article 'The Socialised Penis' (1977).

Stoltenberg argues how 'Refusing to be a Man' means that a male genital functioning, which relies on inevitable or uncontrollable male orgasm/ejacualtion and on the importance of erection, must be rejected. He explains that commonly-held beliefs regarding both male orgasm and male erection are lies, resulting from 'our male-dominated, female victimizing sexual politics' (Stoltenberg 1977: 38). The lie of male orgasm, Stoltenberg explains, is that male orgasm and male ejaculation are perceived as the same thing. His own experience is that these phenomena are actually separate:

> In my experience, orgasm and ejaculaton are not the same. In my experience there is a male orgasm separate and distinct from ejaculation, and these non-ejaculatory orgasms can be multiple. . . . Ejaculation is another phenomenon. Sometimes ejaculation happens also, but I have come to mistrust my conditioning which identifies the so-called 'necessity of ejaculation' as being part of a scenario of male sexual success and satisfaction. In fact and in the truth of my body, ejaculation is something else. I have learned that if I have strived for ejaculation, or put effort into ejaculating in any way, the result is a rather uncomfortable refractory period – which I take to be the body's message that I strove inauthentically to achieve some cultural lie about 'release of sexual tension'.
>
> (ibid.: 38–9)

What Stoltenberg is saying then, regarding male orgasm and ejaculation, is that, physiologically, there are other types of sexual fulfilment and pleasure besides ejaculation and that, indeed, ejaculation in the context of male orgasm may be forced. Similarly, he argues that male erections are culturally defined as an expression of male sexual arousal, but that, in terms of his experience, especially hard erections may be anything but pleasurable. Instead hard erections are about power:

> The lie is that rigidity means arousal, rigidity means power, rigidity means manhood, and rigidity means the urgency for something called 'release of sexual tension'. In fact, I now believe, rigidity is usually a symptom of tension artificially induced (I say 'usually' because I am discounting those rigid erections which occur naturally in males when the bladder is very full).
>
> The truth is that bone-hard erections aren't very comfortable.

They stick out from your body and are painful if bent. And they feel a little dead.

(Stoltenberg 1977: 40)

He concludes that erections 'function in fucking very well, in that they are good for rape. But the idea that they feel good – that they are sensate – is only a cultural illusion' (ibid.).

Thus Stoltenberg is suggesting that in physiological terms male sexuality is a different phenomenon than the way it is typically expressed within the context of western male supremacy. Whether he has actually discovered, or uncovered, a natural male sexuality is speculative. But there is no doubt that in terms of his own experience the expression of male sexuality is primarily a question of learning and not biology. Stoltenberg himself argues that the reason men learn certain types of sexual behaviour rather than others is because, in terms of men's interests of perpetuating male power over women, focus on ejaculation and hard erections is particularly useful. This is also, he suggests, why male sexual 'impotence' is perceived as a problem in our society:

what's called 'impotence' is another internalization of a perverse system of male-dominant cultural values. Men (and women) are taught to believe that a cock is either limp and dysfunctional or erect and functional, and anything in between doesn't have sense unless it's clearly on its way to erection or legitimately on its way to limpness (a legitimacy which can be presumed only if ejaculation has been achieved).

(ibid.: 39–40)

Like Stoltenberg, Litewka discusses the expression of male sexuality as a product of learning within a powered gender context. In his article he describes his attempt to understand the construction of his own sexuality. He became concerned about this when his penis would not erect on three separate occasions when sleeping with women. Usually it always did so. I do not want to discuss his 'impotence' at this point, but will do so later on. At present I want to outline male sexuality as Litewka sees it and examine this in relation to the sexual constructs provided by the sexologists.

Litewka explains that generally sex for men has developed in such a way that it has become 'performance orientated' (and specifically heterosexual). He explains that the general aim is to get an erection and to ejaculate into a woman. In other words, penile penetration is the ultimate conquest. The process leading up to this is also very important. Litewka expresses this process as 'Objectification, and Fixation'. Objectification to make a woman into 'a concept, a lump sum, a thing, an object, a non-individualized category'; fixation on 'portions of the female anatomy' to make her even more distant and unreal (Litewka 1977: 22–4). Most men need this process, he argues, including anti-sexist men, to get an erection, because that is the way they have learnt to do it. Furthermore, objectification and fixation (or fetishisation) of the woman is integral to this dominance/submission scenario, a scenario very similar to that which I identified in my discussion of sexology and also pornography.

So what are the implications of this sexual construct in heterosexual relationships? Litewka discusses this in terms of the three instances mentioned earlier; showing also how in practice men may actually use other sexual means of controlling women rather than merely the process of 'Objectification, Fixation and Conquest'. He explains that he was surprised to experience 'impotence' on three occasions (with different women) because he really wanted to be in the relationships and therefore expected the arousal to give him an erection. As he says: 'I was with women I wanted to be with and who wanted to be with me, when there was mutual attraction and social/political/intellectual compatibility' (Litewka 1977: 19). He tried to understand why he could not have an erection with these particular women. At first he decided that his respect for these women did not allow him to go through the process of objectification, fixation and conquest. But then, discussing it with a woman, he had to agree that his 'impotence' was much more complex than that, and was in fact an insidious attempt at regaining sexual control. It was a result of feeling threatened by women who were feminists, and he held on to *sexual* control as his last bastion of power. He explains this as follows:

> I was able to accept these women on all levels as equals. Except on one level: I was not capable of accepting females as sexual equals. I held onto this bastion of male supremacy with a death-grip. I was willing to deal with these women on a human (rather than male-to-female) basis, except in relating to them sexually, where I still had to deal with them on an objectify, fixate and conquer basis. But since I couldn't objectify them, I rejected

these women rather than give up my last heirloom of maleness. I totally refused to allow them to sexually stimulate or arouse me.

(Litewka 1977: 27)

In order for Litewka to have an erection with women he respected and therefore could not objectify, he thus had to change his sexual behaviour. In order not to be oppressive, his new sexual behaviour was supposed to incorporate getting aroused without exerting power over women, but that is what he could not contemplate. So his reaction was not to be aroused by them sexually in any way, and taking control over the situation once more by making the women feel inadequate at the same time. What Litewka's story implies is that men may behave sexually in very different ways – from super-stud to impotent – and still exert sexual control over women.

What I outlined earlier as the 'sexological construct of male sexuality' is a successful means by which men may sexually control women, but Litewka's story shows that it is by no means the only way. Yet it is the arena of sexual relations which is crucial in the struggle between men and women over power; as Litewka says, the sexual level was the only level on which he could not accept women as equals. In this sense, Litewka's and other anti-sexist men's work, underlines that it is at the level of male–female sexual relations we may locate the dynamic of male domination.[13]

By using some further material from anti-sexist men, I want to explore in greater detail the issue of control through male sexuality which Stoltenberg and especially Litewka identify. I want to focus on two areas: the role of objectification and fetishisation (or 'fixation'), and control through change. By examining the role of pornography in anti-sexist men's lives we can see how these men experience the contradiction of attempting to decrease their power as members of the male ruling class. It is apparent from the literature that many anti-sexist men need to objectify and fixate on women in order to get an erection. They may use sexual fantasies or pornography to achieve arousal with, or without, women. As Litewka points out: 'What pornography does is to create a fertile environment that makes it 'natural' for the imagination to objectify, fixate on, and conquer a verbally or photographically depicted female' (Litewka 1977: 24).

In issue 12 of the *Anti Sexist Men's Newsletter* (1980) a group of

anti-sexist men talk about how pornography makes them feel
sexually aroused. They perceive their feelings as a dilemma since
porn, with its images of degradation and violence to women, is
oppressive to women. Yet they enjoy, and want to be able to
continue to enjoy, the feelings that pornography conjures up in
them, as the following quotes show:

> – I enjoy having pornographic material available when in
> private – although of course it can't be left around in case
> someone finds it, and it can't be bought as that's subsidizing its
> production.
> – I can never quite control the urge to look inside girlie books
> in our local bookshop, but I catch my eyes wandering over those
> black knickers and big tits and buy the sweets for the kids.
> Mixture of self-righteous superiority and hypocrisy, as I would
> not mind a look at the explicit pictures. Fascinated by those
> involving erections with women in all sorts of get-ups. Never
> seen a blue film. Somehow feel ideologically uncertain about
> being caught or being excited by it not to make the effort.
>
> (Reynell 1980: 11)

These men know there is something 'bad' about porn because
they have heard feminist criticism and anger at it, but they do not
really want to stop thinking about it or stop fantasising about
women with 'big tits'. Porn and sexual fantasy is still an integral
part of these anti-sexist men's sexuality. It helps them to objectify
women and fixate on areas of women's bodies so that they can feel
more powerful. It helps them feel that at least they have sexual
power over women when their power is being threatened in other
ways by feminists.

Pornography is thus an integral part of relationships which, at
least some, anti-sexist men are in, even if, as in the case of Paul
Horobin, they are more aware of the oppressive implications. As
he says:

> my eye is still caught by the nudes on the bookstand and I feel
> angry about them invading my life, plying me with images and
> fantasies to throw when I make love with a woman, a whole
> person and reducing me to the rapist.
>
> (Horobin 1980: 12)

I have pointed out elsewhere how pornography, and the objectification it entails and allows, poses a particular problem for

anti-sexist men, because it enables them to continue to oppress women in an invisible way and thus to avoid challenging the basis of their oppressive sexuality (Hester 1984). In this way, heterosexual sex which women consent to is in actual fact a part of women's oppression. It is for this reason that feminists have questioned the viability, for women, of heterosexual relationships. It is not the intention here to suggest that men cannot change. On the contrary, it is possible for men to change, including giving up their power as a group. What the material by anti-sexist men suggests, however, is that even these men are extremely reluctant to give up their power over women, or find this very difficult. This is illustrated further by an article in the newsletter *Achilles Heel*, where it is indicated (unintentionally) how change in men's sexual behaviour can merely hide attempts at further control of women by men.

The article is a transcript of a discussion about male sexuality by a group of men at East London Men's Centre. One of the men, B, describes what happened to him:

> like most men in this room I suppose, the women that I fuck with are mainly feminists and so my approach is always to try and not be your typical male and always taking the initiative and going for a good hard bang – but being gentle and caring, because that's what I thought would be acceptable to a feminist woman. But then I met a woman to whom that approach was a fuck up. It wasn't what she wanted at all and it turned her off me. And we talked about it and it was really a big down for me. I was compared badly with this other bloke she was off with. In fact he's a bit of a male chauvinist but as far as fucking goes that's what she wants.
>
> (East London Men's Centre 1978: 30)

The material suggests that B initially changed his sexual behaviour so that he would stay in favour with feminists. He then decided that being 'gentle and caring' was his new-found sexuality, because it 'was more in tune with my approach to fucking' (ibid.: 30). Feeling quite self-congratulatory that he had tackled his formerly oppressive sexual behaviour, he felt a 'really big down' when he was unable to impose this new sexuality on another woman. His anger at this woman comes out when he talks about the other relationship which she is involved in. Thus he puts her down for having a relationship with 'a bit of a male chauvinist' rather than with him. The guy who usurped B may well be 'a bit of a male chauvinist', but that is not the point. The fact is that B only appears to allow women to act sexually in the way *he* decides is all right or right on. He seems to be ultimately motivated to change by self-interest, that is, wanting to 'fuck with feminists', rather than concern to overcome women's oppression.

In the article the discussion at the Men's Centre continues around what B has said, and about whether he should have told the woman to change her sexual behaviour. Another of the men points out that it is probably 'too domineering' to tell women what to do. But one of the other men present comes up with a very interesting suggestion of how to get round the problem of being obviously dominating, and yet still being able to manipulate women the way they want. He explains how 'Rather than saying "Right, you're doing it wrong" you could say "Well, I like it different" and then see if they do change' (ibid.: 31). In these ways even men claiming to be 'anti-sexist', and thereby anti-women's oppression, are able to impose their (still) oppressive sexual behaviour on women. Anti-sexist men may merely be using more insidious means to control women than do their 'sexist' counterparts.

The material regarding anti-sexist men referred to so far has mainly been written during the 1970s. During the 1980s there appears to have been a move by anti-sexist men away from discussion and description of their personal experience, to discussion of more generalised concepts regarding masculinity and women's oppression (see Brod 1987a; Metcalf and Humphries 1985; Hearn 1987; Eardley 1985; Moye 1985). This trend has been compounded by the development of the 'new men's studies' as an academic discipline (see Brod 1987b). It is interesting to note that in the more recent literature there is a reluctance to discuss the personal links between male sexuality and power indicated in the earlier work. Instead the contributions focus on the detrimental effects which the contemporary construct of male sexuality has on men, and the material tends to suggest that the main benefactors of this oppressive construct is capitalism rather than men (see Moye 1985; Eardley 1985). Indeed, many of the contributions are directly critical of radical feminism in particular, for instance, categorically rejecting Andrea Dworkin's work on male sexual violence as biologically determinist, often without even discussing what her work entails (Carrigan *et al.* 1987; Eardley 1985; Moye 1985).

There is no doubt that masculinity and male sexuality as constructed within contemporary male supremacy has limiting and possibly detrimental effects on men. But focusing on such effects without also looking in detail at the ways men use sexual constructs to maintain power over women, leads the writers concerned to abnegate their responsibility for constructing and perpetuating male supremacy. As I indicated earlier, this has led Andy Moye (1985), for example, to suggest that pornography is possibly more detrimental to men than it is to women. He argues that women are presented in a manner relatively positive to that of men, at least in so-called 'soft porn'. For men, Moye argues, pornography is an attempt to cover up the actual fragility of male sexual identity and it is the capitalist pornographers who are the overall winners. As he explains:

> Ultimately then, the subordination of women to the thrusts of masculine sexuality doesn't pay off, even within the pages of pornography. Men might set the rules, but women are shown to come out 'enjoying it most'. The gap never closes between the magic attempt to possess pleasure in the body of a woman and the continual elusiveness of that pleasure, even while possessing an erection. The whole circular process just spins on and on under its own momentum.

He concludes:

> Being 'in control' of phallic desire allows men the possession of the means of their own alienation; the pornographers are on hand to sell us the message that this is what we most desire.
>
> (Moye 1985: 58)

Despite Moye's intentions, his focus on male fragility in relation to pornography leads him to present actual male experience in a way not dissimilar to that of pornographers. According to Moye, men are fragile rather than strong. This is part of what Jeffreys calls 'the old power game of heterosexual courtship' (Jeffrys 1987: 88), and which Dworkin outlines in terms of men's fear. Dworkin argues that men are afraid that they are unable to maintain power over women, and as a result:

> The fear that what men have suppressed in women will emerge to destroy them makes the control of women an urgent and absolute necessity. Men dare to claim not only that they are

fragile but that the power of women over them is immense and real.

(Dworkin 1981: 65)

By focusing on male fragility, and by not dealing with the question of power in male–female relations, Moye ends up by merely perpetuating existing male supremacist ideas regarding male–female power relations. Despite claims to the contrary, such anti-sexist men are thus presenting a 'backlash' against feminism, rather than support against women's oppression.

Examination of the male anti-sexist material makes apparent that the sexual constructs identified in the sexological literature forms a part of at least some anti-sexist men's sexual practice. The male anti-sexist material also suggests the central importance of objectification and related to this, fetishisation, in the social control and oppression of women and significantly, this is also apparent more generally in circumstances of 'consensual' sex between men and women.

So far in this chapter my analysis has focused on heterosexual relations, presenting such male–female sexual relations as the crucial site of struggle between men and women. But this also begs the question whether sexual relations other than heterosexual, that is, gay or lesbian, are entirely exempt from the oppressive male supremacist power relations, and I will briefly address this.

LESBIANS AND GAY MEN

Sexuality is socially constructed, including lesbianism and homosexuality. This has been increasingly recognised in recent years, partly as a result of the work of Foucault and others in a similar tradition (Foucault 1979, Weeks 1981), and partly as a result of the feminist critique of heterosexuality as an oppressive institution for women (Rich 1980; Leeds Revolutionary Feminist Group 1981; Kitzinger 1987; Dworkin 1987). We must also recognise that people's lives generally are structured and affected by male supremacy, and that male supremacist relations are acted out in practice. Lesbian and homosexual relations are not immune from this context. But, as discussed in Chapter 3, men and women as sex classes have different experiences of living within a male supremacist society, because men generally (whatever their behaviour, economic class or race) are members of the oppressor class while women generally are oppressed. As a result, in political terms, that is, in terms of power, male–male relationships on the one hand and female–female relations on the other are likely to involve somewhat different elements of power. This is why feminists have provided critiques of the maintenance and perpetuation of male power by gay men while arguing at the same time that lesbianism can be perceived as resistance against male supremacy (Hester *et al.* 1980; Stanley 1982; Leeds Revolutionary Feminist Group 1981; Wood 1981; Rich 1980; Jeffreys 1990). The important issue here is not sexual preference, but power. Other differences such as those of race and economic class are also important, but do not detract from the point I am making.

In a study of gay men on the left, myself, Margaret Jackson, Pat Mahony and Jackie Plaster found (by using interviews and examination of literature by the men concerned), that the male–female power relations which are integral to male supremacy are closely reflected, and reinforced, by gay men. We found that the dominant male sexual construct which I have already discussed was important to the self-identity of these men, and that penetrative sex formed an important part of this – as in the case of heterosexually-defined men. We concluded that for gay men on the left, whom we might perhaps have expected to be critical of male power, sex is still essentially about power, and specifically about power in relation to other men (Hester *et al.* 1980: 27). As one of the men themselves pointed out: 'Sex is some form of personal power for me. It is three things: consolidation, it shows you can still do it; confirmation, cementing friendships, etc.; affirmation, *making me three steps higher*' (ibid.: 28, my emphasis). Stoltenberg argues similarly that gay men's relationships tend to incorporate the power-relations of heterosexuality, and links gay male behaviour to sado-masochism, or the eroticisation of power. Such gay male behaviour is directly oppressive to women:

> Gay men do not simply like other men; they have demonstrated through their anti-feminism that they are like other men. Licensed by their movement, which has brought homoerotic sadomasochism out of the closet (but which has not changed much else), the gay male subculture now abounds with neo-Nazi uniforms, torture toys, orgy bars, piss-and-shit shows, fist fucking shows, films and periodicals portraying torture and

mutilation – all of which is tantamount to spitting in the faces of women who are struggling to be free.

(Stoltenberg 1982: 124)

Sheila Jeffreys (1990) has catalogued a vast array of similarly oppressive sado-masochistic behaviour by gay men. The Acquired Immune Deficiency Syndrome (AIDS), which in the West has affected many gay men, has no doubt changed or tempered some of these behaviours. The question is whether they have actually moved away from opressive sexual practices or merely instituted new ones. I would suggest the latter: the practice of safe sex is not necessarily the same as the practice of non-oppressive sex (see also Shiers 1988).

Stoltenberg makes a distinction between sadism and masochism as acted out by men, and sadism and masochism as acted out by women. Following on from Dworkin's analysis of sadism and masochism as 'The eroticisation of violence' and 'the eroticisation of powerlessness' respectively, he argues that it is usually men who are defined as sadistic and women who are defined as masochistic within male supremacist culture. Thus men may at times, with either women or with other men, appear to be acting in a masochistic manner. But this has different implications from masochism as acted out by women. As he explains:

> In some homosexual males, there does exist an erotic drive toward pain and abuse at the hands of other men, but that drive differs significantly from female masochism. Women who are powerless in this male-supremacist culture, are often driven to literal destruction (out of romantic 'love', out of economic necessity), but male homosexuals have the option of eroticizing their powerlessness relative to other men with quite different consequences.

(Stoltenberg 1982: 126–7)

Where heterosexuality is concerned Stoltenberg explains that masochism in men is very rare. Some men might pay women to 'insult or spank them'. But these are not actually masochistic men, instead 'the sexual behaviour of such men is a varient of normal phallocentric domination and economic control' (ibid.: 127). He also outlines the process of eroticisation of powerlessness *between* men, showing again how this differs from the eroticisation of women's powerlessness:

A male homosexual may regard another man as one who possesses more masculinity (which is more power in the culture), and in the course of meeting that man's sexual demands, he may imagine that man's power becoming incorporated into himself. The male homosexual is assumed to be masochistic when he chooses to ingest the masculinity of men who are objectively dangerous, hostile, or violent. But in this woman-hating culture, his longing is not analogous to the female's drive toward destruction because the male homosexual's drive to incorporate manliness functions as a means of dissociating himself from the inferior status of the female – whereas the masochism of a woman functions to fix her in that state.

(Stoltenberg 1982: 127)

In this way male–male relationships are distinctly different from female–female relationships in terms of power, and although mimicking heterosexual relationships, male–male relationships actually involve different power dynamics.

Recognising this distinction between male–male and female–female relationships, in 1979 the Leeds Revolutionary Feminist Group wrote a conference paper on 'Political lesbianism: the case against heterosexuality', arguing that for women lesbianism is a positive political choice and act of resistance against male supremacy.[14] The paper caused a furore because in arguing that sexuality is socially constructed rather than a biological fact, and challenging the taken-for-granted assumption that heterosexuality is natural, it goes on to suggest that all feminists both could and should be political lesbians.[15] A 'political lesbian' is defined, specifically in relationship to men, as 'a woman-identified-woman who does not fuck men' (1981: 5). Prioritising women is thus seen as incompatible with engaging in heterosexual relationships, due to the oppressive construction of male sexuality within male supremacy. In recognition of this oppressive context for women, and the resultant power imbalance between men and women, the Leeds Revolutionary Feminist Group later changed their definition of 'political lesbian' to 'Women who, by withdrawing their energy and support from men, have put women first' and 'In so doing they have found that it is incompatible with sleeping with men' (ibid.: 67).

In a section of the paper entitled 'What heterosexuality is about and why it must be abandoned', the Leeds Group explain in greater detail this reason for emphasising political lesbianism, arguing that in heterosexual relationships men can most intimately and therefore intensively reinforce their oppression of women:

> Only in the system of oppression that is male supremacy does the oppressor actually invade and colonise the interior of the body of the oppressed. Attached to all forms of sexual behaviour are meanings of dominance and submission, power and powerlessness, conquest and humiliation. There is very special importance attached to sexuality under male supremacy when every sexual reference, every sexual joke, every sexual image serves to remind a woman of her invaded centre and a man of his power.
>
> (Leeds Revolutionary Feminist Group 1981: 5)

They conclude that 'it is specifically through sexuality that the fundamental oppression, that of men over women, is maintained' (ibid.: 5). The emphasis of the paper is therefore on woman-identification and withdrawal from sex with men, which, however, does not necessarily mean compulsory sexual activity with women. Recognising that sexual desire is socially constructed, they point out that it is as possible for a woman to desire another woman sexually as it is for her to desire a man.

But, if women are to be political lesbians are they not merely substituting one power relationship for another? This is a crucial question to which the Leeds Group respond that, although relationships between women may exhibit power imbalances, this is by no means similar to the power relations between men and women, because only men are always backed up by their generally superior sex-class position. As they explain: 'the power of one woman is never backed up by a superior sex-class position. Struggles between women do not directly strengthen the oppression of all women or build up the strength of men' (ibid.: 8). However, they also recognise that lesbian relationships may not be a 'rose garden' either: 'Personal perfection in relationships is not a realistic goal under male supremacy. Lesbianism is a necessary political choice, part of the tactics of our struggle, not a passport to paradise' (ibid.: 8). As can be seen, it is not sexual preference which is the important issue here, but political resistance against male supremacy, and it is this political implication which has resulted in much hostility to the ideas expressed by the Leeds Group (see Wood 1981; Kitzinger 1987; Jeffreys 1990). As Jessica Wood responds in agreement with the paper, it is not women making love to women, or sexual preference, which is deemed frightening, but the fact that lesbianism threatens male supremacy at its roots (1981: 54).[16]

In recent years revolutionary feminists have also argued fervently against sado-masochism in lesbian relationships. For lesbianism to be an effective resistance against male supremacy, it is crucial to resist such eroticisation of power between lesbians, including resistance to the acting out of so-called 'butch' and 'femme' roles (see Jeffreys 1987).

Male sexuality, as it is constructed within contemporary male supremacist society, is a means of controlling women socially in the interests of men. While Chapter 4, concerning sexual violence, showed how a specifically violent male sexuality acts to socially control women's lives, the material in this chapter shows in addition that this phenomenon is more generalised, and that male sexuality, both 'normal' and 'abnormal', in heterosexual and homosexual contexts, fulfils the same function. To summarise: in the contemporary socio-historical context, heterosexual relations are crucially important to the construction, maintenance and perpetuation of male power over women, and women's oppression relies on the eroticisation of female subordination. In the following chapters it will become apparent that this analysis may also be applied in other socio-historical contexts.

Chapter 6

The early modern witch-hunts I

INTRODUCTION

The central feature of male supremacy as it exists today is the eroticised inequality between men and women. Taking the early modern witch-hunts as the focus, I will examine how this understanding of inequality between men and women may also be relevant to analysis of historical phenomena.[1] I have chosen to focus on the period of the early modern witch-hunts (during the sixteenth and seventeenth centuries), not only because this has been identified as an important outcome of changes taking place in the early modern and immediately pre-capitalist period, but also for the important reason that the witch-hunts appear to have been directed primarily, and almost exclusively, at women.

The witch-hunt period was a time of major social change where existing social structures, beliefs and relationships were undergoing transformations including, potentially, also men's and women's roles. At that particular time a number of economic, political, legal, ideological and religious factors combined, which allowed and also prompted persecution for witchcraft. I shall argue here that the witch-hunts were an attempt at maintaining and restoring male supremacy within this context.

During the sixteenth and seventeenth centuries, primarily in Continental Europe and Scotland, but also in England and Scandinavia, thousands of people were condemned to imprisonment and death accused of the crime of 'witchcraft'. To make obvious the intensity of persecution at this time, the period has been called the 'witch-craze'.[2] The term 'craze' is in some ways problematic because it implies that the witch-hunts were carried out by crazed individuals in an exhibition of momentary madness

(Burke 1990). None the less, the early modern period does stand out as unique within the history of witchcraft, and it is important therefore, to differentiate this period where *extensive* witch-hunting took place.

Significantly, the witch-hunts were mainly directed against women.[3] In England more than 90 per cent of those formally accused of witchcraft were women, and the few men who were also formally accused tended to be married to an accused witch or to appear jointly with a woman (MacFarlane 1970: 160). In recent years there has been an increasing focus on detailed micro studies in the attempt to examine social relations within local populations, and thus to prepare the ground for a better understanding of the social context of the witch-hunts (MacFarlane 1970, Larner 1983; Karlsen 1987). By their use of contemporary witch trial material, these studies have made increasingly apparent that the specific role of *women* as witches must be explained, and that without such explanation many of the approaches merely help to contextualise, rather than explain, the witch-hunts.

Using a revolutionary feminist approach it may be shown that the witch-hunts provided one means of controlling women socially within a male supremacist society, using violence or the threat of violence, and relying on a particular construct of female sexuality. This specific instance of the social control of women, using the accusation of witchcraft, was a product of the socio-historical context at the time. As a result only certain women – usually older, lower-class, poor, and often single or widowed – were directly affected. To understand why the social control of women took this form at this time we need to examine events leading up to, and taking place during, the witch-hunt period – which in England was largely between the mid-sixteenth and the mid-seventeenth centuries; and we also need to examine reasons for the eventual decline of the persecutions.

The witch-persecutions are a complex phenomenon, and in this brief study it is neither possible nor desirable to cover the subject area in its entirety, but merely to consider what may be deemed important aspects. To initiate the task this chapter briefly considers the issues which may be pinpointed as especially significant to an explanation of the witch-hunts. There will also be an examination of the sources, legislation, and frequency of accusations or prosecutions. The following chapter will examine the period leading up to the persecutions and will also look at the background to the persecutions, including demographic features, important economic characteristics, and the contemporary gender ideology. Finally, Chapter 8 will examine those who were accused of witchcraft and the accusations against them. The case study focuses primarily on the Essex witch-trials due to the existence of fuller records for this area, and where possible material specifically concerning Essex and the surrounding region will be referred to.

EXPLAINING THE EARLY MODERN WITCH-HUNTS: SEX RELATED OR SEX SPECIFIC

Many different approaches have been used to explain the witch-hunts in early modern Europe, but most have not attempted to give reasons why it was primarily women who were accused of using witchcraft. Studies have been carried out on a macro-social level (Trevor-Roper 1969), at a local level (MacFarlane 1970; Larner 1983; Kittredge 1956; Karlsen 1987), and many have used an anthropological approach (Thomas 1971; MacFarlane 1970; Murray 1962, Mair 1969; Marwick 1982). The studies have also focused on a variety of different, and often overlapping, aspects and explanations: that the witch-prosecutions were a product of religious conflict (Thomas 1971; Trevor-Roper 1969; Murray 1962), that influence of ruling-class and/or peasant beliefs was crucial (Keickhefer 1976; Cohn 1975; Thomas 1971; Ginzburg 1983; Larner 1983; MacFarlane 1970), that social strain was an underlying factor (MacFarlane 1970), that the witch-hunts came about through the imposition of a secular state and legal system (Currie 1973; Cohn 1975; Larner 1983), that the development of printing facilitated the rapid spread of the craze (Daly 1979), that social control was an important outcome (Morris 1976; Currie 1973; Daly 1979; Dworkin 1974), that the witch-hunts were a product of the development of male-dominated science and medicine (Ehrenreich and English 1976; Easlea 1980; Merchant 1980), or that it was a product of mass hysteria (Zilboorg 1935). Together, many of these features are indeed important to an understanding of the development of the witch-hunts. But the focus on women must also be explained.

The approaches outlined do tend to have a common theme: that those accused of using witchcraft during the sixteenth and seventeenth centuries (and also the fifteenth century in Europe) were not actually witches in the religious sense. That is, they did not belong to a satanical religion, even if that was often an implicit or even explicit part of the accusations against them. However, there have also been attempts at explaining the witch-hunts phenomenon by recourse to the concept of religious witchcraft (see Murray 1962; Hughes 1965; J. Russell 1972). But such approaches involve some fundamental problems. Margaret Murray's work for instance, which forms the basis for the idea that the witch-hunts were directed at an actual witch-cult, has a tendency to falsify the witch-trial evidence (see Cohn 1975). The women acused of witchcraft during the sixteenth and seventeenth centuries in England (as well as in Europe, Scotland and Scandinavia) were not part of a religious witch-cult. Some of them did indicate that they believed themselves to be witches, but this was largely a result of particular social pressures and expectations.

Another way of approaching the witch-hunt material therefore, besides that adopted by Murray, is to argue that the belief in witchcraft, which people in the sixteenth and seventeenth centuries undoubtedly had, is ideological. Witchcraft may be seen as a means of understanding otherwise incomprehensible natural phenomena such as illness and death (Malinowski 1954). Associated with this may also be the attempt by women to use witchcraft belief as a means of empowerment; that is, to be perceived as more powerful than otherwise socially possible (Daly 1979; Karlsen 1987). In the discussion of the witch-hunts which follows, the belief in witchcraft will be taken as an ideological construct.

But what of the link between witchcraft persecution and women? History as a discipline has tended to omit any description or analysis of male–female relations, and this problem also underlies discussion about the witch-hunts. Historians have either entirely ignored that the accused were women, have merely blamed the accusations on the women themselves, or have perhaps seen women as an important but none the less secondary consideration (see Barstow 1988). Yet feminists are increasingly recognising that women have a unique and distinct position *as women* within historical development and change. This is why feminist historians such as Joan Kelly have suggested the creation of a 'Women's History', which does not merely append 'women' to historical research that is otherwise essentially male oriented, but takes male–female relations as an integral part of that research. Once we examine history in terms of the relative positions of men

and women the outcome is very different fro[...]
orientated) work, because 'the moment one a[...]
are a part of humanity in the fullest sense – t[...]
events with which we deal takes on a wholly dif[...]
meaning from the normally accepted one' (Kel[...]

It is particularly significant that when we take[...]
tions into account, periods generally considere[...] ~~progressive~~ by
traditional historians, such as the Renaissance and the
development of European nation states during the sixteenth and
seventeenth centuries (the period of the witch-hunts), are also
found to be periods when women suffer relative loss of status. In
other words so-called 'progressive change' tends to be progressive
for men, but not necessarily so for women. Therefore, we must
consider how men and women as separate groups experienced the
period of the witch-hunts. For a revolutionary feminist approach,
we must also take into account that male–female relations are
conflictual and probably eroticised.

Of those, mainly feminist, writers who have made male–female
relations a part of their analysis of the witch-hunts, some argue that
the witch-hunts were merely sex related, that 'women' are not the
central issue, while others argue that they were sex specific, that
'women' *are* the central issue. I will argue in agreement with the
latter that the witch-hunts were sex specific, and that they constituted an integral part of conflictual male–female relations at the
time.

SEX RELATED

Christina Larner's work, *The Enemies of God* (1983: 83), is the most
important work which argues that the witch-hunts were sex related
rather than sex specific. Her analysis is a detailed study based on
the Scottish witch-persecutions during the sixteenth and seventeenth centuries with links made to the experiences in both
Europe and England. She sees the question of why women formed
the vast majority of the accused as important, yet only as an
indirect feature of her analysis, concluding that witch-hunting,
although apparently aimed at women more than at men, was not
about woman-hunting (Larner 1983: 92).

Larner places greatest emphasis on ideology, and specifically
the nature of religious ideology, in her explanation of the
development of the witch-hunts in Scotland, as well as in Europe

England. The predominance of women as witches is also in primarily ideological terms. The nature of the legal system is deemed very important, and in England perhaps more so than in Scotland, in helping to explain the course followed by the witch-hunts.

According to Larner, the Scottish witches were, like those in England and rural Europe, primarily poor, middle-aged or elderly women. This was a product of the contemporary stereotype of the witch (similar in Scotland to that identified by Cohn, 1975, in Europe) which directly identified women as witches, such that 'witches are women; all women are potential witches' (Larner 1983: 92). Larner does accept that there is some evidence to suggest that the relationship between witch-hunting and woman-hunting is a direct one. Thus at the level of ideas, and specifically a strongly patriarchal religious ideology, there is a convincing link between witch-hunting and woman-hunting: 'Witch-hunting is woman-hunting or at least it is the hunting of women who do not fulfil the male view of how women ought to conduct themselves' (ibid.: 100). She accepts that the accused were women who presented a challenge to the patriarchally-defined 'ideal woman', because the timing of the witch-hunts fits in with the development of the new religious ideology which placed women in an ambiguous position. However, for Larner, this ideology regarding women was merely a part of a wider assertion of ideological conformity. The female witch stereotype does not provide the reason for the witch-hunts. Thus it is the imposition of what she calls the 'Christian political ideology' which is both more important, and makes the witch-hunts merely sex related but not sex specific.[4]

It is interesting to note that despite Larner's particular emphasis, she points out on a number of occasions how (in Scotland at least) the effect of the witch-hunts must have been to induce a generalised but also sex-specific fear of accusation in certain localities: 'There were periods in 1649 and 1661 when no mature woman in Fife or East Lothian can have felt free from fear of accusation' (ibid.: 197). In this way it was women's lives, rather than men's, which were profoundly affected by the witch-hunts. Furthermore, Larner also links witch-hunting to social control, seeing this form of social control as the most public form ever devised.

Secularisation of the legal system was a crucial precondition for the witch-hunts, and Larner links this to the rise of and imposition of the nation state. She suggests that the establishment of the witchcraft laws in various European countries was another aspect of this process. The effect was 'to centralize and secularize the process of social control in general and witchcraft in particular' (ibid.: 194). The witch-hunts were therefore a specific mechanism for the imposition of the new social order; a new *Christian* social order. But why this imposition of a new social order should take place apparently via women Larner does not explain.[5]

Larner's emphasis is on ideology, but the notion of conflict is at times implicit in her work. With regard to both the emergence of the nation state, and women appearing to challenge male perceptions of appropriate female behaviour, she refers to the overriding importance of (specifically religious) ideology in solving the conflict in favour of the dominant group. What is perhaps odd is that, despite her insistence that the predominance of women as witches is important, and her emphasis on the patriarchal nature of religious ideology, she does not apply these ideas beyond her analysis of the witch stereotype. It is surprising that she does not unite the different parts of her argument regarding the witch-hunts as social control, at the levels of both (gendered) national control over the populace and local control of women. After all, in Larner's own terms the main direction of the control was towards women. The problem here appears somewhat similar to that of the post-structuralists, discussed in Chapter 2, even if Larner's work is not linked to this tradition. Like Weedon (1987), Larner's analysis is focused almost exclusively at the level of ideas. Larner also suggests the existence of a 'plurality' of belief systems, which are not directly tied to a material base:

> The case for a direct relationship between the fantasies, night-mares, religions or ideologies of a given society and its social structure seems quite unproven. . . . In fact the variety of belief systems which can stem from societies with similar social structures seems haphazard and almost unlimited.
>
> (Larner 1983: 202)

There is no doubt that belief systems play a very important part in male–female, as well as other, social relations. What Larner does not allow for, however, is the material implication of such beliefs. In the case of belief in witchcraft, it is specifically men who may benefit because of the direct linkage between witchcraft and the female stereotype which she outlines. I would suggest that belief in witchcraft, as found in England (but also in Europe and Scotland) during the sixteenth and seventeenth centuries, constituted a gendered ideology serving the material interests of male supremacy.

Larner's work is none the less very interesting, partly because it begins to question whether the witch-hunts can be explained in terms of the social control of women. Also because it leads us to question how the nature of the witch-hunts relied on seemingly different sets of interests, both those of the ruling class and of the peasantry. Larner talks about collusion between the lower and upper classes against witches, and despite her insistence that witches are accused as witches rather than as women, we may question whether this 'collusion' was not ultimately directed against women. In other words, whether the lower and upper class men were not united (however unconsciously) in their fight against women, despite different economic class interests.

Since Larner's careful documentation of the witch-hunts in Scotland it has been much more difficult for historians to ignore the importance of women as victims in the witch trials. But her work has also allowed many to avoid tackling the *centrality* of women to the witch-hunts (see Levack; 1987, Scarre 1987). Larner herself acknowledges the need for more research on women's position in society (an area which is lacking to an even greater extent in Scotland than with regard to England). The structural indicators outlined here suggest that such research would probably show how the female witch-stereotype was linked into a structural subordination of women in the early modern period.

William Monter (1977) and Robert Muchembled (1979) both go much further in their analysis of women as witches than most historians. Monter, for instance, sees gender as the reason for the persecutions, arguing that 'witchcraft, as the demonologists had repeatedly insisted, was sex-linked' (1976: 198). Muchembled has made the important point that the witch-hunts persecuted women for their sexuality, and were 'virulently anti-feminist' (Muchembled 1990: 151).[6] Both Monter and Muchembled have also linked the persecution of women as witches to other contemporary examples of female oppression: the increase, for example, in prosecution of women for infanticide and bastardy. Their work, and especially that of Monter, brings us closer to understanding why primarily women were accused of witchcraft, although it is still mainly feminist writers who have placed this problem at the heart of their analysis and consequently see the witch-hunts as sex specific. I want briefly to examine the work of Ehrenreich and English, Daly and Karlsen to show the different aspects which feminist writers have emphasised. Ehrenreich and English link the witch-hunts to the rise of the male medical profession, Daly sees the persecutions as a part of men's sado-ritual oppression of women, while Karlsen focuses on the issue of social control.

SEX SPECIFIC

Ehrenreich and English in their pamphlet *Witches, Midwives and Nurses* (1976) take as a central explanation for the witch-hunts the drive by men, essentially from the upper layers of society, for control of healing. They argue that it was especially during the period of witch-persecutions that medicine was established as the legitimate form of healing, backed by the church and state, while the healing carried out by the peasant wise women was outlawed as heresy. They point out that prior to the fourteenth century, when medicine first started to become established as a profession, the medical needs of the community had been served primarily by female healers or 'wise women'. By conflating the periods of the Inquisition and the witch-hunts, that is the fourteenth through to the seventeenth centuries, Ehrenreich and English suggest that the witch-hunts were part of this four centuries of witch-hunting, albeit with different intensities and manifestations at different times.

They point to three factors which were instrumental in the elimination of the old healing by the male-dominated ruling class. Firstly, the belief, as expressed by the late fifteenth-century text, the *Malleus Maleficarum*, that midwives do harm and that women are sexually insatiable. Secondly, the establishment of the training of doctors in the universities. And thirdly, the nature of healing and medicine themselves.

For Ehrenreich and English the elimination of the witch-healers in favour of male doctors was the most important of these factors and this leads them to conclude that the witch-hunts should be attributed to the male members of the ruling class. The contribution of the ruling class is, of course, also a major focus for Larner (1983), although she provides very different reasons, and does not identify male members of the ruling class as the problem in the way suggested by Ehrenreich and English. While this may be a step forward by Ehrenreich and English, since it allows them to deal with the question why primarily women were accused, their focus on healing and medicine is much too narrow. As will be shown later by the examination of the witch trial material, only very few of the women accused of witchcraft appeared to be either healers or midwives. Indeed, Ursley Kempe in the 1582 trial pamphlet is one of the only women to be mentioned explicitly in the Essex material as a healer. Furthermore, as Larner points out, the main challenge to female midwives by men took place in the eighteenth century, that is, after the witch trials had finished. Also (in Scotland at least), objection to female healers was more prevalent in the towns, which is where male professionals were stronger, rather than in the rural areas where witchcraft accusations were more important (Larner 1983: 101).

In addition it must be stressed that one of the male medics most committed to a male-only profession – William Harvey – actually contributed to the decline of the witch-persecutions through his influence over Charles I. This would not be expected within the parameters of Ehrenreich and English's argument.

Even so, Ehrenreich and English's argument may play a part in a more comprehensive explanation of the witch-hunts, and their analysis, by focusing on the rising male medical profession, also points to the quest by men to control the newly-developing sciences which some have seen as especially important regarding the decline of the witch-hunts (see Easlea 1980; Merchant 1980; and Trevor-Roper 1969).

While agreeing with Ehrenreich and English that woman healers were prominent among those accused of witchcraft, Mary Daly's main argument in her book *Gyn/Ecology* (1979) is that the witch-craze was an attempt at controlling women who were perceived as actively opposing male supremacy, in particular 'women who had rejected marriage (Spinsters) and women who had survived it (Widows)' (Daly 1979: 55). The witch-hunts were an attempt at purifying society of these 'indigestible' female elements, that is, women not assimilated into the patriarchal family. However, women who were seemingly assimilated, such as married women, and often men, were accused too. Daly explains the latter by suggesting that 'the craze had got out of hand', and was also consuming 'the most docile and already socially "digested" women, and, unfortunately, men as well' (ibid.: 185). The witch-hunts were therefore a product of male–female conflict in the particular socio-historical setting of the Christian West in the fifteenth to seventeenth centuries.

Larner (1983) also talks about the accused as those women who were not assimilated and places this in the context of a Christian ideology, but not in terms of male–female power relations centred on marriage and the family, as does Daly. Daly argues that witch-burning may be considered part of what she call the 'Sado-ritual syndrome' bearing a resemblance to the sado-masochistic, eroti-cised construction of power relations between men and women whereby women's sense of self is annihilated (as discussed in the previous chapters). Daly, however, uses the more 'spiritual' phraseology of the negation of the 'self-affirming be-ing of women' (Daly 1979: 111). For Daly access to and conflict around knowledge, and in particular the knowledge of healing, is another important aspect. As she points out:

> I suggest, then, that just as the 'elite' caste who perpetrated the witchburnings was in large measure an aspiring 'intellectual' elite of professional men, so the hated targets were primarily a spiritual/moral/know-ing elite cross-section of the female population of Europe.
>
> (Daly 1979: 184)

This 'elite cross-section of the female population' consisted of women, predominantly from the lower social and economic classes, possessing what Daly calls the 'higher learning' of spiritual wisdom and healing and, as she adds, also possessing 'the highly independent character that accompanies such wisdom' (ibid.: 195). This is where Daly's argument links up to some extent with that of Ehrenreich and English regarding male take-over of the medical profession.

Overall, then, Daly argues that, like Indian suttee or Chinese footbinding, the witch-hunts were directed at controlling women, and in sixteenth- and seventeenth-century Europe this was partic-ularly directed at women who were independent and who had the knowledge of healing. In other words, it was a historically specific instance of sexual violence against women as social control. In this way, Daly provides an interesting link between the revolutionary feminist framework presented earlier and the witch-hunt pheno-menon.[7]

What is also interesting about Daly's perspective is the way she is able to incorporate some of the important features regarding witchcraft accusations and prosecutions which may be identified in relation to the witchcraft material. For instance, there does seem to have been 'an obsession' with female sexual purity in the general literature on witchcraft and also to some extent in the witch trial material. This ideological emphasis was used to justify (at least partly) the prosecution and hanging or burning of 'witches'.

But, there are also some problems with Daly's analysis. A central feature of this is her assertion that single women and widows were taking a stand against male supremacy. Where single women are concerned some of them may indeed have rejected marriage as Daly suggests, but the witch trial material does not lend conclusive proof of this. Some women may merely have been left as single parents by a man promising marriage; and it is also likely that they were viewed as a potential, or actual, financial burden to the other villagers. Thus by remaining single, women might not have been actively rejecting marriage, although by having children out of marriage they were none the less a threat to the male dominant social order, since their very existence undermined the institution of marriage and male control within that.

Daly is correct when she states that the witch-hunts focused on widows as this is borne out clearly by the witch trial material. However, the evidence does not provide the clear-cut explanation which Daly gives when she says that the widow's (and spinster's) 'physical, intellectual, economic, moral and spiritual independence and activity profoundly threatened the male monopoly in every sphere'. By examining the socio-economic situation of widows at the time of the witch-hunts, it can be seen that the accused did sometimes, but by no means always, pose a threat to 'male monopoly', even if at an ideological level women were easily perceived as a threat. As we shall see later, widows generally, at the lower end of the social scale, and especially those with children, seem to have been some of the most financially vulnerable individuals in the community and the parish was often reluctant to provide for them.

Daly's analysis needs to be extended to take this more complex situation into account. In addition, her argument that it was strong women, living outside of marriage, who were the focus of the witch-hunts cannot explain the numbers of married women who actually were involved. Daly makes many important points, but there are problems with her analysis, probably because she uses mainly secondary source material and does not examine any of the trial material.

Karlsen's more recent work, *The Devil in the Shape of a Woman* (1987), provides a much more comprehensive view of the witch-hunts because she also examines primary sources. Her study focuses on the New England experience, and is also of relevance to an analysis of the witch-persecutions in England because the New England situation may be seen as having roots in England, brought across by the English Puritan settlers during the seventeenth century. There are, of course, specific differences attributable to the nature of the two societies, for example, the accused in New England included women from wider social backgrounds than was seemingly the case in England. Even so, in New England, as in England (and also Europe), the accusation of witchcraft was directed primarily at women.

Karlsen argues that it is only by situating the witch-hunts within the context of male–female relations that it is possible to understand the importance of the persecutions in a dynamic relationship to the social structure generally. In her book, therefore:

> We see how witchcraft played a critical role not only in shaping, maintaining, and describing that social structure, but in reconciling men's feelings about women with the demographic, economic, religious and sexual changes of the time. . . . We see witchcraft, finally, as a deeply ambivalent but violent struggle *within* women as well as an equally ambivalent but violent struggle *against* women.
>
> (Karlsen 1987: xv)[8]

Moving beyond Larner's 'stereotype' and to some extent echoing Daly's 'undigestible elements', Karlsen argues that the main reason women were accused of witchcraft (a phenomenon continued in New England to the late seventeenth century), was that they were seen as stepping beyond the role and position assigned to them by men. This included taking a too active, or vocal, part in religious activity otherwise assigned to men; acting in a seemingly independent sexual manner, such as being unmarried, widowed, or having an illegitimate child; and placing themselves in competition with men for economic resources. Any or all of these features were likely to lead to the accusation of witchcraft.

In this way Karlsen presents a picture of the witch-hunts as specifically concerned with male–female conflict. She also shows that the dominant ideology regarding gender relations supported men against women. Since women were generally thought to be inferior to men, if a woman did something to step outside this stereotype, it was thought that she could only have done so by using witchcraft. Male behaviour was not similarly controlled.

While those most vulnerable to witchcraft accusation were undoubtedly women, Karlsen argues that not all women were equally vulnerable. It was women over the age of 40, and especially 'women alone' that is, 'widows, spinsters, separated, divorced and deserted women' (ibid.: 73) who were the most vulnerable. These women were neither defined on men's terms, nor in terms of men, and this was expressed by reference to their sexuality. As Karlsen points out, women over the age of 40 were perceived as no longer having the 'restraint' on their heterosexual behaviour conferred by pregnancy, and single women or widows did not have the 'restraint' of a husband. As a result, in these women, the natural female 'carnal lust' which had been identified in the *Malleus Maleficarum* was particularly likely to be out of control.

The 'excessive' sexual nature of women which led them into sexual temptation with the Devil, was also apparent in seduction or recruitment of others to do the Devil's work. It tended to be other women who were thus seduced, or became 'possessed', and Karlsen points out that while in explicit mentions of possession it is the Devil who seduces the woman, in descriptions of possession there is often an implicitly erotic notion of the 'witch' seducing another woman: 'Descriptions of witches successful in luring women into their ranks sometimes end by appealing to other women's licentiousness' (ibid.: 136). She does not use the term 'lesbianism' but this is surely what Karlsen is implying.[9]

Karlsen shows that women's supposedly sexual natures at times added yet another dimension to the identification of 'witches'. By looking at the possible criminal histories of the women accused, she found that some of these women had previously, often many years earlier, been accused of sexual offences. As she explains:

> Witches were sometimes denounced as bawds or lewd women in the course of their trials, but rarely were the sexual charges specified. Yet when we look at the lives of the accused prior to the accusation, we sometimes find evidence of real or alleged sexual offences.
>
> (Karlsen 1987: 138)

This included fornication and, in some respects echoing the work of Monter and Muchembled, Karlsen suggests that the crimes of having an illegitimate child, abortion and infanticide (all more or less exclusively 'female' crimes) were similarly linked to witchcraft accusations. These crimes might have been seen as women challenging societal rules concerning female sexuality. But, she adds, these particular crimes probably also invoked fears about witches interfering with the natural processes of life and death. It was in this context that suspicion of witchcraft was focused on midwives and healers, although it is difficult to see from the sources exactly how many of the accused may be described as specifically midwives and healers, since 'all colonial women were responsible for the health of their families' (ibid.: 141–2).

Karlsen shows that economic considerations were another important aspect behind witchcraft accusations, and this included women who might be seen to be in competition with men over resources, and especially women who had inherited, or might do so.

Overall, then, Karlsen is presenting a picture of New England 'witches' as women who were perceived as challenging the dominant, Puritan, view of women. Ideological considerations are thus deemed very important, but also tied to material considerations of male–female conflict around power, and control of, or access to, resources. This analysis leads her to argue that the eventual demise of the witch-hunts in New England, in the early eighteenth century, was a product of both male–female relations and the attempt by the ruling class to stop the persecution which was by that time also affecting its own members directly. The development of 'rational' or 'scientific' thought is therefore not, according to Karlsen, the main issue. Instead, part of the answer lies in the fact that increasing numbers of *prosperous* men and women were being accused of witchcraft. And the rest of the answer lies in the structural as well as ideological aspects of male–female relations: the points of conflict between men and women which led to witchcraft accusations remained, but were *reconstructed* to diminish women's apparent power. In other words, the attempts to force women to fit the male ideal of 'woman as inferior' by use of witchcraft accusation was not as effective as the reconstruction of women. The new construction was that of the sexually passive and domesticated woman. The witch-hunts therefore declined eventually because new, and more effective, means of controlling women by men emerged.

Karlsen's work is exciting because it appears to provide not only a comprehensive interpretation of the New England witch-hunts, but also of the witch-hunts as experienced in England. My own examination of the primary sources draws many of the same conclusions. Karlsen's analysis overcomes many of the problems posed by the other approaches to the witch-persecutions since she situates the witch-hunts not only within the social order generally, but more specifically as an instance of male–female conflict within this context. Witchcraft accusations are therefore presented as dynamically related to the social structure and male–female relations within this. Moreover, she implies that witchcraft accusation played a dynamic role in the realignment of male dominance in a situation of social change, presenting this as 'a deeply ambivalent but violent struggle *within* women as well as an equally ambivalent but violent struggle *against* women' (ibid.: xv). Unfortunately, she does not elaborate on the precise meaning of this phrase.

Karlsen also overcomes some of the problems related to the views of Ehrenreich and English, and those of Daly. She does not see male take-over of the medical profession as an important concern, indeed she suggests that it is difficult to determine how many of the women accused of witchcraft were actually healers or midwives. But she also argues that women in this category may have been among those more vulnerable to accusation because they could be construed as interfering with the processes of life and death. Like Daly she argues that it was those women who were perceived as unassimilated into the male-dominated society who were particularly vulnerable to the accusation of witchcraft. This group included widows and single women, who were the most vulnerable, but also many married women who may have been vulnerable for some of the same reasons as women without men.

But while Karlsen provides an analysis that incorporates many aspects of the witch-hunt phenomenon, she does not link this to a more in-depth understanding of the *process* by which the witch-hunts played an important part in the realignment of male–female power relations during the seventeenth century (in New England), even though she suggests that such realignment is an important consideration. This is an aspect which I believe is important to consider and by using the revolutionary feminist framework outlined in earlier chapters (and hinted at by Daly), it is possible to understand more fully the role of the witch-hunts within this dynamic of male domination. I shall return to this theme in the following chapters.

SOURCE MATERIALS FOR THE WITCH-HUNTS

There are three main types of contemporary sources for the period of the English witch-hunts:

1 Court records – largely from the Assize Courts, but also from the quarter sessions, and to some extent from the Church Court and Borough Court. I focus on the Assize records, as the majority of the formal witchcraft accusations are mentioned there and because the secular court was becoming more important at this time.[10]
2 Pamphlets or 'chap books' on some individual trials, of which five still exist for Essex.[11] I examine all of these in some detail.
3 Literature discussing the nature and treatment of witchcraft as well as male–female social relations.[12]

One of the major twentieth-century accounts of the English witch-hunts, Notestein's *The History of Witchcraft in England from 1558 to 1728* (1968), is based almost exclusively on literary sources and pamphlet material. Since these sources only cover a small number of trials, Notestein obtained a very partial view of the extent of formal accusations of witchcraft. Ewen's slightly later work *Witch Hunting and Witch Trials* (1971)[13] was a study and listing of some of the court records, in particular the Assize Court indictments[14] for witchcraft from the Home Circuit. This work listed 790 such indictments for the Home Counties. Notestein and Ewen's work taken together form a more useful picture of the English witch-hunts. However, in terms of Essex specifically, MacFarlane's detailed study (1970) supercedes both of these earlier works, and MacFarlane has found more Assize Court indictments than did Ewen. None the less, Ewen's work is useful as it lists Assize Court indictments between 1564 and 1663, which, combined with MacFarlane's additions, gives the fullest picture possible of the frequency of formal accusations. Ewen also discusses Assize Court procedure as well as providing information regarding other courts.

Recently James Cockburn (1978 and 1982) has researched and published the entire Assize Court records for Essex in the Elizabethan and Jacobean periods. These records, while providing little additional material to that outlined above, give a means of comparing indictments for witchcraft or sorcery with indictments for other crimes during the period of greatest witch-hunting intensity. Cockburn's work is also more accessible as he has translated the Assize Court records into English, where they were previously in Latin.

The court records generally give us an idea of those formally accused of witchcraft, that is, witchcraft legally defined as a crime (see section below on legislation). From the Assize Court records we can usually tell who the accused were, what they were accused of, and how they were sentenced. Unfortunately these records are by no means complete, although especially comprehensive ones do exist for the Home Circuit, and in particular for Essex.15

The contemporary pamphlets for Essex (and elsewhere) are a useful source from which to examine the witch-hunt phenomenon in greater depth. They may be used as a supplement to the court records, often providing detailed accounts of evidence given in court and information regarding the accused and their accusers otherwise merely listed in indictments. As MacFarlane outlines:

> The pamphlets. . .give added information about those involved in prosecutions, their age, wealth, personality and relationships: they indicate how witchcraft was believed to work, the power of cursing, the use of spells and familiars; they reveal the motives ascribed to witches and the actual incident which was believed to have prompted the bewitching.
>
> (MacFarlane 1970: 81)

The close fit between the pamphlet material and the Assize Court records leads him to suggest that the pamphlet writers 'were accurate and almost certainly eye-witness reporters' (ibid.: 85). The pamphlets were written by individual men (never women) present at the trials, possibly the court scribe or even the judge himself. Such is thought to be the case with the 1582 pamphlet from Essex, which is probably written by Judge Darcy (see MacFarlane 1970: 85). The pamphlet about the 1612 Lancaster trial was written by a lawyer, Thomas Potts (1613) actively involved in the case (Summers 1971: 27).

While the pamphlet material is closely related to the indictments listed in the Assize Court records, we must also recognise that they are the accounts of men who were not themselves among the suspected witches. We do not know how the accused actually perceived their accusation and trial, beyond the inferences made by the pamphlet writer. Furthermore, all the pamphlets being discussed here were (according to their introductory sections), written as statements against witchcraft. They supported the judgements rather than the individuals accused of witchcraft. The introductory sections of the pamphlets generally suggest that they were written as a warning so that others would be deterred from also following the Devil. The pamphlets are therefore presenting a particular perspective regarding both the witch-hunts and gender relations. It can perhaps be assumed that the pamphlets provide a perspective not dissimilar to the dominant ideology regarding both gender and religious belief, and it is in this context that the pamphlets must be viewed.[16]

Regarding dissemination of the pamphlets' message it is quite possible that they had a popular appeal, due to their chatty style and sensational titles. There are often woodcut pictures of the women accused, their supposed familiars, and in a few instances those executed are shown hanging on the scaffold. The printing press, of course, was invented before the witch-hunts. Daly identifies this as a particularly important factor in the spread of the European witch-hunts, arguing that it had the dual function of placing the educated elite in the role of 'experts', and also presenting popularised versions of the witch-hunting message to the general populace through wood-cuts and engravings (Daly 1979: 192). It has been suggested that the English pamphlets were probably written for the London literary market (MacFarlane 1970: 81). But the readership may also have been more widespread than this because of the emphasis during this period on people generally, or at least men generally, learning to read the Bible (Gittins 1985: 44). Both the Bible and the pamphlets were printed in English, indicating a generalised rather than specialised readership.

The five witch trial pamphlets from Essex are mainly from the earlier part of the witch-hunts, and in this sense do not represent the trials throughout the whole period, that is between 1560-1680.[17] Four of the five pamphlets relate to trials in the sixteenth century, during the reign of Elizabeth I (1566, 1579, 1582, 1589), and the remaining pamphlet relates to a trial towards the end of the witch-craze period (1645).[18] It has been suggested that two of the trials written about in pamphlets, those in 1582 and 1645, may be regarded as exceptional in the context of the Essex trials generally (with or without pamphlets). This is because there were a large number of defendants in both of these trials and they came from only a small area, while otherwise the accused in any one trial tended to be from a greater geographical area. Both the 'exceptional' trials involved individuals who were especially keen to seek out witches: Judge Darcy in the 1582 trial, and Matthew Hopkins in the 1645 trial. The 1579 trial pamphlet is perhaps the most representative of the Essex witch trials (MacFarlane 1970: 85).[19]

There is a wealth of literature written at the time of the witch-hunts dealing with, amongst other relevant topics, witchcraft, women's place in the social order, and religious beliefs. This material will be considered in the following chapters.

LEGISLATION

While a witchcraft statute of little significance existed during the reign of Henry VIII, the first important witchcraft law was placed on the statute books in 1563, soon after Elizabeth I became Queen.[20] It has been suggested that this piece of legislation came about because it was feared that witchcraft would be used as a means to dethrone the Queen. Mary Queen of Scots was said to be involved in such an anti-Elizabeth plot (see Notestein 1968: 18–19). The 1563 law saw witchcraft as a serious offence involving the following penalties:

1 Bewitching an individual to death warranted the death penalty (hanging).
2 Other use of witchcraft or sorcery to injure people or animals warranted one year's imprisonment for a first offence, and the death penalty for a subsequent offence.

Most of those who were brought to trial for witchcraft were either acquitted or imprisoned, and those sentenced to death were hanged. In Europe and Scotland the death penalty was carried out by burning, and it is often thought that the same applied to England. But this is not the case. In England 'burning to death' was only the penalty for treason, or petty treason. Treason was defined as threat to, or murder of, the monarch by his/her subjects, and petty treason was murder of the master or mistress by his/her servants, and murder of a husband by his wife. Thus in England a woman would be burnt to death if she was deemed to have used witchcraft to kill her husband, employer, or monarch.[21]

James I had a new witchcraft law, harsher than the previous, placed on the statute books in 1604, and this law remained in force until 1736 when the witchcraft legislation in England was repealed. James's law extended the use of the death penalty to instances where evil spirits had been used to cause harm, and thereby placed much greater onus on the accused having 'spirits' or 'familiars'. This change came about because of the wish, by the judiciary, for stricter standards regarding proof of witchcraft:

> what they now wanted was sworn evidence that the witch kept a familiar or bore the devil's mark on her person; most decisive of all, they hoped for her free confession that she had entered into a pact with Satan.
>
> (Thomas 1971: 575)

To us this might seem rather odd 'proof', but for many Jacobean judges familiars were an actuality, as was the Devil. Like the Elizabethan law, James's laws also had imprisonment as the penalty for other use of witchcraft, extending this to the death penalty for a second offence.

The particular nature of the crime of witchcraft is very important. This varies between England and different European and Scandinavian countries, for instance, in Europe the direct linkage with Satanism is important (Ankarloo and Henningsen 1990: introduction). Unlike crimes such as theft or robbery, witchcraft was not merely a crime or sin related to an individual person – although that is often how it appeared in the English trials – it was a crime directly against God, because the perpetrator sided specifically with the Devil. Perhaps by inference, it was also a crime against *man*kind because of the way men were seen as being closer to God than women, reflected within the church as well as political hierarchies. As a secret crime (its similarity to poisoning), witchcraft made the usual judicial procedure – giving evidence, obtaining confession and use of two direct witnesses – unlikely: 'It was only possible to testify to motives and effects, not to witness the actual act of witchcraft or the invisible way in which this force operated' (MacFarlane 1970: 16). As a result the Justices were instructed that 'half proofes are allowed, and are good causes of suspicion'; and it was also 'lawful to give in Evidence matters that are no ways relating to that Fact, and done many years before'.[22]

NUMBERS

Use of witchcraft to cause harm was one of the major crimes throughout the Elizabethan and Jacobean periods. In Essex during Elizabeth I's reign it was the third most common crime after theft and burglary; and during James I's reign it came fifth after theft, burglary, homicide/infanticide and highway robbery.[23] MacFarlane similarly points out that at the Essex Assizes only trials for thieving were more frequent than trials for witchcraft, leading him to conclude that witchcraft 'was no peripheral, abnormal crime, but of central importance' and 'There were few years when indictments did not occur' (MacFarlane 1970: 30). Use of witchcraft was the main crime committed by women during this period (Monter 1977).

The number of executions for witchcraft, primarily of women, which took place throughout the witch-hunt period in England have been estimated by Ewen at 'less than 1000' between 1542 and 1736 – that is, between the passing of the first witchcraft statute and the repeal of the last (Ewen 1971: 112). This involves a much smaller amount of woman-murder than that experienced in continental Europe or Scotland.[24] In Essex, in the village of Hatfield Peveril – one of the densest areas of persecution – there were about 15 accusations of witchcraft reaching the courts over a period of 30 years, in a population of approximately 550 to 650. Out of these 15 or so individuals, six were found not guilty, two were hanged for the offence of witchcraft, and the rest suffered either penury or prison (MacFarlane 1970: 95). But while the figures may seem small, they are none the less significant and 'witchcraft prosecutions were of central importance in village life' (ibid.: 32).[25]

The vast majority of witchcraft cases coming before the courts occurred in England during the reign of Elizabeth I, that is between 1563 and 1603. The numbers do, of course, refer to *recorded* figures, and the real figures, including those accusations of witchcraft not ending up in court, were probably much larger. It might seem surprising that Elizabeth allowed many fellow women to be imprisoned or murdered for the crime of witchcraft during her reign, and somewhat ironic that the only rule by a *female* monarch during the witch-craze period saw the greatest number of cases. However, Elizabeth's rule is not characterised by positive legislation or other support for women. She has been described as an 'honorary male' who 'having established herself as an exceptional woman, did nothing to upset or interfere with male notions of how the world was or should be organised' (Heisch 1980: 53). As with Margaret Thatcher and other exceptional women today, Elizabeth was able to act as a monarch contrary to the view of women at the time, because she continued to express her support of the prevalent gender ideology. She was able to remain unmarried, for instance, by becoming the one respectable alternative allowed: a *virgin* queen, married to England in the way nuns were married to God (ibid.: 50).

During James I's reign, from 1603 to 1620, the recorded figures for witchcraft accusations were much lower than those in the Elizabethan period. The underlying trend was of a decrease from then until the repeal of the witchcraft legislation in 1736, although accusations of witchcraft seem to have continued at a local level until the twentieth century, and indeed also precede the witch-hunt period (see Hole 1947: Chapters 11 and 12).

It is perhaps surprising that the number of prosecutions should have continued to decrease during James's reign, because of his instrumental role in fuelling the Scottish witch-hunts during the 1590s. As King of Scotland, James wrote *The Daemonology* (1597), stressing that witches did indeed exist, that they were a threat to the social order, and that they should preferably be eradicated. He had come to these conclusions after witchcraft had supposedly been used to harm his bride-to-be, Anne of Denmark, and himself (Robbins 1959: 277; Larner 1984). James, however, had always maintained some scepticism regarding witches' supposed powers, believing that fraud or delusion was often involved in 'bewitching', and was consequently involved in facilitating the decrease in prosecutions towards the end of his reign (Hole 1947: 186).

The decrease in prosecutions continued until the time of the Civil War, during the 1640s, (preceding the English Commonwealth), when circumstances did seem to change for a while. Tensions were heightened as the war for supremacy of Parliament versus King progressed. Religious beliefs and conflicts were intensified, and during the Civil War the usual judicial processes were disrupted, making it easier to get round the judges who were otherwise increasingly sceptical about the existence of witchcraft. During this period there was also an apparent challenge to the status quo with regard to gender relations as a number of radical religious sects emerged which often had women in more prominent and important roles than was allowed within the established Church (Kelly 1986: 6 fn4). The particularly massive increase in the formal accusations for Essex during the 1640s was also due to the involvement of Matthew Hopkins, the self-styled 'Witchfinder General' who, for a fee, found and provided evidence for the existence of large numbers of 'witches'.[26] Hopkins (and his assistant John Stearne) managed, during only a few years, to bring about the death of a couple of hundred women, and also a few men. Hopkins wrote a book justifying his activities, called *The Discovery of Witches* (1647), partly based on James I's earlier work and also reflecting some of the ideas concerning witches expressed in the earlier *Malleus Maleficarum* (1486). Despite large numbers of accusations there was not a total compliance with Hopkins's work. In some places there was objection to what he was doing and a woman in Essex who rallied supporters against Hopkins's assistant was eventually let off from the witchcraft accusation against her (Notestein 1968: 192).

This chapter has provided an introduction to the early modern witch-hunts. In the next chapter I examine the contextual background to the persecutions, including the period leading up to the hunts, demographic, economic and ideological features during the period; and the eventual decline of the phenomenon.

Chapter 7

The early modern witch-hunts II

PEASANT BELIEFS AND THE INQUISITION

Two aspects of pre-witch-craze Europe may be considered a particularly important basis for the witch-hunts: peasant beliefs regarding the existence of witches; and the establishment by the ruling class of an inquisitorial apparatus. Norman Cohn argues that it was the alteration of traditional peasant beliefs and incorporation of these into the beliefs of the ruling class (and especially the clergy), combined with change in the legal system via the inquisitorial process, which provided the necessary elements for the European witch-hunts to take off.[1] In other words, actual witch-*hunting* relied on peasant beliefs, but could not have occurred without the intervention of the upper echelons of society. I will examine these issues before going on to look at the main period of witch persecution.

The belief in *maleficium*, that is, doing harm by occult means, has been shown to have a long history among the European and also the English peasantry (see Thomas 1971). According to Cohn (1975), such beliefs can be identified in historical documentation stretching back to the fourth century and persisting during the Middle Ages. He distinguishes between sorcery and witchcraft, because 'sorcery' refers to general techniques while 'witchcraft' denotes particular powers residing with only certain individuals, and the witches could use their powers, or substances, objects, gestures or spells to carry out their supposedly evil deeds. However, although sorcery and witchcraft were known in pre-witch-hunt Europe as distinct concepts, these forms of *maleficium* were also perceived to overlap (ibid.: 148).

During the medieval period the practice of maleficium was

thought to cause a range of adverse conditions, including the death of humans and animals, illness similarly, destruction of crops, storms, and male impotence. All of these effects were later, during the witch-hunting period, attributed to the Devil. For instance, in England the Essex clergyman, George Gifford, wrote in the sixteenth century that 'it is common opinion when there are any mighty winds and thunders with terrible lightnings that the Devil is abroad' (Gifford 1593).[2] It is especially interesting that within the medieval tradition of belief it was usually or mainly *women* who were perceived as possessing the necessary occult powers for the practice of *maleficium*. It also appeared to be specifically women who believed themselves to possess such power and tried to use it (Cohn 1975: 153).

Cohn cites numerous instances from the Continent of action being taken informally against suspected witches centuries before the formal witch-hunts. All the cases cited are of women, and they were murdered by their accusers. For example: 'In 1128 the burghers of Ghent disembowelled a suspected witch and paraded her intestines through the village' (ibid.: 154).

And a further example from 1090 bearing much resemblance to the later witch trials:

> Three indigent women were rumoured to be 'poisoners' and 'destroyers of people and crops'. They were seized by the mob and subjected to the ordeal of immersion in water; next, though the ordeal gave negative results, they were repeatedly flogged to make them confess; finally, though they did not confess, they were burned alive on the banks of the river Isar.
>
> (Cohn 1975: 155)

This suggests that the accusation of witchcraft was probably traditionally used as a means of controlling women.[3] But in this earlier period, in England at least, the intense persecution to be seen later in the sixteenth and seventeenth centuries was not apparent (Thomas 1971: 461).

At least part of the upper classes, the clergy, also believed in *maleficium*. However, in pre-witch-hunt Europe, the Church's view was somewhat different from that of the peasantry, since the Church associated such occult practices with non-Christian religion, and specifically paganism. The Church took for granted, as did most of the rest of society, that occult practices were both possible and could lead to miracles. But for the Church, occult

practices were also inherently pernicious because they were perceived as anti-Christian; they were 'evil devices by which the
demons tricked human beings into opposing God' (Cohn 1975:
156). In this sense sorcery and witchcraft came to be seen as
heresy, and ultimately as allegiance with the Devil.

Cohn identifies 1320 as a crucial moment in history when the
link between sorcery, heresy and ultimately also witchcraft, was
formally established. As he points out:

> In 1320, the Pope, disturbed by reports that were reaching him
> concerning the practice of ritual magic at the papal court at
> Avignon itself, decided that the time had come to clarify and
> define the relationship between magic and heresy. . . . Hence-
> forth the Inquisitors were empowered to act against practitioners
> of ritual magic as heretics.
>
> (Cohn 1975: 176)

Thus the Inquisitorial procedure was installed in Europe, with its
concomitant shift in the judicial process – from a situation where
the onus of proof was on the accuser, to the situation where the
onus of proof was on the accused. The Inquisitorial judicial
process also allowed torture to procure confessions, and minimal
use of evidence (see Lea 1906). This was a similar format to that
used later in the witch trials where evidence was also minimal, even
hearsay. Moreover, heretics were allowed to give evidence against
each other, as occurred later in the witch trials and probably led to
many extra and erroneous accusations being made, partly because
the accused wanted to save their own skin. Another aspect of the
trials was the age of the witnesses; in the trials of the Inquisition a
witness as young as ten years old is recorded (Maycock 1926: 147),
while later, in the witch trials it was relatively common in some
areas to have child witnesses.

It is important to realise that the Inquisitorial apparatus merely
provided a backcloth to the witch-hunts rather than the actual
framework for prosecution (Tedeschi 1990). Also, we must distinguish between the English and European situations. The legal
system in England was different from that in most of Europe, and
England did not experience the Inquisitorial trial process. These
differences were instrumental in producing a less intense witch-
prosecution in England than in Europe or Scotland, although with
respect to use of evidence and witnesses there were general
similarities.

It was the fact that in the Middle Ages ritual magic involved *demons* which led to the charge of heresy, although the references to demons in ritual magic had previously been contained within the terms of Christianity, without any hint of Satanism. As Cohn explains, in ritual magic

> The demons are not to be worshipped but, on the contrary, mastered and commanded; and this is to be done through the power of God who created all spirits as well as all human beings.
>
> (Cohn 1975: 169)

None the less it was the link made by the ruling class between sorcery or ritual magic and heresy which also placed the notion of *maleficium* in a new and sinister light, paving the way for the witch-hunts. It was the authorities who created the idea of a Satanic pact:

> left to themselves, peasants would never have created mass witch-hunts – these occurred only where and when the authorities had become convinced of the reality of the sabbat and of nocturnal flights to the sabbat.
>
> (ibid.: 254)

This relates specifically to the European experience, but it might also provide a rationale for the more individualised witch-hunts in England. Cohn suggests that although in the English trials there was little mention of Satanic pacts, and hardly any torture to procure confessions, the existence of witch-hunts in England still depended on the attitudes of, and intervention by, the authorities (ibid.: 253). Thomas, on the other hand, argues that in England the witch-hunts relied more specifically on the attitudes and activities of the peasantry, while on the Continent the persecution of witches as Devil-worshippers inevitably started from above. In England the initial force was the fear of *maleficium*. It therefore emanated from below (Thomas 1971: 463).

With regard to the European Inquisition, it is interesting to note that the accusation of 'heresy' often involved accusation of what may be seen as deviation from the Church's doctrine or ideology regarding gender and sexuality. Groups which elevated women's social status, such as the (mixed) Albigensians who were also accused of homosexuality, and the (single-sex) Beguines were persecuted, as was Joan of Arc, who was accused of wearing supposedly 'male' attire (Karlen 1971; Clark 1981; Lea 1906;

Dworkin 1987). This focus on 'deviant' sexuality is also at the heart of most of the writings on witchcraft. The European works including the *Malleus Maleficarum* (1496) express this equation most forcefully, though it is apparent in English writings and accusations of witchcraft. Both the English, and especially the European, writings point to the supposedly more deviant nature of women's sexual behaviour, and specifically to the belief that women are sexually insatiable (or 'over-sexed') and therefore more likely to have sexual relations with the Devil than are men (see Merchant 1980: 132–8).

I will now move on to examine the Tudor and early Stuart periods and outline the reason why England in the sixteenth and seventeenth centuries experienced the phenomenon of witch-hunts. The position of women in the social order at that time relative to men is an important consideration.

THE WITCH-HUNT PERIOD

As indicated earlier, during the sixteenth and seventeenth centuries England (as well as Europe) experienced great changes and a major restructuring of society. Very briefly, changes were occurring from a Catholic, tenant-farmed, and monarch-ruled social structure, to Protestantism, greater reliance on wage labour and greater influence by Parliament. The population was increasing at a rapid rate. The law was being transferred from ecclesiastical to secular administration, that is, from enforcement by the Church to enforcement by the state, although the Church (Protestant) continued to form the basis of the state. These changes led to tensions and conflicts, and made society appear unstable (see Pennington and Thomas 1978; Hill 1975). Some of these changes will be discussed in greater detail below.

Changes in the population were a significant feature of the early modern period and resulted in significant pressure on resources, and it has been suggested that 'The changing balance between population and resources affected the largest numbers of individuals in the most visible fashion' (Houlbrooke 1984: 27). The population, decimated during the fourteenth century by plague, showed a marked increase from the late fifteenth century to the late seventeenth century, doubling during this period. As Houlbrooke explains:

Following a period of stagnation, a hesitant growth of the
English population began after 1470 from a probable level of a
little over 2 million, which gathered strength in the early
sixteenth century. It then grew to 3 million by 1550, over 4
million by 1600, and by the 1650s was fluctuating around 5 1/4
million. . . . Thereafter, it fell gently and remained below 5
million for much of the late seventeenth century.

(ibid.: 27)[4]

This enormous increase in population affected both cities, towns
and villages, although towns and cities absorbed a greater share,
especially London, which as a result placed greater demands on
the surrounding areas for foodstuffs and other supplies (Amussen
1988: 7). The changes appear to have come about initially through
a lowering of the mortality rate and a high but falling fertility rate
(Houlbrooke 1984: 27–8).[5]

The rapid increase in population contributed to the major
increase in the number of poor at the time. Significantly, in terms
of the witch-hunts, the population increase was most intense
between 1560 and 1630, which was also the main period of witch-
persecution in England. Regarding men and women, there were
more women than men in the overall population throughout the
period concerned; although in certain localities such as London
this was reversed (Houlbrooke 1984: 67).

During the sixteenth and seventeenth centuries, just as today,
marriage was seen as a primary institution. (Religious doctrine and
ideology concerning marriage will be discussed later.) By contrast,
the timing of marriage was different in the earlier period: the
lower classes married very late, while for the upper classes
marriage tended to occur earlier, below the age of seventeen. The
difficult economic circumstances of the times meant that it tended
to be financially impossible for people from the lower classes to
marry until they reached their late twenties (Stone 1979: 44).
Regarding financial constraints on marriage, it is interesting to
note that there appears to have been a direct relationship between
real wage rates and the incidence and timing of marriage, such
that when wage rates increased so did the rate of marriage and vice
versa. As Houlbrooke outlines:

Both real wages and marriage rates fell sharply during the later
sixteenth century, with only one short interruption. The
marriage rate revived for a time between 1566 and 1581 in

response to a short-lived improvement in real wages. Real wages reached their nadir in the early seventeenth century and began to rise very slowly thereafter. A readjustment of expectations took place only slowly after the long period of falling wages had come to an end, and the rate of marriage went on falling, albeit more unevenly, till after the middle of the century.

(Houlbrooke 1984: 67).

Where the upper classes were concerned, early marriage was often financially and politically advantageous, especially with regard to the eldest son, and daughters generally. During the period under consideration there was, however, a change towards slightly later marriages for the upper classes, as well as an increase during the seventeenth century of peers remaining unmarried, although the precise reason for this is unclear (ibid.: 65–6).

Overall, the sex ratio and marriage pattern as described, particularly that among the lower classes, had an important effect. It resulted in a population with large numbers of unmarried people, especially women, and women possibly living outside the direct control of men (Wall 1981).[6]

GENDER RELATIONS AND THE ECONOMY

Consideration of the economy is important with regard to the witch-hunts phenomenon, since not only were changes taking place within this sphere, but there may also have been a relationship between accusation of witchcraft and competition between men and women around resources.

There is some general agreement amongst historians and social scientists that the sixteenth and seventeenth centuries were part of the period that saw the transition from feudalism to capitalism, characterised by petty commodity production (Saville 1969; Middleton 1979; Hilton 1975). This largely pre-industrial period exhibited various capitalist and industrial, as well as feudal features of production (Middleton 1985). Within the context of this book, it is important to ask what the links were between male–female relations and the capitalist economic development taking place at the time. It is therefore useful to briefly examine the sexual division of labour during the sixteenth and seventeenth centuries, and also to consider the possible existence of a sex struggle within production.

There has in recent years been some consideration of these questions (see Hamilton 1978; Zaretsky 1976; and Middleton 1981), and a few earlier works considering, in some detail, women's role in pre-capitalist production also exist (Clark 1982; Pinchbeck 1977). It has been argued by most of these sources that the period of pre-capitalism and early capitalism saw a deterioration of women's role in production. This is a similar argument to that generally presented by the Marxist contributors to the Domestic Labour Debate who see the pre-capitalist period as one of gender equality, with capitalism bringing inequality between men and women (see Hester 1988). Chris Middleton, who calls this type of explanation the 'Critical-Pessimistic Tradition', suggests that it is an oversimplistic, as well as somewhat confusing, view of gender relations and the economy in early modern England. As he explains: 'I think it can be shown that the effects of the process of transition from feudalism to industrial capitalism were both more complicated and uneven than the 'critical-pessimistic tradition' generally suggests' (1985: 182).[7]

What is especially interesting about Middleton's critique, is the indication that it was specifically men who became predominant in the occupations which were foremost in the development of the earlier feudal production and also in the development of capitalist production (Middleton 1979, 1985). Both these modes of production developed at the expense of 'sexual equality', that is, at the expense of women. Male–female relations therefore played a vital role in the formation of these modes of production, and this may also be related to the struggle for livelihood, as well as the resultant power between the sexes. Middleton himself does not actually question why men should procure prominent positions in production. This is a major weakness of his overall analysis, but does not, however, detract from the important points which he does make regarding gender relations and the economy.

In the context of gender relations and economic activity, it may also be useful to reiterate the point made by Sylvia Walby (1986), which was discussed earlier (see Chapter 2). She suggests that when there are changes in the economic sphere, such as changes in production methods, conflict around male–female power relations also take place in order to ensure male dominance. We may therefore expect to find a realignment of male–female power relations in the sixteenth and seventeenth century due to the major changes taking place in the economy at that time. Walby's point thus underlines Middleton's findings, but it also goes further by emphasising gendered power relations more specifically.

In addition to the economic questions outlined, it is also important to consider the implications of the rapidly growing population mentioned earlier. During the sixteenth and seventeenth centuries the distribution of those working on the land was changing. Initially as a result of the growing population, and later also due to enclosure of common land, a group of landless peasants was being created. It is important to note that in Essex extensive closure had already taken place by the time of the first effective Witchcraft Statute in 1563, thus indicating the development of an increasingly capitalistic agricultural sector (see Saville 1969: 266–7). Moreover, witchcraft prosecutions were concentrated in the areas where enclosure *had* taken place (MacFarlane 1970: 154). This factor has led MacFarlane to observe that: 'if the Essex pattern is general, it may be that witchcraft was related to the problems of a growing population pressing on already enclosed land' (ibid.: 155). Clark (1982) has suggested that women were more directly and adversely affected by enclosure than men because it was women who tended to use common land for grazing.

We should also note that Essex was considered one of the most advanced and prosperous counties in England by contemporaries of the early modern period. One reason for this relative prosperity may have been the growing population of London, with the resultant effect of an increase in demand for supplies from Essex. However, prosperity was by no means evenly spread, and the enclosure of common land tended to only increase the wealth of landowners, while at the same time creating an increasing sector of landless wage-earners. Spufford (1974), for instance, has estimated that by 1660, towards the end of the witchcraft prosecutions, over half of the population of the neighbouring county of Cambridgeshire was landless. Together, these factors and those above may suggest that there were links (however tenuous) between the developing capitalist economy, male–female relations, and the witch-hunts.

The picture which emerges is of a growing proportion of the population with no land to work, and who were likely to become part of the increasing body of poor, the beggars and vagrants whom Elizabeth I legislated against in the late sixteenth and early seventeenth centuries (see Beier 1983). The associated Poor Laws placed responsibility for the poor on the local communities in which they lived. Vagrants and beggars could also be moved on from village to village, with no one wanting to take responsibility for them. Housing was part of this problem of the poor, and Alice Clark points out how: 'It was often necessary to compel unwilling overseers to build cottages for the impoverished poor and [significantly] for widows' (Clark 1982: 74–5).

In recent years there has been an increase in research specifically on women and the economy in the sixteenth and seventeenth centuries (see Charles and Duffin 1985; Roberts 1985; Amussen 1988; Crawford 1983; Hartman and Banner 1974; Bridenthal and Koonz 1977; Lewenhak 1980; Prior 1985). Alice Clark's *The Working Life of Women in the Seventeenth Century* (1982) remains useful as one of the most detailed studies of this period, despite the criticisms of her work.[8] Her data indicates quite clearly that it was men who were particularly concerned to be involved in the more profitable areas of economic development in this pre-capitalist period.

So what was women's position in the changing economy relative to that of men? Generally, it may be concluded that women were in a less advantageous situation than men, especially within the peasantry and amongst artisans and traders – the areas that were particularly relevant to the emerging capitalist economy and also the group amongst whom witchcraft accusations predominated. Evidence of women's work suggests that there was a struggle between the sexes around making a living, which also had the overall effect of ensuring that men rather than women obtained the better positions in, and thus overall control of, the new capitalist economic structure. Overall, male supremacy was maintained within the developing capitalist era, and women's relative dependence on men ensured.

In general it may be seen that there was a sexual division of labour during the sixteenth and seventeenth centuries (as well as prior to this), in which women were centred more exclusively on production within the household and on the family holding than men. Since the feudal economy was based on the household as the unit of production, women played a recognised and important role in production whether as managers of their husbands' estates or as labourers, and they were also involved in the economy as merchants and in crafts and trades (Lewenhak 1980: Chapter 7). Evidence suggests, contrary to the views of the 'critical-pessimists' that the sexual division of labour was in existence when the household was the unit of production, and, more significant, that there was a sexual division of responsibility and control in relation to production with men dominating these aspects (ibid.; Crawford 1983; Gittins 1985). Women did play a more direct role in pre-capitalist production than they were to do later, but not necessarily an equal role with men. Relative to men, during the sixteenth and seventeenth centuries, women were in various ways squeezed out of 'important' areas of production, or out of important positions in production for surplus rather than for subsistence. This also implies that women did not play a significant role in the more 'competitive' areas of the economy.

The sexual division of labour applied to women across the social classes. There was a distinction between classes, however, such that women of the upper classes were concentrated on the production of the household throughout the period in the capacity of 'managing', while peasant, artisanal and trading women were involved in extra-household productive activities as well (Kelso 1978). This meant that women of the upper classes played a less 'important' role in the development of capitalism than the other groups of women mentioned, and women of the lower classes and the rising middle class were seen as 'productive' throughout. However, overall, it was men who dominated the embryonic areas of the development of capitalism, and hence the form that this mode of production took (Clark 1982).

While the trends outlined above applied to both married women and single women and to widows, it is important to note that financial independence tended to be dependent on marital status. Women on their own, particularly widows, were more likely to be financially independent than married women. This was because married women were subordinate to their husbands (as reflected in the law) and under their husbands' control financially. Widows might inherit their husbands' land, property and/or craft or trade, and unmarried women might occasionally inherit their fathers' land and property or engage in other productive activities (Stenton 1957; Watkins 1984). Thus in the period covering the witch-hunts, women's work was largely defined by the institution of marriage. For example, a woman could only practice a craft alongside her husband, taking on his craft, or in her own right as a widow or as a single woman living in her father's household (see Amussen 1988: Chapter 3).

To look at these trends in greater detail with regard to women from the lower classes (those most affected by the witch-hunts) I will refer to examples from the textile industry, brewing and peasant labour. Firstly, the textile industry, which was also of particular importance to Essex. The textile industry grew considerably during the witch-hunt period, and MacFarlane has noted that the textile areas were also centres of prosecutions, although by no means the only such centres (MacFarlane 1970: 149). The wool trade and textile industry was very important in sixteenth- and seventeenth-century England, and also crucial to the development of capitalism. It was women who did all the spinning of thread for the weavers, hence the term 'spinster' for the women making their living by spinning. This was work which was badly paid but could, none the less, provide women with a livelihood: 'Though these wages provided no margin for the support of children it was possible for a woman who could spin the better quality yarns to maintain herself in independence' (Clark 1982: 115). In other words, it was possible for the single woman or widow without children to support herself in this way. Indeed the word 'spinster' increasingly denoted single women.

While women spun the yarn, the weavers were increasingly men. 'Women were excluded from cloth weaving on the grounds that their strength was insufficient to work the wide and heavy looms in use' (ibid.: 103). Only as the widow of a weaver could a woman carry out this trade, and even take on apprentices. However, such apprentices might not be accepted by the Company of Weavers (the trade organisation and extension of the earlier guilds) in the same way as apprentices trained by men, thus again highlighting women's relatively inferior position (Lewenhak 1980: Chapter 7).

Brewing was another important industry, because beer was the staple drink of men, women and children at most meals. Women did the brewing needed for immediate consumption by the household, and prior to our period, women also brewed for sale. But during the sixteenth century brewing changed from a female to male profession. Excluding women from brewing occurred alongside the separation of brewing from the sale of beer, which was a policy pursued by the government with the object of simplifying the collection of taxes, and supposedly to better the quality of the beer brewed. As a result of brewing was, by the early seventeenth century, restricted to those designated 'Common Brewers' who obtained a monopoly on production. Importantly, it was men who became Common Brewers, thereby winning this lucrative trade while women lost out. Clark concludes as a result that 'The closing of the trade of brewing to women must have seriously reduced their opportunities for earning an independence' (Clark 1982: 228). Again it was only widows who appeared able to carry out this trade by inheriting it from their husbands.

The peasant or labouring woman without ownership of land was likely to be in an even worse situation, and most likely to need support from the Parish. As a single woman she could go into service, and would be able to exist on her combined earnings and keep. But once married and with children she could no longer remain in service and was only able to earn a very low wage from farm labour – paid at a lower rate than that given to men. She might further supplement her wages by spinning. Furthermore, where she could live might be in dispute as a result of her financially precarious position. For instance:

> Normally she was transferred to the parish where her husband was bound as a servant for the term of one year, but the parish objected to the settlement of a married man lest his children became a burden on them.
>
> (Clark 1982: 88)

Indeed, if the wife was also a mother, she became wholly dependent on the parish for support if her husband died or deserted her (ibid.: 89).

Overall, then, women were finding it difficult throughout the period to make a living and their income was generally lower than men's. If single they might find work as servants, if married, they were dependent on their husbands. But if widowed they could be in either a threatening or vulnerable position, sometimes able to carry out a trade or craft left them by their husbands, but if unable to do this more likely to be dependent on others for financial support. Alternatively, widows might end up owning land, and proportionately women lower down the social scale inherited larger amounts of land than their aristocratic sisters (Amussen 1988: Chapter 3). Generally, however, women at the lower end of the social scale, widowed and with children seem to have been some of the most vulnerable individuals in the community. Since women in the peasantry tended to marry late, precisely because of problems of financial security, older women were also likely to have young children.

By looking at the material concerning socio-economic changes in the sixteenth and seventeenth centuries, it begins to become apparent that those accused of witchcraft also tend to be those who were among the most vulnerable in the economy, that is, labouring women, widowed and possibly older, and poor. Or otherwise those in competition with men for work in lucrative areas, that is, women carrying out a craft or trade, and more specifically, widows, who were more able to do so. These important issues will be revisited later in relation to the trial material.

IDEOLOGY AND MARRIAGE: EXPECTATIONS AND SOCIAL CONTROL

Examining the contemporary gender ideology aids our understanding of the witch-hunt phenomenon and shows how women were perceived as innately different and inferior to men in the early modern period. This ideology appeared to be prevalent at both a village level and among the literate middle and upper classes. At the core, despite changes over time, was not only the notion of male superiority and female inferiority, but also a specifically sexualised construct of women. It was this apparent 'sexual' nature of women which made them distinctly different from men. It eroticised women's apparent inferiority and also legitimated and justified their control by men. The result was that women were in a general sense seen as naturally deviant in relation to men and the male-dominated society, and were perceived to be especially prone to the ultimate deviance of siding with the Devil in what was a God-fearing and strongly religious society.

By contrast, men were not defined so exclusively in sexual terms. As Amussen observes, 'men complained of being called thieves, drunkards and blasphemers, as well as critical assaults on their social standing', which included that of cuckold (Amussen 1988: 102). But they were not construed sexually. Altogether, these ideological constructs placed men in an advantageous position, and allowed a sexual double standard of male and female behaviour whereby the same act was construed more detrimentally for women.[9] I would suggest that these constructs were not essentially different from the current gender ideologies discussed earlier in relation to today, and similarly allowed men to be seen as naturally supreme in a context of male–female conflict over power.

The Catholic Church's view of women, which formed the

dominant ideology regarding gender before and towards the beginning of the witch-hunts, was based on the Creation story in Genesis. Eve was conceived from the rib of Adam and was therefore considered inferior to him. Eve, representative of womankind, had also sinned in the Garden of Eden, thus making all women by nature sinful. It was particularly female *sexuality* that made women sinful; women were considered sexually insatiable and led men into damnation through association with their bodies. This view was to remain dominant until the end of the witch-persecutions, as indicated by John Sprint's *The Bride-Woman's Counsellor*, a sermon preached towards the end of the seventeenth century. Sprint argues that woman was responsible for the Original sin, and as a result he suggests that: 'tis but fair and just, that she, who hath been so greatly instrumental of so much Mischief and Misery to Man, should be actively engaged to please and comfort him' (Sprint 1709: 6–7).

The quote from Sprint also suggests the change that was to take place over the sixteenth and seventeenth centuries towards a greater emphasis on women's role as dutiful wife. Indeed the change in (upper class) gender ideology, which devalued women in a different but equally oppressive way, appears to have played a very important role in facilitating the eventual decline of the persecutions, as Karlsen also suggests with regard to New England. As shall be discussed in greater detail below, the 'new ideology', changed the perception of women from that of 'powerful and threatening witch' to that of 'hysterical woman', thereby emphasising women's (subordinate) place in marriage.

During the sixteenth and seventeenth centuries, marriage as an institution was an extremely important part of the social order, perhaps even more so than it is nowadays (Ingram 1987). The household, based on the nuclear family, was the focus for production and consumption, for accumulation and transmission of property, and it was seen as the foundation of social order and political authority.[10] Ingram, for instance, observes that:

> Tudor and Stuart philosophy regarded the rule or 'government' of the householder over his wife, children and servants as analogous to that of the prince over his subjects: royal and patriarchal authority were mutually validating reflections or natural manifestations of a distinctly ordered hierarchy.
>
> (ibid.: 125)

Thus the seventeenth century writer William Gouge described the family as 'a little church, and a little common-wealth' (in Bridenbaugh 1968: 32). Marriage was, therefore, a central institution which everyone was expected to embrace at some time in their lives. The great importance of marriage and its corollary, the establishment of new households, meant that not merely the potential husband and wife but also their families and possibly others, took part in deciding who should marry. As a result, dominant societal views also frowned upon those who did not uphold the 'marriage bond', and extramarital sexual activity was abhorred as a sin against God (ibid.: 125).

Marriage was not merely central to sixteenth- and seventeenth-century society, alongside sexual behaviour it was also perceived differently for men than for women. There was a clear double standard operating, and this relied on distinctly sexual constructs. We can see this by examining writings about marriage, and also by looking at the situations where men, and especially women, were not considered to be acting according to marital expectations, as exemplified in the Church Court or 'Bawdy Court' depositions (Ingram 1987; Hair 1972; Amussen 1988; Hill 1964).

There was an obvious concern with marriage amongst the literate elite during the witch-hunt period, with many books and pamphlets written about men and women's expected role in marriage and the household (see Woodbridge 1986). The general message was that of women's inferiority to men, and resultant unequal position of the sexes in marriage where the man should be the undisputed head. One such text, *The Lawes Resolution of Women's Rights* (1632) was a treatise compiled during Tudor times (but only published later) which explained women's social status. According to this, it was because of 'Adam's sin' that women should be excluded from public office:

> Women have no voyse in Parliament, they make no lawes, they consent to none, they abrogate none. All of them are understood either married or to bee married and their desires ar subject to their husband. I know no remedy though some women can shift it well enough. The Common Law here shaketh hand with Divinitie. . .
>
> (in Bridenbaugh 1968: 28)

These ideas were echoed by both Puritans and Anglicans, exemplified by the following Puritan treatises: William Gouge's *Of*

Domesticall Duties (published and reissued in 1622, 1634 and 1636) and Daniel Roger's *Matrimonial Honour* (first published in 1642, and reissued 1650); and the Anglican treatises: *Helpe for Domesticke Discipline* (1615) by R.R., and the anonymous *Discourse of the Married and Single Life* (1621). Bridenbaugh suggests that the only real difference between these texts was the 'refreshing brevity' of the Anglican treatises (1968: 31).

None the less, there was some change in the general view of marriage over the witch-hunt period. The period from the early sixteenth century to the end of the witch-persecution saw the important change in religious dominance from Catholic to Protestant/Puritan. This included the change of ideology regarding marriage from the Catholic Church's view that marriage was a necessary evil, to that of the Protestants, and especially Puritans, who moved towards a much more positive view of marriage. The Catholic Church had condemned sex, within as well as outside marriage, as sinful, and saw instead celibacy and virginity as the highest forms of existence. Within this doctrine, it was women who were the repositories of all sin and evil, and men would be tainted by their close presence. None the less, procreation was necessary, and hence women were forced into marriages in which they were obliged to service their husbands sexually. The story of the patient Griselda who fulfilled all her husband's horrific demands, was held up as the ideal of wifely virtue (see Sullerot 1979: 1–4). For Protestants, and especially Puritans, marriage was not perceived in this way, because marriage was no longer merely for the fallen, for those who could not attain celibacy or virginity throughout their lives. As Schucking observes, 'The Puritans recognised marriage as being essentially a sharing of spiritual–sensual experiences' (1969: 38). Women were active among the Puritan reformers and often supported this new form of marriage to escape the brutality of former times (see O'Faolain and Martines 1979: 206).

But despite these changes it may be argued that the basic male–female power relation had not actually changed. Husbands continued to exert and maintain firm control over wives within the Puritan marriage, on the one hand as the spiritual heads of the family, and on the other hand by the specific form of the heterosexual act. Flandrin, for instance, outlines the requirements given by the Protestant clergy for the heterosexual act and for what he sees as the continuation of male control:

Coition was only truly 'natural' and 'conjugal' when the woman lay on her back, with the man on top of her, because, they asserted, this position was the most favourable to procreation, and probably, above all, because it symbolised masculine domination and the fertilising gesture of the tiller of the soil.

(Flandrin 1979: 162)

What had taken place, then, was a change in the ideology concerning the form of marriage and its place within the social order. But it is important to recognise that one means of maintaining male power over women had merely been exchanged for another.

Despite the apparent changes, the focus by the Catholic Church on women's inherently sexual and therefore sinful natures had not been lost either. As Carolyn Merchant (1980) points out, a constant theme in the literature throughout the witch-hunt period is women's unruliness, and specifically her sexual unruliness. She cites Robert Burton, who, in his book *Anatomy of Melancholy* (1621), asserts that women, both young and old, are more sexual than men, something he obviously perceives as a problem:

Worse [lust] is in women than in men; when she is. . . an old widow, a mother long since. . . she doth very unseemly seek to marry; yet whilst she is so old a crone. . . a mere carcass, a witch, scarce feel, she caterwauls and must and will marry again, and betroth herself to some young man.

(in Merchant 1980: 182)

Similarly, according to Burton, young women eagerly partake in sexual intercourse as soon as they reach puberty. What is particularly interesting with regard to the witch-persecutions is Burton's focus on *widows* as 'oversexed'. He also presents another, and related, contemporary topic: the dominant idea that widows should not remarry. Miranda Chaytor, for example, points out how there was local pressure to stop widows remarrying:

Remarriage was not only economically unnecessary, it was also socially discouraged: ritualised hostility to second marriages (charivari, Katzenmuzik, rough music) has been widely documented and convincingly explained, for the woman who married again had a number of groups to appease. First she had to placate her dead husband and his kin; then there were the children (hers or her husband's) whose property expectations might be compromised by the new marriage; and third, the

young single women in the community may have resented her
for having taken an eligible husband from the pool.

(Chaytor 1980: 43)

Thus the underlying factors for discouraging widows from remarrying may have been directly material, although the pressures
were expressed in terms of an expressly sexualised ideology. Yet
widows did remarry for various social and economic reasons
(ibid.: 44).

As I have shown, the notion that women were essentially sexual
and therefore prone to sin was at the heart of sixteenth- and
seventeenth-century gender ideology. This is also reflected in
women's social reputations, which were again based on
perceptions of their sexual behaviour. Women's reputation and
hence social standing was much more easily threatened than
men's. Amussen for instance, points out that:

> The position of men in the social order of their communities
> was a product of a complex combination of sexual behaviour,
> familial relations and relations with their neighbours. Women's
> reputations were far more narrowly rooted in sexual behaviour.

(Amussen 1988: 103)

In particular, women sought to dissociate themselves from charges
of being a whore, of cuckolding their husbands, of bearing illegitimate children, and of keeping a 'bawdy house'.

During the period of the witch-hunts, therefore, women were
perceived as more likely to be sexually deviant than men because
women were by definition sexually deviant. And sexual deviance
was defined in opposition to marriage as the only appropriate
place for any sexual activity to take place. As a result, bearing an
illegitimate child, fornication (heterosexual intercourse outside
marriage), and incest, were illegal and punishable through the
Church Courts (Ingram 1987; Amussen 1988; Hair 1972).[11] Interestingly, pre-nuptial fornication, that is, heterosexual intercourse
prior to marriage, was also an offence, but greatly lessened by the
eventual marriage of the individuals concerned. It is important to
note how women often ended up accused of fornication and
illegitimacy without having intended either. Precisely because the
penalties, both legally and socially, were high for women who had
committed either of these offences, it may be expected that
women did not commit them willingly. Amussen, for instance,

points out that: 'Many of the women who became pregnant alleged that they consented to sexual relations only after a promise of marriage; given the treatment of bastard-bearers, they undoubtedly relied on the promise' (Amussen 1988: 116). As we shall see later, one of the alleged witches apparently used witchcraft to get herself out of a similar predicament.

Women were supposed to be under the control of their husbands and hence cuckolding their husbands, that is, going with other men, and by association dominating them, was considered deviant behaviour. This was often dealt with by the local community (both women and men, but especially men) by 'charivari' or 'rough music'. According to Amussen:

> The most fully documented charivari in East Anglia in Wetherden, Suffolk in 1604, was directed at Nicholas Rosyer and his wife, who had beaten him one evening when he came home drunk from the alehouse. There is no other allegation of his behaviour in that case, and the charivari was organised and carried out by men.
>
> (Amussen 1988: 118)

The woman concerned was stepping out of her role as defined by men, and as Amussen concludes: 'Men, not women, were concerned with the phenomenon of the domineering wife'.[12]

THE 'POPULAR CONTROVERSY'

The 'popular controversy' over women was a debate concerning women's position in society taking place among the educated middle classes and rising bourgeoisie during the same period as the witch-hunts.[13] It is illuminating about the views of women at the time, and shows clearly the eroticised notions of female inferiority which were prevalent. Wright (1935) suggests that the reason behind the controversy was the apparent threat to men posed by women's activities. The 'activity and boldness of women, especially women of the middle classes, aroused the ire of conservatives, who vented their displeasure in pulpit and pamphlet' (ibid.: 466). The controversy was fuelled by the ascendancy of women (Mary and Elizabeth I) to the highest position in the land, the position of monarch, and the reign of Elizabeth was especially significant.[14]

The debate covers a number of themes: whether women are naturally inferior to men; whether women should be married and so under the control of a husband; and the issue of cross-dressing. The attacks on women came from men and the more positive responses probably came primarily from women, although it is in dispute who actually wrote the different pieces (see Shepherd 1985; Woodbridge 1986).

Following the increasingly dominant Puritan ideology at the time, the attacks on women had as recurring themes that women not only seduce men and are generally unchaste, but are also vain and embezzle their husband's money. Some of the first writings appeared in the 1540s, in the years leading up to the witch-hunts. The first and one of the most popular was the *Schole House of Women* (circa 1542) by Edward Gosinghill, which according to the author was 'a diatribe against the vanity, talkativeness, extravagance, faithlessness, and general frailty of women from Eve to Jezebel' (in Wright 1935: 468). Gosinghill suggests that despite the apparent failing of women, men need women – and in particular for sex, which women lure men into by kissing 'with open mouthe. . . tongue to tongue' (in Woodbridge 1986: 26).

While men wrote the attacks on women, both men and women wrote in defence of the female sex. In 1542, Robert Vaughan wrote a reply to the *Schole House of Women*, entitled *A Dyalogue defensyue for women*. As well as defending various other aspects of women's nature, *A Dyalogue* attacked the double standard of morality to which women were subjected: 'the author. . . holds that women are not more to blame than men for unchastity, since the latter besiege them with solitations and exert all their vaunted intelligence to bring about their capitulation' (Wright 1935: 468). This was a point expressed by many of the defending authors.

While works such as the *Schole House* labelled all women as unchaste, some of the writings claimed only to attack those women who were actually unchaste, thereby creating the separate categories of 'good' and 'fallen' women. About 1500 Abraham Vele published *The deceyte of women, to the instruction and ensamble of all men, yonge and olde, newly corrected*, which beseeched 'all ye good honest women, and vyrgins be not myscontent' (in ibid.: 471), but which at the time gave a warning to husbands to keep their wives under control, in the form of a pictorial warning of the cuckolded husband. The title-page has a picture presenting a woman astride her spouse, who is on all fours with a bridle in his mouth, and she is flogging him with a three-lashed whip.

The most popular of all the attacks on women, and the most intense part of the controversy, was the work by Joseph Swetnam, entitled *The Araignment of Lewd, Idle, Froward, and unconstant Women: or the vanitie of them, choose you whether. With a commendacion of wise, vertuous, and honest Women. Pleasant for married Men, profitable for young Men, and hurtful to none* (1615). This pamphlet went through at least ten editions, showing its great popularity. Again we find that women are accused of 'leading a proud, lazie, and idle life, to the great hindrance of their poore husbands' (Wright 1935: 487). Women are extravagant and become ruined by their idleness:

> For commonly women are the most part of the forenoone painting themselves, and frizling their haires, and prying in their glass like Apes, to prancke vp themselues in their gawdies, like Poppets, or like the Spider which weaues a fine web to hang the flie.
>
> (ibid.: 487)

Unlike the other writers, Swetnam even questions whether men should marry these potential Apes and Poppets; but if they must, then he suggests that they marry a maid of seventeen who is 'flexible and bending, obedient and subiect to doe anything' (ibid.: 487). Swetnam thus expresses the need, above all, for husbands to keep control of their wives.

While Swetnam's misogyny rages throughout the pamphlet, he acknowledges that men themselves may not be altogether pure. However, he is not prepared to dwell on this because, he reckons, men should stick together 'for it is a very hard winter when one Woolfe eateth another. . . and a most unkinde part it were for one man to speake ill of another' (Swetnam 1615: 64).

There are a number of criticisms of Swetnam's work, probably all by women.[15] Ester Sowrenam is one of the authors. As a result of the obvious pseudonym[16] Shepherd (1985) wonders whether this was actually a male writer, although concludes that it probably was a woman. Ester Sowrenam wrote a criticism of Swetnam's work in which she refutes his arguments by careful reference to religious writings, entitled *Ester hath hang'd Haman: or an Answere to a lewd pamphlet, entitled 'The Arraignment of Women'* (1617). Swetnam may say that women are crooked due to the nature of the rib from which they were fashioned, but Sowrenam replies cleverly that: 'if Woman receaued her crookednesse from the rib, and consequently from the Man, how doth man excell in crookedness, who hath more of these crooked ribs?' (Sowrenam 1617: 3). Similarly the serpent in the Garden of Eden who tempted Eve was a male, because the form of the Devil is always seen to be male (ibid.: 7), and as a result Sowrenam argues that it is men who prey sexually on women rather than the other way round. In this way Sowrenam presents a similar picture to that found by Amussen (1988) in relation to the Church Court prosecutions of women for sexual offences – that it was the sexual double standard integral to male–female power relations, rather than women's 'oversexed sexual natures', which resulted in the large number of illegitimacy cases during the witch-hunt period.

In the late 1630s there were a couple of works by John Taylor entitled the *Divers Crab-tree Lectures* (1639) and *A Junior Lecture* (1639), which were satires on the husband and wife theme. Instead of merely writing a tirade against the female sex, Taylor uses female characters to express his criticisms of women, for example, a character called Mary Make-Peace. What is particularly interesting is the reply to Taylor, written by two individuals signing themselves spinsters. The work, entitled *The Women's Sharpe Revenge* (1640), might actually have been written by Taylor himself (Shepherd 1985). Unfortunately, nothing is written about Iona Hit-him-home and Mary Tattle-well, although the writings could suggest that they are middle-class urban females, and perhaps tradeswomen (George 1973: 152). Shepherd, however, suggests that it is merely Taylor attempting to increase sales of his pamphlets. The pamphlet reads very differently if written by either Taylor or the 'two spinsters'. If the former, then the pamphlet seems to provide a scathing satire of the defence of women. If written by women, then the pamphlet appears a radical tract indeed.

The pamphlet stresses that women were not created, even if men think so, to be men's slaves but to be men's equals. Furthermore, women might even be better than men with regard to precisely those things men say women are not, namely 'Chastity, Charity, constancy, Magnanimity Vallour, Wisedome, piety, or any

Grace or Vertue whatsoever' (in George 1973: 152–3). Iona Hit-him-home and Mary Tattle-well also suggest that if men think women to be so terrible, then they should leave women alone rather than insist that women be their wives (ibid.: 153). Women marry mainly because they want to have children, rather than because they want to be wives, and would not end up living with men if they did not have to:

> Surely if there had been any lawful way for them to have had Children without Husbands, there hath beene, and are, and will bee a numberless number of women that would or will never be troubled with wedlocke, nor the knowledge of man.
>
> (ibid.: 172)

Finally, the issue of cross-dressing and the 'masculine woman' bears out the same findings. After James I became king in the first decade of the seventeenth century (1603), there was an increase in misogynist literary attacks and women's clothing was criticised, in addition to their apparently unchaste behaviour. It was the wearing of 'masculine' clothes by women that many men, including James I, abhorred – a fashion increasingly popular during the late sixteenth and early seventeenth century. The King attempted to suppress this phenomenon, through the clergy, and a contemporary letter written by John Chamberlain (1620) notes:

> Yesterday the bishop of London called together all his clergie about this towne, and told them he had expresse commandment from the King to will them to inveigh vehemently against the insolence of our women, and theyre wearing of brode brimed hats, pointed dublets, theyre hayre cut short or shorne
>
> (Wright 1935: 493)

Rudolf Dekker and Lotte Van de Pol suggest that cross-dressing by women was prevalent in the early modern period, finding 'fifty authentic cases. . .in the seventeenth and eighteenth centuries in Great Britain' (1989: 1).

Faderman suggests that some women actively wanted to look like men in order to gain male prerogatives and freedom, freedoms including 'self-sufficiency, freedom to wander unmolested, freedom to explore occupations more varied than those open to women' (Faderman 1981: 52). It is perhaps not surprising that there were attacks on such 'masculine' women since they represented women's entry to male preserves. At the same time it is important to note that this aspect of the popular controversy at least indicated that women were actively trying to overcome the constraints of living in a male supremacist society.

The most important pamphlet at the time condemning 'masculine' women was entitled *Hic Mulier: Or, The Man-Woman: Being a Medicine to cure the Coltish Disease of the Staggers in the Masculine-Feminines of our Times* (1620). The author's concern was that women acting out of their assigned role would bring disgrace to women as a sex, let alone to the families of the women concerned. Both married and unmarried women or widows dressed in masculine attire. Some women managed to disguise themselves so well that they were mistaken for men, and the actress, Mary Frith, even lived quite openly as if the latter (Faderman 1981).[17]

The reply to *Hic Mulier*, entitled *Haec Vir: Or the Womanish-Man: Being an Answere to a late Booke intituled Hic Mulier* (1620) reflected this ambition of many women to be independent from men. As the author says:

> you say wee are barbarous and shameless, and cast off all softness, to runne wilde through a wildernesse of opinions. In this you express more cruelty then in all the rest. . . we are free-borne as Men, haue as free election and as free spirits, we are compounded of like parts, and may with like liberty make benefit our Creations.
>
> (Wright 1935: 496–7)

Overall, there are a number of important aspects to the attacks against women in the 'popular controversy'. The pamphlets attacking women argue that women's place is in marriage, where they are under the will of their husbands. They stress the need for husbands to control their wives so that they are not unchaste, which women are prone to be, according to the writers. Furthermore, by presenting women as generally weak and inferior the pamphlets seemingly attempt to curtail the independent activities of the women who are encroaching upon 'male' areas of economic activity and power generally. By contrast, the pamphlets written in defence of women argue strongly that women are neither weak nor inferior, but are only placed in such a position by men. Indeed, most of the authors suggest that it is precisely men who are the problem.

DECLINE OF THE WITCH-HUNTS

It is often argued that the 'Scientific Revolution' and the concomitant emphasis on 'reason', taking place largely during the
seventeenth century, played a part in the decline of the witch-
hunts by negating witchcraft belief amongst the ruling class
(Easlea 1980; Trevor-Roper 1969; Thomas 1971; Merchant 1980).
Hugh Trevor-Roper, for example, in his classic study of the European witch-hunts, argues that the persecutions eventually declined
because the 'scientific' revolution of the seventeenth century
brought with it an entire change in ideas regarding witchcraft:
'what ultimately destroyed the witch-craze. . . was the new
philosophy, a philosophical revolution which changed the whole
concept of Nature and its operations' (Trevor-Roper 1969: 108).
The belief in witchcraft was thus no longer feasible.

What is in dispute, however, is why and in what way it became
appropriate for the witchcraft belief to be negated, and in
particular the importance of male–female relations to this. Carol
Karlsen (1987), for instance (as outlined earlier), argues that the
development of 'rational' or 'scientific' thought is not the main
issue. She emphasises instead the construction of a new gender
ideology, arguing that the new construct of the sexually passive
and domesticated woman emerged as an effective alternative to
witchcraft accusation as a means of socially controlling women.

Brian Easlea (1980), focusing on the English example, also
considers male–female relations, albeit less centrally. He suggests
that the new 'mechanical philosophy', became an appropriate
alternative to previous explanations of natural phenomena, such
as the idea of natural magic (on which 'witchcraft' can be seen to
have relied), because it provided legitimation for the developing
social order, while at the same time stressing the continuity of
Christianity. He points out that the new philosophers provided an
explicitly male-dominated approach. Francis Bacon, for instance,
using obviously gendered language, argued that their method
would inaugurate the 'truly masculine birth of the Universe', and
stressed that 'Nature' must be conquered and harnessed to give up
'her' secrets through the use of experimental method. He intended to establish the 'Dominion of Man over the Universe' (ibid.:
128–9). Easlea also explains how, according to the seventeenth-
century mechanical philosophers, men were equated with 'reason'
and 'rationality' but women were deemed incapable of reason

because they had 'soft' and 'delicate' brains (ibid.: 140–2). The result was the ideological conceputalisation of women as nature and men as culture, which has remained in some form to the present day (Jordanova 1981).

In this way it may be argued that the decline of the witch-hunts was an integral part of the establishment of the seventeenth-century social order. Partly, as a result of the change in ruling-class ideology associated with the new 'mechanically' rather than 'organically' orientated social order (Merchant 1980), and crucially, the changes in gender ideology which increasingly saw women as passive rather than active. Instead of actively dangerous female witches, therefore, the dominant view became that women were merely passive vessels of procreation, without even the means to reason. The gender ideology remained based on natural or biological definitions, but the content changed.

The change in gender ideology and its implication for witch accusations may also be identified by examining the work of the contemporary writers who were sceptical about witchcraft, such as the Dutchman Johann Weyer (1563) (whose anti-witch-hunting work was also known in England), and especially that of Reginald Scot (1584). It is thought that Scot wrote his treatise against witch-hunting at least partly as a result of the 1582 trial in Essex. Those accusing women of being witches were presenting women as active, while those defending women against such accusations were presenting women as passive. Yet both accusers and defenders relied on the naturalistic assumption that women were naturally weak and gullible (Merchant 1980). Rather than women's apparent weakness and gullibility being seen as a reason to convict them, as texts such as the *Malleus Maleficarum* tended to do, sceptics such as Weyer suggested instead that women's natures led them to be victimised by the Devil. As a result he argued that the fault lay with the Devil and not with the women concerned.[18]

Weyer based his naturalistic, or biologistic, views of women partly on humoural theory which saw women as 'melancholic' and hence tending to be 'wrathful'. Similarly, Reginald Scot, who also defended women against witchcraft accusation, presented 'melancholy' as the reason women believed themselves witches. But, unlike Weyer, Scot was also sceptical about the reality of demons, and argued that women who believed they saw demons were actually ill:

Reginald Scot . . . maintained in his *Discoveries of Witchcraft* (1584) that the melancholy that affected witches attacked their brains and depraved their senses and judgement. If a witch's mind and will had not become corrupted and confused, she would never make voluntary confessions of such deeds. A woman so weakened in body and brain could then imagine herself to be a witch who could do strange, impossible things. This was particularly likely to happen after menopause, 'upon the stopping of their monthly melancholic jinx or issue of blood'.

(Merchant 1980: 142)

In this way Scot was suggesting that especially post-menopausal (and therefore older) women were likely to become 'ill in the head', and therefore to perceive themselves as witches.

Both Weyer and Scot wrote their anti-witch-hunting treatises during the height of the witchcraft prosecutions, and their work was heavily criticised at the time. For example, James I wrote his *Daemonology* (1597) as a refutation of Scot's work (Robbins 1959: 277). None the less, the ideas they were expounding were later to become part of the dominant (if not prevalent) view of witchcraft. The example of the Royal Physician William Harvey provides an interesting bridge between these two situations (see Keynes 1966; Merchant 1980).

Harvey was physician to both James I and Charles I, and influenced these monarchs' belief in witchcraft. Harvey himself did not think that women could be either 'witches' or 'bewitched', but instead attributed these phenomena to 'hysteria' and the product of a 'dysfunctional womb'. Keynes (1966) cites one instance of a woman who believed herself to be a witch, but whom Harvey showed otherwise. Harvey visited the woman, 'who dwelt at a lone House on the borders of the Heath', pretending to be a wizard himself. Assuring the woman that they were thus 'brother and sister', he asked her about her familiar and the woman brought him a toad. While the woman was out of the room, Harvey dissected the toad and found it to be quite ordinary. The letter in which this episode is mentioned continues as follows:

A woman had a tame toade, which she believed to bee a spirit and her familiar; the toad upon disection proved an arrant naturall toad, and had really eaten milk, and not in appearance onely, therfore there are no witches.

(Keynes 1966: 214).

Thus Harvey did not believe in witches, and instead sought the explanation of this apparent phenomenon in what he saw as women's natural, and potentially defective, make-up.[19]

Through his eminent position as Royal Physician and member of the Royal College of Physicians, Harvey was able to enforce his views and thereby stop a number of 'witch' prosecutions directly as well as affecting other cases indirectly during the reign of Charles I (ibid.). But his apparent support of women accused of witchcraft actually relied on notions of women's inferiority, as did the anti-witch-hunting views of Weyer and Scot.

The work of Ehrenreich and English (1976), outlined earlier, argues that male take-over of the medical profession was a central reason for the witch-persecutions. I would refute this centrality, because the example of William Harvey's role in enabling the decline of persecutions shows otherwise. Harvey, through his membership of the Royal College, was directly involved in stopping women practising as midwives. In his role as censor Harvey also dealt with illegal, largely female, practitioners of medicine (Webster 1979). However, it is important to recognise that Harvey, with his stress on women's inferiority, was involved in *both* countering witchcraft accusations and attempting to stop women's involvement in medicine and midwifery.[20]

In this chapter it has been suggested that certain contextual features, notably demographic, economic and ideological, in addition to male–female relations, enable us to situate the witch-hunts and aid explanation of this phenomena. This context provides a background to the following chapter, which examines more closely who the accused were and the accusations against them.

Chapter 8

The accused and the accusations against them

THE ESSEX WITCH TRIALS

This chapter focuses on the nature of those accused of witchcraft in sixteenth- and seventeenth-century England and the accusations against them. As indicated previously, some of the main sources for the witch-hunt phenomenon are the contemporary court records, in particular from the Assizes, and also the contemporary pamphlets about individual trials. These sources, especially the pamphlets, will be of central importance to the discussion in this chapter. As I pointed out earlier, the records are often incomplete. In the case of Essex, however, the primary source material is unusually good and affords an opportunity to consider the details of specific cases.

Generally it can be seen that controlling the use of witchcraft became a central concern of Elizabethan and Jacobean village life (MacFarlane 1970). Once accused of using witchcraft the label of 'witch' was also virtually impossible to shake off. Even if a woman accused of witchcraft was acquitted, she might well be accused of another crime of witchcraft at a later date. Such was the case of Margaret Welles (or Gans) who was acquitted in 1579 after being accused of using witchcraft to cause murder. She appears in the records of the next Assizes accused of bewitching a pig, though again acquitted. Similarly Elizabeth Frauncis, accused in 1566 of using witchcraft to cause injury to a fellow villager, was imprisoned for one year. She was again accused and found guilty of causing injury by witchcraft in 1572, when she was once more imprisoned and also placed in the pillory. In 1579 she was tried for the last time, convicted of using witchcraft to murder, and hanged. (The testimony of Elizabeth Frauncis in particular will be examined below as a part of the discussion of the trial pamphlets.)[1]

It is clear from the Essex material that witchcraft accusation was aimed not only at women, but at a particular group of women. Those accused tended to be poor, but not necessarily the poorest in the community; and a disproportionately large number of widowed or unmarried women were affected. There was also a strong tendency for the accused to be older women, usually over 40 years of age. These 'witches' were accused of various crimes which were closely related to the everyday life of people in the Essex villages, ranging from injury or murder of people and animals, to producing bad harvests or stopping milk from churning to butter.

From the Assize Court records for Essex we can see that at least 90 per cent of those formally accused of using witchcraft were women, and Alan MacFarlane has suggested that of these at least 40 per cent were widows (MacFarlane 1970: 160–4). This constitutes a disproportionately high number of widows among the accused if we compare the figure to that of widows in the village population as a whole – which, as indicated in the previous chapter, tended to be between 10 and 20 per cent. But it is often difficult to tell with accuracy whether the women concerned were single or married or what they did for a living.[2] Most of the women in the court records are referred to as 'spinster', and this could mean that they were either single or married, but carrying out the trade of spinster, that is, spinning. From the seventeenth century the term 'spinster' officially began to be used to denote 'single woman' (see *Oxford English Dictionary* 1975). Even so, it may be concluded that the total number of unmarried or widowed women probably constituted over 50 per cent of the accused.

Regarding the economic class position of the women accused of witchcraft, our main indicator is often the husband's occupation, since the records list this rather than that of wives, although in fact very few occupations are listed overall. By examining the Assize Court records for Essex between 1560 and 1680, MacFarlane is none the less able to list the occupations for the husbands of 49 'witches'; which are as follows:[3]

Labourer	23
Husbandman	11
Yeoman	4

Beer Brewer	1
Tailor	4
Weaver	1
Shoemaker	1
Sailor	2
Mason	2

My own examination of the Assize Court records has in addition revealed an accused 'witch' called Sarah Godfrie, whose husband John Godfrie was a glover (see Cockburn 1978: case 1084). The vast majority (80 per cent) of husbands of the accused were in agricultural work, whereas the victims' menfolk, and male victims, were less likely to be so, and instead were small artisans and tradesmen, thus suggesting that 'Witches seem to have been poorer than their victims' (MacFarlane 1970: 150). There may of course be problems in using the husband's occupation as the measure of a witch's social standing, since not all of the 'witches' were married. None the less, as the previous discussion regarding women's position in the economy indicates, wives and widows were likely to be closely associated with their husbands' livelihood, and wives and widows formed the bulk of the accused.

The witch trial material, both Assize Court records and trial pamphlets, helps us to see who the accused were, and to begin to understand the possible reasons for the accusation of witchcraft against these particular individuals. It presents a complex picture, with various different levels of interpretation, both in terms of what actually took place and of the ideological slant given to events by the pamphlet writers. The pamphlet writers themselves seem to have believed in the use of witchcraft. Interestingly we find, at least according to the writers, that some of the women accused also believed in witchcraft to the point of using it as a means of empowerment. Some women deny that they had used witchcraft, while yet other women appear not to have believed in witchcraft wholeheartedly, and give what we might consider more rational explanations for their activities.

Reading through the pamphlets and Assize Court indictments, two main areas regarding the accused are apparent: who the accused were, and the evidence against them, although who they were also appears to have been used as a form of evidence and the areas therefore overlap. In terms of the accused the following categories seem to be important: sex, marital status, age, and whether other kin have been accused. In terms of 'evidence' I would suggest the following categories: liaison with the Devil, economic conflict or activity, and sexual 'deviance' (see Table 8.1). I shall refer to these aspects when outlining the individual trials, and also in the summary discussion towards the end of the chapter.

I will now take a closer look at the accused and the accusations against them by focusing on the five Essex pamphlets still in existence. Outlining and comparing the pamphlets has its problems, however, because they vary greatly in length, and depth of detail, and this needs to be taken into consideration.

THE 1566 PAMPHLET AND WITCH TRIAL[5]

The examination and confession of certaine wytches at Chens- forde in the Countie of Essex before the Quenes maiesties Judges, the xxvi daye of July Anno 1566.[6]

Three women were accused of witchcraft at this trial and all of them appear to be using witchcraft as a means of empowerment: to obtain a rich husband, and various commodities, to get their own back against their husbands or neighbours, or to kill their husbands with whom they quarrelled. The most important evidence against them is 'proof' of having familiars as this is deemed to show their liaison with the Devil. The accused are: Elizabeth Frauncis, wife of Christopher Frauncis, who 'bewitched John the infant son of William Auger of Hatfield Peverel so he became paralysed' (witchcraft) (Cockburn 1978: case 273); Agnes Waterhouse (or Mother Waterhouse), a 63-year-old widow, who 'bewitched William Fynee at Hatfield Peverel so that he lingered. . . and then died' (murder by witchcraft) (Cockburn 1978: case 274); and Joan Waterhouse, 18-year-old spinster and daughter of Agnes Waterhouse, who 'bewitched Agnes Browne of Hatfield Peverel, spinster, so that she lost the use of her right arm and leg' (witchcraft) (Cockburn 1978: case 263).[7] Of these indictments, only that of Joan Waterhouse is mentioned directly in the pamphlet.

The pamphlet, written by a John Phillips, begins with an introduction giving praise to God and denouncing the Devil (by reference to biblical and classical texts). There is a poem telling people to gather round to hear the tale of the three witches; and

Table 8.1: Summary of evidence against the accused mentioned in Essex Pamphlets

Name	Date of trial	Outcome of trial	Age	Marital status	Other kin accused	Experience of economic conflict	Liason with the Devil (familiar or witches' marks)	Different types of sexual 'deviance'
Elizabeth Frauncis	1566	P		Wf	2	1	1	4
Agnes Waterhouse	1566	H	63	Wd	2	1	1	1
Joan Waterhouse	1566	N.G.	18	S	2	1	1	
Elizabeth Frauncis	1579	H		Wf		1		
Elleine Smithe	1579	H		Wf	1	1	1	
Margery Staunton	1579	Free			1	1		
Alice Nokes	1579	H		Wf			1	1
Ursley Kempe	1582	H		S		1	1	1
Ales Newman	1582	P		Wf		1	1	1
Elizabeth Bennet	1582	H		Wf			1	2
Ales Hunt	1582	N.G.		Wf	2		1	
Cysley Celles	1582	P		Wf		1	1	
Ales Manfielde	1582		63	S			1	
Margaret Grevell	1582	N.G.	55	S			1	
Elizabeth Eustace	1582	N.G.	53					
Annys Herd	1582			S			1	1
Joan Robynson	1582							1
Margery Sammon	1582				2			
Annys Glascocke	1582	P		S			1	
Joan Pechey	1582		60 +	Wd		1		1

Name	Year	Sentence	Age	Status				
Joan Cunny	1589	H	80 ±[4]	Wd	1		1	3
Joan Upney	1589	H		S	1		1	
Joan Prentice	1589	H		S	1	1	1	
Margaret Moone	1654	H		Wd			1	
Elizabeth Clarke	1654	H		S			1	1
Elizabeth Gooding	1654	H		Wf		1	1	1
Anne Leach	1654	H		Wd	1		1	
Hellen Clark	1654	H		Wf	1		1	
Rebecca West	1654	N.S.		S	1		1	
Anne West	1654	H		Wd	1		1	
Mary Greenleife	1645						1	
Mary Johnson	1654	P		Wf			1	
Marion Hocket	1654	H		Wd			1	
Sarah Hating	1654	H		Wf			1	
Elizabeth Harvie	1654	H		Wd			1	
Rose Hallybread	1654	D.I.G.	65 ±			1	1	
Joyce Boanes	1654	H		Wf		1	1	
Susan Cock	1654	H		Wf	1	1	1	
Margaret Landish	1645	H		Wf			1	
Rebecca Jones	1654	H		Wd		1	1	
Johan Cooper	1654	D.I.G.		Wd			1	
Anne Cate	1654	H		S	1	1	1	

Key

Wf – Wife	S – Spinster	H – Hanged	N.S. – No Sentence
Wd – Widow	P – Prison	N.G. – Not Guilty	D.I.G. – Died in Gaol

Source: Adapted from Hester (1988).

we are told that these witches had turned away from God to be with Satan. The pamphlet then outlines the testimonies of the three witches, including the confessions of Elizabeth Frauncis and Mother Waterhouse. Elizabeth Frauncis was found guilty and imprisoned; Mother Waterhouse found guilty and hanged; and Joan Waterhouse found not guilty. The three women are all from the village of Hatfield Peveril, and there are close connections between them. Not only is Mother Waterhouse the mother of Joan, but it transpires from a later pamphlet (1579) that Mother Waterhouse and Elizabeth Frauncis are sisters. They also have a spirit or familiar in common, called Sathan, and this is central to the trial. This spirit variously appears as a white cat with spots, a toad and a dog with or without horns.

Elizabeth Frauncis is questioned first and says that she learnt 'this arte of witchcraft' from her (now deceased) grandmother, Mother Eve, also of Hatfield Peveril. She was then 12 years old. Mother Eve told her to renounce God and to give herself to Sathan instead, through the white cat with spots, Sathan. She was to feed Sathan the cat with bread and milk, and to keep him/it in a basket. Elizabeth wanted Sathan to make her rich and spoke to him about this:

> When this Mother Eve had given her the cat Sathan, then this, Elizabeth desired firste of the sayde cat (callinge it Sathan) that she might be ryche and to have goodes – and he promised her she shoulde – askinge her what she would have. . . (for this Cat spoke to her as she confessed in a strannge holowe voice)
>
> (Ewen 1971: 317)

First of all she asked for sheep, and Sathan obliged by bringing 18 black and white sheep into her pasture. But they all eventually disappeared, although 'She knew not howe'.

She then asked Sathan to procure her a rich husband, Andrew Byles. But this was not fulfilled in the way she had wanted. As the pamphlet continues:

> when she had gotten these shepe, she desired to have one Andrew Byles to her husband, which was a man of some welth, and the cat dyd promise she shold, but that he sayde she must fyrste consent that this Andrew shuld abuse her, and she so did. And after when this Andrew has thus abused her he would not mary her, wherfore she willed Sathan to waste his goodes, which

he forthwith did, and yet not beyng content with this, she willed him [Sathan] to touch his [Andrew's] body whych he forthewith dyd whereof he [Andrew] died.

... when this Andrew was dead, she doubting her selfe with childe willed Sathan to destroye it, and he bad her take a certayne herbe and drinke it, whych she did, and destroyed the childe forthwyth.

(ibid.: 317–18)

In other words, Andrew agreed to marriage only if Elizabeth would have sex with him beforehand. But despite her agreement to this, in the end he did not want to marry her, and left her pregnant. She got her own back by using witchcraft to make him impotent[8], and eventually by having him killed. She also managed, by the use of herbs, to procure an abortion. As discussed in the previous chapter, 'pre-nuptial fornication' was a common prelude to marriage and as a result many women were already pregnant on their wedding day; but fornication without marriage was a punishable offence. This, together with the other financial and social burdens of having an illegitimate child, probably led to Elizabeth's wish to have an abortion. I have suggested elsewhere that the pamphlet story of Elizabeth Frauncis presents a very plausible scenario of a women's life, and one that we would also recognise today (Hester 1990). Whether or not the pamphlet record of Elizabeth Frauncis's trial represents her actual experience, the events mentioned, and the way they are mentioned, can be seen to be a product of a society where men dominate women. In this context we can expect that it is women who tend to be financially dependent on men, and would therefore find a rich husband advantageous; it is women who are left with the responsibility for pregnancy; and it is women who are sexually abused by men rather than the other way round.

But to continue with the pamphlet: having failed to marry Andrew Byles, Elizabeth asked Sathan to get her another husband and he suggested Frauncis, who was unfortunately not as rich as Andrew. Sathan again wanted her to consent to sex: 'willynge her to consent unto that Frauncis in fornycation which she did, and there of conceaved a daughter that was borne within a quarter of a yere after they were married' (Ewen 1971: 318). So Elizabeth Frauncis was also involved in pre-nuptial fornication with Frauncis, her eventual husband, and was consequently six months pregnant when they married. But as she did marry this was perhaps not perceived as especially sinful or deviant. Unfortunately after they were married 'they lived not so quietly as she desyred, being stirred (as she said) to much unquietness and moved to swearing and cursinge'. The child especially seemed to be a problem and Elizabeth asked Sathan to kill her when she was about six months old, which he did. She also asked Sathan to make her husband lame, which he did in the following way:

> It cam in a morninge to this Frauncis shoe, lying in it lyke a tode, and when he perceived it puttinge on his shoe, and had touched it with his fote, he being sodenly amased asked of her what it was, and she bad him kil it and he was forthwith taken with a lamenes wherof he can not be healed.

(Ewen 1971: 318)

In this way Sathan, the white cat with spots, changed into a toad, so as to carry out his task of laming Frauncis more effectively.

In the pamphlet Elizabeth also describes how she rewarded Sathan by giving him a drop of blood every time he did anything for her, 'by prycking herselfe, sometime in one place and then in an other, and where she pricked her selfe there remayned a red spot which was styl to be sene' (Ewen 1971: 318). This red spot was the 'witches' mark', proof of her association with Sathan the cat as well as Satan the Devil.

The pamphlet continues with Elizabeth Frauncis's testimony, saying that eventually, after 15 or 16 years, she gave the cat to Mother Waterhouse, her neighbour, who was 'a poore woman' and would have a better life through him. Elizabeth asked for a cake in return, and then instructed Mother Waterhouse in the manner she herself had been taught by her grandmother. The examination and confession of Mother Waterhouse then follows.

Mother Waterhouse explains that once she had received Sathan the cat, she wanted to see 'what he coulde do' and asked him to kill one of her own pigs, which he duly did. She rewarded him with a chicken and a drop of her blood, and these were also to be the reward for further deeds. In order to obtain the drop of blood she would prick her hand or face and let him suck the blood, and 'the spots of all the which priks are yet to be sene in her skin' (ibid.: 319). She then outlines the various deeds she had Sathan carry out for her. She had Sathan kill three of Father Kersye's pigs because she was offended with him. When she fell out with widow Gooday she had Sathan drown her cow; and similarly killed her neighbour's three geese when she fell out with her as well. (There follows a long catalogue of incidents.) She was said to have destroyed her own 'brewing' because she wanted peace and quiet. She was denied butter by someone and caused her to lose the 'curdes'. Sathan killed certain individuals for her, namely her (male) neighbour because she had fallen out with him and his wife; and also her husband, whom she had had killed a year previously, because they lived 'unquietly' together. Thus, like Elizabeth Frauncis, she was thought to have killed her husband because they quarrelled.

Apparently, when she wanted Sathan the cat to do anything for her she would say her Pater Noster in Latin. She also did this to turn Sathan the cat into a toad, a desire based on poverty as she explains:

> she kept the cat a greate while in woll in a pot, and at length being moved by povertie to occupie the woll, she praied in the name of the father and of the sonne, and of the holy ghost that it wold turne into a tode, and forthwith it was turned into a tode, and so kept it in the pot without woll.

> (ibid.: 320)

It is worth noting that, being 63 years old in 1566, Mother Waterhouse's childhood and young adulthood would have been spent in a Catholic environment, since the Protestant Reformation did not take effect until the reign of Henry VIII during the 1530s. She was therefore likely to have learnt to 'say her Pater Noster in Latin', not because she was a witch, but as part of her upbringing. But 'popery' was seen by many, and Puritans in particular, as involving witchcraft: 'Popery, in the words of Daniel Defoe, was "one entire system of anti-Christian magic", and the Pope for the Elizabethan lawyer William Lombarde was the "witch of the world"' (Thomas 1971: 69). It is therefore not surprising that saying prayers in Latin was given as one of the signs that Mother Waterhouse was a witch.

Finally, she says that Sathan had forewarned her of her eventual apprehension as a witch and suggested that she would be hanged or burnt shortly. It should be recalled that in England 'witches' were hanged for murder, and only burnt if treason or petty treason was involved, the latter including a wife murdering her husband. Despite mention of killing her husband, this did not, however, appear to influence the outcome for Mother Waterhouse. While she was indeed found guilty of using witchcraft to murder, she was hanged rather than burnt. (The final evidence against her is outlined below, after the testimony of Joan Waterhouse.)

Joan Waterhouse is the last of the accused to be questioned. According to the pamphlet she had once seen 'the thinge' like a toad and heard her mother (Agnes Waterhouse) call it Sathan, but she was adamant that she had not learnt the art of witchcraft even though she had had the chance to do so the previous winter. Yet she did once try to 'exercise' Sathan while her mother was away. With her mother absent, she did not have any bread and consequently went to the neighbour's child to ask for some bread and cheese, but she was not given as much as she wanted. As a result, when she came home she called Sathan as she had seen her mother do, and he came to her from under the bed; this time 'in the lykeness of a great dogge'. She asked him to scare the neighbour's girl who had denied her the bread and cheese, and offered him a red cock for his labours. But he said no, requesting instead that she give him 'thy body and sowle' (Ewen 1971: 320). Being afraid, she agreed to this. Sathan then went, in the form of 'an evyll favoured dogge with hornes on his head', to scare and haunt the neighbour's girl. So, Joan Waterhouse apparently did not use Sathan to any large degree, but by thus testifying to the existence of Sathan she unfortunately helped to convict the other two women.

There is a 'Second Examination and Confession' of both Mother Waterhouse and her daughter Joan regarding the neighbour's girl, Agnes Brown, in the final part of the pamphlet. Mother Waterhouse confesses to having had a white cat, and getting this cat to destroy her neighbour's cattle, to kill a man, and to turn himself into a toad. She also testifies that Joan, her daughter, had used Sathan in the form of a black dog to make Agnes Brown afraid. Agnes Brown is apparently brought in at this point and provides a very elaborate description of Sathan, saying he is a thing: 'lyke a black dogge with a face like an ape, a short tail, a cheine and a sylver whistle (to her thinking) about his neck, and a peyre of hornes on his head' (Ewen 1971: 322). Sathan told Agnes Brown he wanted butter, but she replied that she could not give him any. When he had gone she told her aunt about the incident, who sent for the priest, and he told her 'to praye to God, and cal on the name of Jesus'. When Sathan came to her again the next day she 'spake in the name of Jesus, and Sathan replied that she spoke 'evyll woordes in speakyng of that name'.

Agnes Brown's testimony suggests that she then saw Sathan return to her another couple of times, but because she spoke Jesus' name he would go away again. It is interesting to note that using prayer was seen as an effective antidote to the Devil in pre-Reformation times, but was no longer considered entirely effective by Protestants (Thomas 1971: 493–9). This tension is perhaps reflected in Agnes's use of Jesus' name and prayer.[9]

Agnes did not see Sathan for a while, until very recently, when he came 'with a kniffe in his mouthe' and asked if she were not dead. He threatened to kill her by thrusting the knife through her heart, and she asked him to put down the knife. This he refused, saying 'he wolde not depart from his sweete dames knyfe as yet'. Asked 'who was his dame' he nodded and wagged his head to Mother Waterhouse's house (Ewen 1971: 323). In this way Agnes Brown delivers the penultimate incrimination of Mother Waterhouse. But Mother Waterhouse attempts to deny that the knife is hers and also reiterates that Agnes Brown is lying when she says that Sathan has a face like an ape. As a means of resolving this problem of the form taken by Sathan, the attorney asks Mother Waterhouse to make Sathan appear before them, but she says she cannot because she no longer has power over him. Finally the attorney asks of Mother Waterhouse 'when dyd thye cat suck of thy blood'. 'Never', she replies, but the jailer lifts up the 'kerchief' on her head and makes visible 'divers spottes in her face and one on her nose', that is witches' marks. When asked the question again she replies 'not this fortnight', thus providing, albeit by inference, the final piece of evidence against her.

THE 1579 PAMPHLET AND WITCH TRIAL[10]

A Detection of damnable driftes, practized by three Witches arraigned at Chelmisford in Essex, at the late Assizes there holden, whiche were executed in Aprill, 1579.[11]

In this pamphlet there is a focus on everyday borrowing and lending as an important basis of witchcraft accusation. We also find that men and women's deeds are interpreted differently. It is specifically women's tasks that are construed as leading to witch-craft rather than similar tasks carried out by men, thus suggesting that it is the sex of the individual rather than the task itself which is the more important. Elizabeth Frauncis from the 1566 trial appears again, and is apparently the main suspect. There are also some interesting examples of economic conflict, of the use of ritual magic, and of conflict around adultery. Having familiars, or at least witches' marks, is again important.

According to the Assize Records, ten women and one man were formally accused of witchcraft at the 1579 trial (Cockburn 1978: cases 1024, 1044, 1047, 1055, 1056, 1063, 1084, 1085, 1092 and 1093), but only four of these are actually mentioned in the pamphlet. The four in the pamphlet are Elizabeth Frauncis (as in 1566 pamphlet), who 'bewitched Alice Poole, spinster, wife of Richard Poole of Hatfield Peveril, so that she died' (murder by witchcraft) (ibid.: case 1024); Elleine Smithe, who 'bewitched Susan Webbe, aged 4 years, so that she died' (murder by witchcraft) (ibid.: case 1044); Mother Staunton, spinster/wife, of Wimbish who 'bewitched a white gelding (£3) and a cow (40s.) so that they died' (witchcraft) (ibid.: case 1063); and Mother Nokes, spinster/wife, of Lambourne who 'bewitched Elizabeth Barfott to death' (murder by witchcraft) (ibid.: case 1047).[12]

It is not clear who wrote the pamphlet, but like the 1566 pamphlet it has an introduction which warns the reader about Sathan, saying that he can catch people unawares. It tells the reader to stop 'suche Devilish deedes' and to protect themselves with prayer. The pamphlet then goes on to discuss the four witches. The material is presented in a different way from that of the 1566 pamphlet; only the supposed testimony of Elizabeth Frauncis is given, whereas the other three merely have evidence given against them by a variety of others. Of the four accused, Elizabeth Frauncis is found guilty and hanged, Elleine Smithe and Alice Nokes similarly, while the indictment for Margery Staunton is found to be insufficient.

Elizabeth Frauncis provides the first 'testimony', which is presented as her confession. The main item is her supposed problem with Poole's wife, her neighbour. She asks to borrow 'some olde yest' from Poole's wife, but is denied this. She decides instead to ask for yeast from Osborne's wife and on her way she curses Poole's wife for her denial and 'hadde a mischief to light uppon her'. While she is thus engaged, a spirit appears very noisily, white in colour and like a small ragged dog (there is a picture of this creature in the pamphlet). She asks the spirit to go and plague Poole's wife 'in the head', in return for a crust of white bread. After this, Poole's wife 'was grevously pained in her head', and according to the testimony, has remained so ever since. In this way

Elizabeth Frauncis implies that she has merely hurt Poole's wife, and not actually killed her as the indictment suggests, although she is still found guilty of murder. Elizabeth Frauncis then goes on to incriminate others. Firstly, Elizabeth Lorde whom she knows poisoned John Frauncis's servant seven or eight years ago. Secondly, Widow Lorde whom she says bewitched Joan Robertes to death through a piece of apple cake. In addition she says she knows that Mother Osborne is a witch because she has 'witches markes', and indeed Elizabeth reckons they are similar to those of the previously hanged Mother Waterhouse (from 1566 trial), saying that they are 'nippes', that is, nipples.

The evidence against Elleine Smithe is as follows. It immediately becomes apparent that Elleine Smithe's mother, Alice Chaundeler, was also accused of witchcraft and was indeed executed for this crime some years previous.[13] Elleine inherited some money from Alice, which Alice's widowed husband, John Chaundeler, has now demanded for himself. It transpires that Elleine Smithe and John Chaundeler (her stepfather?) have fallen out over his demand for the inheritance, and Elleine has warned him that it would have been better if they had not. John Chaundeler dies, and before his death states that Elleine bewitched him such that he could not eat or digest meat.

Two further examples of Elleine's witchcraft then follow, both concerning her support and protection for her children. Firstly, her thirteen-year-old son is refused 'an almose' from John Estwood, and as a result Elleine Smith apparently bewitches him so that 'the said Estwood was taken with very greate paine in his bodie'. Moreover, as he sat by his fire a rat ran up the chimney, and fell down as a toad. When he placed this toad in the fire it burnt with a blue flame, and when it was buried Elleine 'Smithe was in a greate paine and out of quite'. Secondly, Elleine Smithe's daughter has fallen out with Widdow Webbe's daughter. Elleine steps in, striking Webbe's daughter so that she languishes and eventually dies. According to the indictment, it is for this deed of killing four-year-old Susan Webbe that Elleine Smithe is convicted. Apparently, immediately prior to her death, Susan Webbe cries continually 'awaie with the Witche, awaie with the Witch', and the following morning Widow Webbe thought she saw something like a black dog going out of her door, whereafter 'she fell distraught of her wittes'. The final piece of evidence against Elleine Smithe comes from her own son, who says that she has three spirits: Great

Dicke who is kept in a wicker bottle, Little Dicke who is in a leather bottle, and Willet who is kept in wool. A search of the house is ordered, and the places where these spirits are kept are found, which is evidence enough, although the spirits 'were vanished awaie' and not to be found.

The evidence against Mother Staunton is then presented, including eleven separate incidents. Most of these incidents result from the refusal of various individuals to give in to Mother Staunton's demands for items such as leather thongs and milk. It is interesting to see how, because she already has a reputation as a witch, her behaviour is also construed to *be* that of a witch.

Three of the incidents mention the same individual, Thomas Prat, and the evidence begins with these. Mother Staunton, visiting Thomas Prat, tells him that a knave has beaten her because he thought her to be a witch. Thomas Prat, plus John Farrow and Thomas Swallowe who are also present at Thomas Prat's house, endorse that she is not a witch. But when Mother Staunton and Thomas Prat fall out at a later date, Prat 'raced her face with a Nedle', and thereafter became tormented in his limbs, thus suggesting he had been bewitched. In their third encounter, Mother Staunton went past Thomas Prat's house with some grain. He wanted some of this for his chickens, and snatched it from her. But after his chickens had eaten it, three or four dozen of them died, again suggesting she had bewitched them.

The pamphlet then moves on to catalogue the various incidents regarding items being refused Mother Staunton. Firstly, she asks for yeast from Richard Saunder's wife, but when refused this, she walks away murmuring something. Subsequently Saunder's young child becomes ill, and the cradle rocks mysteriously without the baby in it. A similar pattern is repeated when Mother Staunton is denied 'diverse thynges' from Robert Petie's wife, with Petie's child becoming ill. And again a child becomes ill because Mother Staunton is denied a piece of leather and something else (not specified) from William Torner. The next piece of evidence concerns refusal of Mother Staunton's demand for a bottle of milk from Robert Cornell's wife. After the refusal Mother Staunton swops one of her own bottles for that of Cornell's, and then comes back later to demand her own bottle back. She is denied once more because Cornell's wife thinks she is a witch. Mother Staunton then makes a circle on the ground with a knife outside Cornell's door, saying, when asked, that it is a 'shitting house' for herself.

She departs, and thereafter Cornell's wife becomes ill, swelling as if pregnant but to bursting point. She is apparently still not in good health by the trial. This instance of making a circle on the ground with a knife is interesting because of the possible links with earlier ideas about magic. Although Mother Staunton calls her work a 'shitting house', these elements of drawing circles and using knives are also important features found in contemporary and pre-witch-hunt descriptions of ritual magic or sorcery (see Cohn 1975: 170–72).

Mother Staunton is also refused a leather thong from John Hopwood, and according to the pamphlet, this leads to the death of his gelding. It is for this instance of supposed witchcraft that Mother Staunton is indicted. She is also 'denied her demannde' by John Cornell, the younger (presumably related to the other Cornell mentioned earlier), and as a result his cattle no longer give milk but give 'gore stinkyng blood'. Furthermore, Mother Staunton is not allowed to carry out an errand by the vicar's wife while the vicar is away. Subsequently her child becomes ill, but when the vicar returns the child becomes well again; thus suggesting a triumph by the good vicar over the evil Mother Staunton. Finally, Mother Staunton is denied something by Robert Lathouse who does not like her 'dealying'. After her departure, twenty of his pigs die; and he burns one 'whereby as he thinketh, he saved the rest', though his cow also dies. This is the end of the evidence against Mother Staunton who, despite the variety of evidence against her, and her prior reputation as a witch, was apparently let free because her indictment was considered insufficient.

This leads us onto the evidence against Mother Nokes, the final 'witch' to be mentioned in this particular pamphlet. Despite the outcome of this case, which was conviction and hanging, the actual indictment is not mentioned among the other instances of witchcraft presented against her. Like Elleine Smithe, Mother Nokes gives support to her daughter, in this case against a youth (servant to Thomas Spycer) who snatched cloves from the daughter's pocket. He would not give the cloves back and that was when his limbs became paralysed. He sent the cloves back, but this apparently did not undo the paralysis because the pamphlet describes how his master had to carry him home in a wheelbarrow.

The next incident mentioned appears to be concerned with adultery. Mother Nokes has said that her husband 'laie with one Taylor's wife of Lamberd Ende', and she appears to fall out with this woman rather than her own husband. This Taylor's wife had a 'Nurse Childe', that is she was a wet-nurse, and Mother Nokes warns her that the baby will die, which is what happens. Someone else testifies that he has reproved both Taylor's wife and Mother Nokes after church, and tried to make them friends again. But Mother Nokes, fuming, replies that 'She cared for none of them all, as longe as Tom helde on her side, meanyng her Feende'. In other words, she was alright as long as her spirit stuck by her.

There appears, moreover, to be some antagonism between the 'reconciliatory' man mentioned above and Mother Nokes. This same man had a servant who did not answer a question from Mother Nokes while at his plough. She went away, but later the plough horse's head swelled and the horse died. The incidence finishes as follows:

> His maister at first supposyng that it came by a strype, was greatly offended at the ploughman, but afterwardes understandyng of Mother Nokes goyng by, and the circumstance afore mentioned, went to the said Mother Nokes and chid and threatened to have her to her answere, howbeit the horse died.

Thus it was assumed that the fault lay with Mother Nokes.

THE 1582 PAMPHLET AND WITCH TRIAL

> A True and Just Recorde of the Information, Examination and confession of all the Witches, taken at S. Oses in the countie of Essex: whereof some were executed, and other some entreated according to the determination of lawe.[14]

The overall impression from the 1582 witch trial pamphlet is of a largely female community accusing each other of witchcraft, often as a result of transactions between them such as borrowing, lending and buying various household items and food. There is an obvious arbitrariness of the deeds that lead to the accusation of withcraft, such that both borrowing and lending, giving and taking may have this consequence. For instance, Grace Thurlowe owes money to Ursley Kempe, but it is Ursley who is accused of witchcraft; while on another occasion Ursley is accused of witchcraft when her son is refused scouring sand by Annis Letherdall. As was noted earlier, it is especially important who the accused is. The pamphlet clearly suggest that being female makes a person particularly vulnerable, but within this category certain women also appear more likely to be accused than others, and Ursley Kemp is one of these. Interestingly, many of the suspects initially deny the accusations against them, or even deny that things that have happened are due to witchcraft at all. But eventually they are forced to confess through pressure from the judge, the use of a jury of women to search for witches' marks, or other 'over-whelming' evidence concerning familiars provided by their own children. There are some interesting instances of sexual 'deviance', including what appears to be incest and also lesbianism. In addition, the accused often deny that they have used withcraft, and they apparently do not all share a belief in witchcraft.

The Judge, Brian Darcy, had connections in the area as his family owned property or church presentations in the villages where the accused lived (MacFarlane 1970: 85). Significantly, Darcy's father, Lord Darcy, was thought to have been bewitched to death previously, possibly by Ursley Kempe who is the major suspect of this trial. The pamphlet mentions thirteen accused, all women, while the Assize Records only mentions nine of these women. In one of the two copies of the pamphlet in the British Library there is an appended list of the accused with the appropriate indictments and a list of the women's spirits, where relevant.[15] We know from the Court Records that three of these women were found not guilty, that two were hanged and three were imprisoned.[16]

The introductory section of this pamphlet discusses witchcraft and sorcery in even stronger terms than in the previous examples. The author argues that hanging is not a heavy enough sentence, and that witches should be burnt as they were in other countries. The pamphlet is extraordinarily long being of approximately one hundred pages.[17] It contains both testimonies taken against the accused and statements from the accused regarding the evidence cited against them, as well as testimonies taken in the court setting.

The main suspect in the 1582 trial is without doubt Ursley Kempe, and there is an especially large body of evidence presented against her. She is also one of the two 'witches' executed (according to existing Assize records). Ursley Kempe appears to be a spinster, partly because this is recorded in the Assize Records and also because she appears to have her maiden surname. (Her brother is mentioned in the pamphlet as Lawrence Kempe.)

Evidence is presented against her by Grace Thurlowe, who works for Judge Darcy, by Annis Letherdall, and by Thomas Rabbet who is Ursley's illegitimate son. Many of the other accused women also incriminate Ursley Kempe, and Ursley confesses to her various crimes at a number of points in the pamphlet, speaking in court, privately to Judge Darcy, and from prison. The story of Ursley Kempe is particularly interesting, and will be outlined in some detail.

It transpires from the pamphlet that Ursley Kempe is recognised as a wet-nurse and healer by the local community, and she ministers to Grace Thurlowe's ill child who becomes better. But Ursley and Grace (according to Grace Thurlowe's testimony) fall out after the birth of Grace's latest child because Ursley has not been allowed to nurse it, that is wet-nurse it. Grace implies that as a result Ursley kills the child. According to Grace, Ursley Kempe had also been angry that she had not been given the job of tending to Grace during the latter's pregnancy and birth. As a result Ursley appears to have made Grace lame and Grace warned her that she will accuse her of witchcraft. Ursley replied that she can unwitch but not bewitch, which Grace, however, suggests is part of the same thing:

> Take heed (said Grace) Ursley, thou hast a naughtie name. And to that Ursley made an answere, though shee coulde unwitche shee could not witche, and so promised the saide Grace, that if she did sende for her privily, and send her keeper away, that then shee woulde shew the saide Grace, how shee shoulde unwitch herselfe or any other at any time.

– the 'keeper', of course, being the Devil. Later Grace becomes lame in her legs again, and Ursley appears at her house without being sent for. Ursley offers to help Grace get over her lameness if she pays Ursley 12 pence, to which Grace agrees and becomes well again. However, Grace never pays any of the agreed sum, nor the alternative payment of cheese that Ursley suggests. Consequently Ursley and Grace fall out yet again, and Grace becomes lame once more. Grace does get better from time to time, but on those occasions her child 'is tormented'.

Annis Letherdall's evidence against Ursley Kempe suggests that she, like Grace Thurlowe, sees Ursley 'to be a naughtie beast', that is, probably a witch. Annis Letherdall will not give scouring sand to Ursley's son who has been sent to obtain this, in return for which

Ursley 'would give her the dying of a payre of women's hose'. Subsequently Annis's child becomes ill and Ursley is blamed. But it is the evidence against Ursley Kempe provided by her eight-year-old illegitimate son which is particularly incriminating. This son, Thomas Rabbet, says that Ursley has four spirits, naming them as Tyffin, Tyffey, Pygine and Iacke: 'Tyffey is like a little grey Cat, Tyffin is like a white Lambe, Pygine is black like a Toad, and Iacke is black like a Cat.' Apparently he has seen his mother giving them beer to drink and white bread or cake to eat; and says that at night time they all come and suck blood from her arms and other parts of her body. When questioned further by the Judge, Thomas Rabbet adds that he has seen Ursley give Mother Newman the earthen pot in which she keeps her (Ursley's) spirits, and that he has heard Mother Newman mention to his mother that she has 'sent a spirit to plague Johnson to death, and an other to plague his wife'.

In a later part of the pamphlet Ursley Kempe provides her testimony, and it transpires that at one time she was lame herself, and was told by Cocke's wife that she was bewitched, but also how to unwitch herself. For the unwitching she learnt to use the following elaborate 'medicine':

> take hogges dunge and Charvell and put them together and holde them in her left hand, and to take in the other hande a knife, and to pricke the medicine three times, and then to cast the same into the fire, and to take the said knife and to make three pricks under the table, and to let the knife sticke there; and after that to take three leves of sage, and as much as herbe John (alias herbe grace) and put them into ale, and drink it last at night and first in the morning. . .

Ursley then used this same medicine for Page's wife and Graye's wife both of whom were also lame and had been, as she thought, bewitched.

What can be seen from the evidence against, and testimonies of, Ursley Kempe is that she seems to consider herself to be a 'white witch', that is, someone who can spot ill health associated with witchcraft and also has means of countering it. The medicine she uses is made out to contain both counter-witchcraft and healing properties. It is, however, a very short step between such white witchcraft and the black witchcraft of which she stands accused. Judge Darcy was particularly keen to make Ursley confess to the charges against her, and promised her 'favours' if she does so (as indeed he also does to others later). Consequently she confesses that she does have the spirits suggested by her son, that she has used them to kill Grace Thurlowe's child, Annis Letherdall's child and John Stratton's child. Furthermore that she has given her spirits to Ales Newman who uses them to do deeds she, Ursley, wants. She also incriminates the other woman who is eventually executed for witchcraft, Elizabeth Bennet, whom she says has two spirits called Suckin and Lyerd. Ursley has been told this information by her own spirit Tyffin. Ursley also goes on to incriminate some of the other women accused of witchcraft, namely Ales Newman, Ales Hunt and Annys Glascocke, saying that they all have spirits. It transpires that part of this 'confession' has been procured by Judge Darcy by talking to or coercing Ursley in private.

Possessing spirits is a critical aspect of this trial, and those women accused of witchcraft who try to deny that they have such spirits are ordered by Judge Darcy to be searched for witches' marks by a small group of women. It has been suggested that this is the first evidence of such a 'jury of women' being used to search for witches' marks (MacFarlane 1970: 85). Only one of the women searched in this way is found not to have witches' marks. (See Table 8.1 for list of accused and spirits attributed to them.) Annys Glascocke, Joan Pechey and Joan Robynson did not in the end confess to having spirits, but Annys Glascocke was searched and found to have spots and was subsequently found guilty of witchcraft and imprisoned. It is noteworthy that Annys Letherdall was one of the 'witch-mark finders', and as her child was supposedly killed by Elizabeth Frauncis she could be deemed to have a vested interest in her position.

As in the earlier trial pamphlets, children of the accused gave evidence against their mothers. Thomas Rabbet, the eight-year-old son of Ursley Kempe, has already been mentioned. In addition Cysley Celles's son, Henry, said his mother was a witch and had two spirits or imps. Her younger son John, aged seven-and-three-quarter years, testified similarly. Annys Herd's illegitimate daughter Annis Dowsing, aged seven years, also gave evidence against her mother, saying that her mother had lots of imps:

> She hath in one boxe sixe anices or Blackbirds: being asked of what colour, she saith, they be white speckled, and all black, and she saith, the she hath in another boxe, vi, spirits like Cowes

(being asked howe big) she saith, they be as big as Rattes, and that they have little short hornes and they lie in the boxes upon white and blacke wooll. . .

Ales Hunt's daughter, Febey Hunt, was another child (aged eight) to give evidence against her mother, again producing a seemingly fanciful story about how her mother had spirits in the shape of 'little things like horses'.

Another, this time adult, child of an accused woman, Ales Newman, also gave evidence against his mother. What is interesting about this instance is the suggestion that Ales Newman had an incestuous sexual relationship with him. As the pamphlet indicates Ales denies this allegation:

> This Examinate being charged to have willed her sonne Phillip Barrenger, beeing of the age of xxiii yeares to lye in bedde with her, denyeth that she hath so doone, other then shee hath willed at some tymes to lye uppon the bedde at her backe.

But the son does not agree, as the pamphlet continues:

> But the saide Phyllipe beeing examined, confesseth and saith, that manye times and of late hee hath layne in naked bed with his owne mother, being willed and commanded to doe of her.

Unfortunately we do not know who is correct (or whether this situation is mere fabrication by the pamphlet writer).

There are other instances of what may be termed sexual 'deviance'. It has already been mentioned that both Ursley Kempe and Annys Herd had illegitimate children. Furthermore, Elizabeth Eustace's daughter is called 'lewd'. But a particularly interesting case is perhaps that of Elizabeth Bennet, the other woman hanged besides Ursley Kempe, who appears to be having a lesbian relationship with William Bonner's wife.

William Bonner testifies against Elizabeth Bennet, and accuses her of killing his wife or at least making her very ill, and this appears to be a product of the two women being lovers and spending much time together, that is, what we would now call lesbianism. As the pamphlet states:

> The said William Bonner saith, that the said Elizabeth Bennet and his wife were lovers and familiar friendes, and did accompanise much together: and saith that since Candlemas last his wife hath complained of a lamnesse in her knee, and that

sithence also shee hath been much troubled. And saith also that not ten daises past the saide Elizabeth Bennet being with his wife, she beinge sickely and sore troubled, the said Elizabeth used speeches unto her, saying, a good woman, how thou art loden, and then clasped her in her armes, and killed her [sic]: Whereupon presently after her upper lippe swelled and was very bigge, and her eyes muchsunken into her head, and she hath lieu sithence in a very strange case.

So William Bonner is saying that Elizabeth Bennet 'bewitched' his wife. But how exactly can we interpret this? Was Bonner's wife love sick? Had she caught herpes or suchlike from Elizabeth? Or was Bonner jealous? There are, however, difficulties involved in con- textualising this instance, because hardly any research has been done with regard to lesbianism and the sixteenth century.

The way the reference is made in the pamphlet perhaps suggests an association between 'deviance' and lesbianism, and research carried out with regard to *male* homosexuals in this period would indeed support the idea of such sexual behaviour being seen as deviant (Bray 1982). The extremely limited research on lesbians in this period has suggested that women loving each other was neither sexual nor deemed threatening (Faderman 1981),[18] and yet the terms 'lovers' and 'familiar friendes' might suggest a more sexual relationship. For instance, spirits or imps were called familiars precisely because their relationships with the 'witches' were perceived as physically intimate and with possible sexual connotations, as also exemplified by the familiars 'suckling of teats' or 'nipples' on the witch.

The mention of Elizabeth Bennet's association with Bonner's wife constitutes only a small part of the evidence against her. Elizabeth was also called 'olde trot, old whore, and other lewde speeches' by her neighbour William Byet, whom she supposedly killed as a result of this and previous rows by using a spirit called Suckin. And most of the pamphlet material is concerned with whether or not she confesses to having two spirits or familiars called Suckin and Lyerd, whom she initially denies the existence of. Apparently Elizabeth also fell out with Byet's wife, who put a pitchfork through one of Elizabeth's pigs. She is condemned for killing Byet's wife, but denies this, saying that Suckin, the spirit, did this without her knowledge. In the final analysis the case of Elizabeth Bennet probably tells us that a woman who was a lesbian was accused of witchcraft. The trial material appears only incidentally to mention her relationship with Bonner's wife and it is not clear what bearing this had on the accusation against her, although the pamphlets generally tend to mention only what is considered relevant 'evidence' to an accusation of witchcraft.

In addition to Ursley Kempe and Elizabeth Bennet, Ales Newman appears to be the other main character of this trial. The accusation against her provides an interesting example of how the poor attempted to manage in the village, and it also provides a stark contrast of evidence whereby Ursley Kempe argues that Ales definitely has and uses spirits while Elizabeth Bennet interprets the same event in an altogether more 'rational' manner. Ales Newman is accused of killing weaver Johnson, the 'Collector appointed for the poore', because he is unable to give her the money she needs as her husband is ill. Ursley Kempe testifies that Ales does indeed kill Johnson using Ursley's own spirits. This is endorsed by Thomas Rabbet (Ursley's son who also happens to be Ales Newman's godchild) who states that 'he had heard [Ales] to tel his mother that she had sent a spirit to plague Johnson to death, and an other to plague his wife'.

By contrast, Elizabeth Bennet denies that Ales Newman has sent a spirit to plague Johnson, or his wife. She provides an account of the incident which suggests she was herself present at the time, and saying that Ales was (justifiably) greatly angered by the denial of the money and used 'harded speeches' against Johnson as a result:

> that shee being at Johnson's to have woll to spinne, he being a clothmaker, of whom she had many times worke. At that present mother Newman being come tither, she this examinate saith she hard the sayd Mother Newman to desire Johnson to give her xii.d. saying: her husbande lay sicke, whereunto she heard him answere that hee woulde gladly helpe her husbande: but that he had laide out a greate deale more then he had received, saying, he was a pore man and hee, his wife and familie, might not want for the helping of her husban, saying that hee coulde not helpe her with any, untill he had collected more moeny, wheupon shee departed, and used some harde speeches unto him, and seemed to be much angrie.

Despite Elizabeth Bennet's denial that Ales Newman used spirits against Johnson, there is no doubt that the implication of cursing, as in 'used some harde speeches unto him', was an important aspect of evidence against Ales.

Johnson's role as collector for the poor probably placed him in a position believed to be vulnerable to bewitching, as the case of Joan Pechey also attests. Ales Hunt, who is herself accused of witchcraft, testifies against Joan Pechey to the effect that Joan has at least cursed and probably bewitched Johnson, the reason being that Joan was not happy with her Christmas handout:

> one the said Joan two or three dates before Christmas last, went to the house of Johnson the collector appointed for the poore, whereas she the said Joan received beefe and bread, the which the Examinat saith, shee hearde to bee of the gift of the said Brian Darcy. And this examinat saith that the said Joan going homewardes, murmured and found great fault at Johnson, saying he might have given that to a gyrle or another and not to her, saying the bread was to hard baked for her, and that she then seemed to be in a great anger there withall.

In this way, Joan Pechey is presented as an old widow, who is both thankless and cursing.[19]

THE 1589 PAMPHLET AND WITCH TRIAL[20]

> The Apprehension and Confession of three notorious Witches, Arraigned and by Justice condemned and executed at Chelmesforde, in the Countye of Essex, the 5. day of Iylue, last past. 1589.

Altogether there are eleven separate individuals mentioned as suspects in the Assize Court records, of whom all but one are women, and the male defendant is related to an accused woman.[21] Three of the eleven were executed for witchcraft, and it is only these three women who are discussed in the trial pamphlet. They are Joan Cunny, Joan Upney and Joan Prentice.[22]

In the pamphlet central importance is given to spirits or familiars. All three women are accused of having spirits, and the evidence against them catalogues the use of these, mainly against people but also against animals. Joan Cunny is said to have four spirits named Jack, Gyll, Nicholas and Ned, and two in the form of frogs, who are all pictured in the pamphlet. Joan Upney has three spirits altogether although at different times, two of them in the form of moles and one in the form of a toad. Joan Prentice's spirit is described as a ferret called Bidd. The way the women are seen to obtain their spirits is particularly interesting, showing the direct, and probably sexual, link assumed to exist between the Devil and the accused, and also showing the way both spirits and witchcraft skills were thought to be handed on from woman to woman.

Joan Cunny learnt the 'Arte of Witchcraft' from Mother Dumfrye, who taught her an elaborate ritual to make the spirits appear. This ritual involved drawing a circle on the ground, and praying to Sathan who is described as 'the cheefe of the Devills'. As will be recalled, Mother Staunton in the 1579 pamphlet also drew a circle on the ground as a part of what she called her 'shitting house', and this act was known to be a common part of sorcery or ritual magic. Joan Cunny's ritual made two 'spirites' appear within the circle she had drawn, and they offered to do what she wanted in exchange for her soul, to which she assented. That the spirits appeared *inside* the circle is possibly a distortion (if unintentional) of the use of this 'technique' by sorcerers, who would stand inside the circle in order to protect themselves from the demons who would appear *outside* (see Cohn 1975: 172).

Joan Upney obtained a spirit from another 'witch' called Justain Kirtle. This spirit stayed with her for about a year before being 'consumed away' (perhaps in similar manner to the disappearance of Elizabeth Frauncis's sheep in the 1566 trial pamphlet). Joan was then given two more spirits which stayed until recently, when she herself had run away 'because she heard John Harrolde and Richard Foster say she was a "witch"'.

The third woman discussed in the pamphlet, Joan Prentice, says in her 'confession' that the Devil first appeared to her as a dunnish coloured ferret with fiery eyes, as she was getting ready to go to bed. The ferret asked for her soul, but she refused, saying that her soul belonged to Jesus Christ, although when the ferret asked her for some blood she gave it willingly, offering her left forefinger from which he suckled some blood. On other occasions, the ferret would return and suck her cheek, always when she was getting ready for bed. Thus stress on the spirit always appearing at bedtime appears to underline the sexual attachment which was thought to exist between the 'witch' and the Devil. In the English trial material this link tends to be mentioned indirectly and implicitly, as in this case. The Continental material, on the other hand, with its focus on Satanism, is much more explicit about sexual activity between the women and the Devil or his 'angels'.

The pamphlet, which is quite brief, does not say why Joan Upney used her mole and toad familiars to suck Harrold's wife to death and pinch Foster's wife, the latter being the indicted offence. The implication is, however, that it was in retribution for John Harrolde and Richard Foster calling her a witch. Joan Cunny used her familiars on many occasions to hurt 'divers persons' over the past twenty-six years because she fell out with the individuals concerned or those associated with them. Joan Cunny also put her spirits at her daughter's disposal, for instance, when her daughter fell out with Father Durrill and 'gave him cucled speeches', that is called him a cuckold.

Joan Prentice, who appears to be Joan Cunny's mother, is described in the pamphlet as one of the women from the Alms House of Hinningham Sibble. She uses her spirit to nip and kill Sara Glascocke, child of Master Glascocke who had refused her alms the previous day, although she attempts to lessen the offence by suggesting that she only wanted Sara Glascocke nipped, but the spirit went too far. On another occasion, when she wanted wood, Joan Prentice had used her spirit to uproot a tree by creating a wind. The High Sheriff, whose tree it was, attested that the oak had indeed been blown down at a time of otherwise great calm. It appears significant that Joan Cunny is described in the pamphlet as living lewdly, and with two lewd daughters and two illegitimate sons, the eldest aged 10 or 12. She may thus be placed in the category of sexually 'deviant'. Again we see illegitimate children used against their mother, to testify. Her two sons were called by the judge to give evidence as she was not prepared to confess to all of the accusations. As the pamphlet points out: 'the Judge of the Circuits very wisely with great inesight, called in the two bastard Children before mentioned.' As a result Joan Cunny confessed all. The eldest of the boys also provided evidence against Joan Prentice, his 'Grandam', that is, his grandmother.

The final part of the 1589 pamphlet describes the three accused being taken to their place of execution. Once there, an attempt is made to make them repent their sins, and as a result Joan Upney shouts that the Devil has deceived, and 'she seemed very sorry for the same, and died very penitent, asking God and the world forgiveness, even to the last gaspe, for her wicked and detestable life'. She was killed despite her public repentance, and there is a picture of the three hanging on the scaffold.

THE 1645 PAMPHLET AND WITCH TRIAL[23]

A True and Exact Relation of the Several Informations, Examinations and Confessions of the late Witches, arraigned and executed in the County of Essex.[24]

The four witch trial pamphlets discussed so far were all from the late sixteenth-century Elizabethan period. The fifth pamphlet refers to a trial half a century later, during the English Civil War of the 1640s. The intervening period had seen an increasingly sophisticated and sceptical discussion about witchcraft among the literate elite, and in some ways this is also echoed in the 1645 witch trial pamphlet.

The 1645 trial was built around the investigations by Matthew Hopkins into the existence of witches in Essex, which he largely carried out in order to make money (Summers 1971: 28). Hopkins himself wrote a pamphlet, *The Discovery of Witches* (1647), as a result of criticism regarding the 1645 trial, and it is useful to relate this to the trial pamphlet. In his work, Hopkins sets out to justify his witch-hunting activities, and thereby provides us with an account of at least part of the ideological background to the 1645 witch trial. One of the particularly interesting aspects is his suggestion that witches met together regularly to worship the Devil and to plan their devilish deeds, thus indicating that he thought a Satanic coven was in existence. Besides the 1612 trial in Lancaster, the mention of Satanism in the English trials is otherwise unusual. Related to the idea of Satanism, and echoing the Continental persecutions, the 1645 trial also included explicit mention of a *sexual* pact between witches and the Devil.

Talking about the beginning of his work as witch-finder, Hopkins explains how:

The Discoverer never travelled far for it, but in March 1644 he had some seven or eight of that horrible sect of Witches living in the Towne where he lived, a Towne in Essex called Manningtree, with divers other adjacent Witches of other towns, who every six weeks in the night being alwayes on the Friday night had their meeting close by his house, and had their several solemne sacrifices there offerred to the Devill. . .

In other words he came across a coven of witches in Manningtree that apparently met every six weeks, on a Friday night. He goes on to describe how these 'witches' were intially sought out by him because he heard one of them talking to her imps. He also discusses the torturous means used to see whether they definitely were witches, including stopping the accused from sleeping over a number of nights (and presumably days) so that the witnesses may see her familiars. Sleeplessness is a form of torture, although Hopkins denies this. Hopkins also used the water ordeal, which was based on the assumption that water as the holy substance of baptism would refuse a witch and receive someone not a witch. In other words, if a suspected witch was thrown, hands and feet bound, into a pond, she would float if guilty and sink if innocent. Hopkins wrote in support of this in his pamphlet, and the water ordeal was also discussed by James I in his *Daemonologie* (1597). Satanism and use of torture were a central part of the 1645 trial pamphlet. Having familiars was also very important.

According to the Assize Court records, 35 women were indicted to appear before the Court in 1645. Of these, 19 are directly mentioned in the trial pamphlet, which was written by H.F. MacFarlane observes that of the 35 brought to trial: 'nineteen were almost certainly executed, nine died of gaol fever, six were still in prison in 1648, and only one, a woman from another part of Essex, was acquitted and escaped free'(MacFarlane 1970: 134). The outcome of this trial was therefore much more extreme than the trials mentioned in the Elizabethan pamphlets, where a sizeable proportion of the accused were set free. Of the women mentioned in the 1645 pamphlet, 14 appear to have been executed, one imprisoned, 2 died in jail, and no sentence or outcome is given for the last two.[25] Apparent testimonies of the accused and others giving evidence against them are outlined. A large number of individuals (largely male) provide evidence against the accused, including Matthew Hopkins and his assistant John Stearne. The 'evidence' includes that obtained by watching the accused during periods of enforced sleeplessness.

The introduction to the pamphlet contains a very long, and much more philosophical debate regarding the nature of witchcraft than the Elizabethan pamphlets. This argues that the Devil cannot create, and has power merely to make witches believe things to be true that do not really exist, such as the transformation of witches into animal forms, or causing witches to fly. Only God, it is stressed, has the power to create. Thus:

> it may be demanded, whether a spirit or Devill can cause such a transmutation of the bodies of witches into those severall shapes and forms of Cats, Dogges, Birds and other creatures, as is often reporte, where Witches and Sorcerers have lived. The answer is, that it is impossible in nature, and in the ordinary unchangeable course of all things created by God, that one individual and continued substance or entire thing should be wholly divided from it self, and yet be itself; for there can be no wall or transmutation of one substance, or nature into another, but either by creation or generation. Now creation is the worke of an infinite power, and therfore of god alone.
>
> (H.F. 1645: preface)

The reason, therefore, why 'witches' should be punished is because they have allowed themselves to be taken in by the Devil.

It is revealed that many of the accused incriminated each other, and the pattern of these incriminations suggest that separate groups of women knew each other. Elizabeth Clarke, Anne West, Rebecca West, Elizabeth Gooding, Anne Leach, and Hellen Clark formed the basis of the most important group. Rose Hallybread, Joyce Boanes, Susan Cock and Margaret Landish formed a second, while Marion Hocket, Sarah Hating and Elizabeth Harvie formed yet another. The first two of these groups also appear to have organised their supposed witchcraft together, meeting to worship their familiars, as also indicated by Matthew Hopkins in his pamphlet. When Matthew Hopkins visits Rebecca West in gaol, she confesses that at this meeting she was also married to the Devil.

Another important feature of the 1645 trial was, as mentioned above, the possession of spirits or familiars. As I discussed earlier, the period between the Elizabethan pamphlets and the 1645 pamphlet had seen the imposition of the new and more strongly-worded Witchcraft Statute of James I, which saw the possession of spirits as a specific and obvious sign of witchcraft, and such ownership was therefore an offence warranting the death penalty. Consequently many of the indictments given in the Assize Court records after this period merely involve the witchcraft-related crime of entertaining evil spirits. Every one of the women mentioned in the 1645 trial pamphlet accused of witchcraft is described as having spirits, imps or familiars which are often named. Elizabeth Clarke, for instance, who was watched for several nights by a team including Matthew Hopkins and John Stearne, was seen to have five spirits: Holt, Jarmara, Vinegar Tom, Jack and Sugar, and one other. (There is a picture of these in Hopkins's pamphlet.) Some of the accused were searched for witches' marks, and Anne Leach was found to have teats in her 'privie parts', or genital area, where the imp supposedly sucked. Mary Greenleife was similarly found to have teats in her 'secret parts' which were apparently not like haemorroids but like the 'bigges' that witches are known to have.

In *Discovery of Witches* Hopkins explains how it is possible for someone skilled, such as a midwife, to tell the difference between 'naturell excressencies' (including haemorroids, piles, and child-bearing) and teats that are for imps to suck. There are three main ways to tell these different marks apart: the place they are found, which differentiates them from haemorroids or marks left by child-bearing; that they are insensitive; and that they may change shape or suddenly appear or disappear depending on when the 'witch' suckles her familiar (Hopkins 1647: 4). This is why Hopkins reckons that the marks have to be searched for thoroughly, to have pins forced through them to measure sensitivity, and the accused watched closely for at least a day and a night to see if the 'teats' change shape.

Just as the 'witches' marks' were found in obviously sexual areas, notably the genitals, sexual 'deviance' also tends to be sex directly between the witch and the Devil. Matthew Hopkins, giving evidence against Elizabeth Clarke, for instance, reports that :

> the said Elizabeth confessed shee had had carnhall copulation with the Devill six or seven yearses; and that he would appeare to her three or foure times in a weeke at her bed side, and goe to bed with her, and lye with her halfe a night together in the shape of a proper Gentleman, with a laced band, having the whole proportion of a man, and would say to her, Besse I must lye with you, and she did never deny him. . .
>
> (H.F. 1645: 2)

John Stearne, giving further evidence against Elizabeth Clarke, apparently endorses this story. It is important to note that beyond sexual relations with the Devil, implication of sexual 'deviance' is not as prevalent in this trial account as in the earlier trial pamphlets. Only Elizabeth Gooding is directly called a lewd woman, although Anne Leach had also been accused of being a naughtie woman by Mr Bragge some 30 years previous, and as a result had sent an imp to kill two of his horses.

Reasons why the accused used witchcraft to kill and maim are not dwelt on to any large degree, beyond being seen as a product of their allegiance with the Devil. Elizabeth Clarke is apparently given an imp by Anne West in order to obtain a husband who should maintain her ever after, thereby showing similarity with the case of Elizabeth Frauncis in 1566. Elizabeth Gooding wants to buy some cheese on credit from Robert Taylor, but he refuses. She comes back later with the requisite money and buys the cheese, but Robert Taylor's horse becomes ill and eventually dies. A group of women comprising Rose Hallybread, Joyce Boanes, Margaret Landish and Susan Cock are all refused a sack of chips by Robert Turner's servant, and as a result, they all kill this servant. There is also the separate, and interesting, incident of Susan Cock and Margaret Landish who together kill six or seven of Mr Mannocks's pigs, because his wife has refused Susan Cock poor relief, telling her that she was a young woman, and able to work for her living. Finally, Anne Cate uses witchcraft to kill George Parby's child because Parby's wife denies her milk, and she also kills Samuel Ray's wife, this time because Ray's wife has refused Anne the two pence owed to her.

In addition to the 1645 trial, Hopkins was responsible for a number of other large witch trials in East Anglia. But, as Summers records, there was increasing opposition to Hopkins' activities and 'it is possible that after say, 1646, his activities entirely surceased' (1971: 45). According to his assistant, Stearne, Hopkins died 'peacibly, after a long sickness of a consumption' (ibid.: 45), the following year, although this is in dispute, and it has also been said that Hopkins was eventually himself accused of witchcraft. Whatever his end, Hopkins's horrendous activities allowed large-scale murder of women, although also bringing to the fore some of the many contradictions in witchcraft belief at the time.

Overall, the pattern revealed regarding the accused in this particular trial is similar to that of the earlier trials, albeit with greater emphasis on spirits or familiars and direct sexual liaison with the Devil. I will now move on to discuss this general pattern of who is accused and the reasons for those accusations.

CONCLUSION

The most consistent feature of the individuals accused of witch-craft is without doubt their sex. With very few exceptions all the accused were women, and this emphasis is expressed even more strongly in the trial pamphlets where all of the accused mentioned are women. We may conclude that the use of witchcraft can be seen to have been associated specifically with women, as indeed it also tended to be, amongst the peasantry at least, in earlier centuries (see Chapter 6). But why women? And why only *certain* woman? By looking at the other aspects of the trial material, and situating them in the context outlined earlier, the answer to this question becomes clearer.

Both marital status and age of the accused tell us more about the women who were accused. The figures obtained from the pamphlets endorse those quoted earlier, that is, that married women predominated, although widows and unmarried women generally constitued a disproportionately large number of the accused. The figures from the pamphlets (which are incomplete) are 10 widows, 15 wives and 11 spinsters for the total numbers of defendants mentioned in the pamphlets (see Table 8.1). Accor-ding to the figures available, widows thus constitute over a quarter of the accused while wives constitute just under half, and spinsters between a quarter and a third. This is a smaller proportion of widows than that mentioned by MacFarlane, who, it will be recalled, suggested a figure of 40 per cent widows for the total available trials and other records for Essex as a whole. However, in terms of the pamphlets, the proportion of widows convicted and executed is about 40 per cent.

MacFarlane suggests that because a large number of 'witches' were widows this suggests that 'widowhood was a serious problem in Elizabethan villages' (MacFarlane 1970: 164). Unfortunately he does not say why exactly widows might be a problem. My discussion earlier in Chapter 7, however, suggests that widows might be especially vulnerable to witchcraft accusation because they were (as Robert Burton, 1621, pointed out) especially prone to sexual deviance. They were also likely to be either poor and therefore a burden on the community, or in direct competition with men in work inherited from their husbands. Most of the women mentioned in the pamphlets appear to have been poor, but some also had an inheritance, such as Elleine Smithe in the 1579 trial pamphlet.

Listing the precise ages of the accused is very difficult because most of the ages are not mentioned, although it is at times possible to infer the ages of the women concerned by taking into account their children, their mothers and other more impressionistic aspects. The women whose ages are mentioned in the pamphlets tend to be either young (18 years) or old (63, 63, 55, 53, 60, 65 and 80 years) (see Table 8.1), and many of the others may be inferred to be around 40 years or at least 40 years. Thus the accused do tend to be women of 40 or over, even if those executed are not always the oldest. We must also consider the link between age and marital status, because spinsters, who according to the pamphlet figures are probably least likely to be convicted and hanged, are also likely to be young – as in the case of Joan Waterhouse in the 1566 trial. In this sense the link between harsher trial sentence and greater age is strengthened. Carol Karlsen (1987) has made very similar findings with regard to New England.

Women over the age of 40 were vulnerable to witchcraft accusation, partly because they were no longer carrying out their main role (according to Puritans), that of childbearing. The oldest were unlikely even to be caring for children (ibid.: 71). Older women, if widows, might also be seen as even more out of male control sexually than other women (see Chapter 7). Age might also have posed special problems of financial support within villages. MacFarlane suggests, for instance, that age might have posed special problems of financial support within villages:

> Pressure on economic resources and growing unease at the neighbourly values of village society . . . naturally tended to cause friction with the older inhabitants who, by their very presence, made demands on younger village families. The problem of the aged was likely to be particularly acute when methods and ideals of charity were changing as they seem to have been in this period.
>
> (MacFarlane 1970: 164)

In addition, age had 'mystical power' associated with it which could be used to do evil (ibid.: 167). In the cases of Susan Cock (1645 trial) and especially Ales Newman and Joan Pechey (1582 trial), relief of the elderly poor probably did play a part in the accusations of witchcraft, suggesting that attitudes to the poor, but also conflict over resources, may have been important considerations.

Of the other four categories, the most prevalent is liaison with the Devil, that is, the accused had spirits or were in any other way associated with the Devil – as mentioned by the accused themselves or by others. And this remains the most prevalent category even if the more extraordinary 1645 trial pamphlet, focusing almost exclusively on evidence of liaison with the Devil, is ignored (see Table 8.1). In general, what I have called 'liaison with the Devil' appears as sin rather than heresy, as we might expect in the English context (see also ibid.: 189). The accused were not (except perhaps in the 1645 trial) questioned about any possible involvement in organising against the Church, and it is clear from the pamphlets that some of the 'witches' attended Church.

Significantly, 'liaison with the Devil' appears to offer certain individuals a means of bettering their lives, for example Elizabeth Frauncis and also Mother Waterhouse in the 1566 trial, and a means of retribution against those who have not fulfilled their wishes. 'Liaison with the Devil' by the accused also seems to provide an explanation of death and disease, of both humans and animals. What the pamphlet material suggests is the existence of a set of beliefs whereby certain individuals thought themselves able to call upon special powers, and whereby the same individuals were expected to be able to do so. These beliefs, seem closely related to the much older ideas concerning witchcraft and sorcery outlined by Cohn (1975), where it was thought possible to obtain special powers by the use of particular techniques (involving circles and knives) and by calling forth demons. There are a few instances in the pamphlets of such special techniques being used, and the spirits or familiars are Devil-related demons. As was noted earlier, among the peasantry the ability to thus obtain and use special powers was seen to rest specifically with women.

Kin relations are also important. The pamphlets describe in a number of instances, concerning a third of the defendants mentioned, that the accused learnt the art of witchcraft from her mother or another older woman. In this way the 'technique' of obtaining special powers including the spirits or familiars themselves, was perceived to be handed on. The pamphlet material also appears to assume that this process would take place only among female kin, such that daughters of 'witches' would be thought to have learnt to use witchcraft, as exemplified by Joan Waterhouse (1566), Ales Hunt and Margery Sammon (1582), Rebecca West and Hellen Clark (1645). Kin relations thus appear to have identified certain women as 'witches' but this does not apply to all of them.

The association of witchcraft with death and disease also provides interesting insights into the witch-hunt phenomenon. Contemporary writers such as Reginald Scot (1584) and George Gifford (1593), suggest that witches were blamed for only certain illnesses, Scot arguing that these were 'sudden diseases', and Gifford arguing to the contrary that they were 'lingering diseases'. But MacFarlane points out that the symptoms ascribed to witchcraft were very diverse and in general no particular diseases were specifically linked to witchcraft. Most illness did not in fact appear to be linked to witchcraft at all (MacFarlane 1970: 178–82). As a result, he suggests that it was the nature of the social relationship between the victim and the accused rather than the particular nature of the illness which resulted in an accusation of witchcraft. In other words, illness or death was explained by witchcraft only if the individuals concerned had prior reason to fear the use of witchcraft against them, such as being cursed by the suspect or having denied her certain items. While this is useful, I would suggest that we also need to take into account that social relations are specifically gendered. In other words, illness or death are attributed only, or largely, to tasks or behaviour carried out by women, not by men. This is similar to the point made by Delphy (1977) regarding male–female social relations in present-day France (see Chapter 2).

This brings us on to the category of 'economic conflict', a category which includes various forms of dispute around borrowing, lending, buying, selling, begging and obtaining work, as well as other matters concerning someone's financial well-being. Over half the cases mentioned in the pamphlets involved at least one incident of what I have termed economic conflict, and this played an important part in witchcraft accusations (see Table 8.1). The crimes, on which accusation was based, were not real 'crimes' at all, but a means of explaining unpleasant events in the village. It was the general belief in supernatural powers which placed events in the lives of the villagers within the context of witchcraft, rather than the particular events themselves. A common pattern, according to the pamphlet material, involved the suspect asking someone from another household (usually a woman) for food, other household items and even money. When refused this, the refuser or her/his family, would subsequently suffer death or illness. On many occasions the onset of death or illness would be accompanied by the sighting of one of a range of domestic or rural animals construed to be a 'familiar'. Altogether, these events (refusing the suspect, illness/death and sighting of 'familiar') would provide ample evidence of witchcraft having been committed. Both demanding something and being demanded of led to the accusation of witchcraft, and the sex of the accused is especially important. In general women who were accused of witchcraft made demands of others (both men and women), but men could make similar demands with the women still ending up accused. This situation can be seen in the case of John Chaundeler who demanded Elleine Smithe's inheritance, in the case of Thomas Prat who took grain from Mother Staunton, and when Thomas Spycer's servant snatched cloves from Mother Nokes's daughter.

It has already been pointed out that in Essex the density of accusation was greatest in the more prosperous areas, areas which had also experienced enclosure. It will also be recalled that 'witches' tended to be poorer than their victims, a point borne out by both pamphlet and other material (see MacFarlane 1970: 149–50). It may be added that the conflict with regard to resources would be likely to favour those who were both better off and had a higher social status, and that they might also want to reduce the potential threat from others encroaching on their standing. This may help us to understand why the category of 'economic conflict' is considered directly important in almost half of the cases mentioned in the pamphlets. This does not, however, explain why women in particular should be affected by witchcraft accusation. The question of male–female relations and the economy, which I discussed in Chapter 7, is important here, as it situates the 'economic conflict' found in accusations of witchcraft within the wider, specifically gendered, economic context. During the sixteenth and seventeenth centuries there were attempts to curtail women's economic activities in favour of men in lucrative areas such as brewing (Clark 1982). Women were expected to be both financially dependent on men and economically inferior to them, and would be considered 'deviant' if they overstepped this definition.

Finally, the category of sexual 'deviance' needs to be considered. Instances of sexual 'deviance', ranging from calling the accused 'lewd' to fornication (with men and the Devil), incest and lesbianism are cited in relation to about one-third of the cases mentioned in the Essex pamphlets. If the 1645 trial pamphlet is ignored, this figure approaches one half of the cases mentioned. These figures suggest that not conforming to dominant societal views regarding sexual behaviour might be a contributary factor to accusation for witchcraft.

MacFarlane, who looks at the formal, Church Court accusations for sexual deviance suggests that only very few women were formally accused of both 'sexual offences' and witchcraft, and concludes that sexual deviance is not a particularly significant feature in the identification of witches. But MacFarlane's rather positivistic approach regarding this issue obscures the potential importance of sexual 'deviance' in the identification of witches. As he himself indicates, the contemporary witch sterotype included lustful behaviour and leading 'a lewd and naughtie kind of life' (ibid.: 158), and as I pointed out earlier, what is especially important about these features is their specific association with women rather than men (see Chapter 7). It was largely because of their proneness to be seen as sexually deviant that women were generally perceived as a 'problem' in sixteenth- and seventeenth-century society. We can therefore not ignore the sizeable number of women who, in the trial pamphlets, were associated with sexual deviance, nor that this category may have been another aspect of the identification of certain women rather than all women as 'witches'.

This is of course complex, because women as a category were generally perceived to be prone to sexual deviance, and we may therefore expect such accusation. But, not all women were actually accused in this way. It may be that women perceived as more sexually deviant than others were also more prone to witchcraft accusation, as Karlsen (1987) has also suggested for New England. Combined with the other features already outlined (regarding marital status, age, whether other kin had been accused, liaison with the Devil, and economic conflict), this led to only certain women being formally accused.[26]

This chapter concludes my general discussion of the early modern witch-hunts. In the next and final chapter I shall draw together the main aspects of this material and the revolutionary feminist approach outlined earlier.

Chapter 9

The conclusion

The maintenance and perpetuation of male domination over women relies on an eroticised construct of inequality between men and women, where male and female sexualities are constructed as both different and unequal. Fundamentally, sex and power are merged. This becomes apparent when we look at the issue of male sexual violence against women, and examine male sexuality and male sexual practice. Within the system of male supremacy men thus have power over women by virtue of being perceived as 'naturally' superior to women, but it is a system of social domination rather than natural inequality, and therefore has to be socially maintained through the eroticisation of male–female relations generally, and also by the use, and threat of, male sexual violence against women. What makes male supremacy especially enduring, is the way these mechanisms are eroticised or made 'sexy' and acted out in heterosexual relations, thereby appearing both 'natural', 'normal' and 'consensual'.

Where the witch-hunts in sixteenth- and seventeenth-century England are concerned, this revolutionary feminist framework provides new insights. Largely because it helps to explain why women were the primary targets of the persecutions, but also because it enables us to take into account the many disparate elements involved. For an analysis of the witch-hunts the following points need to be considered: that the accused were nearly all women; that they constituted a particular group of women, tending to be older, unmarried or widowed, and poor; that women tended to accuse and incriminate each other; and that ruling-class intervention was essential for the witch-hunts to become established, as well as for it to eventually decline. In addition, the witch-hunts must be situated within the general social changes taking place during the sixteenth and seventeenth centuries.

Overall, the witch-hunts were an instance of male sexual violence against women, relying on a particular sexual construct of female behaviour. The hunts were a part of the apparently ongoing attempt by men to control women socially, and to reimpose the male-dominated status quo in a period of many changes including economic restructuring and pressure on economic resources. In other words, the witch-hunts of the sixteenth and seventeenth centuries were a part of the 'dynamics of domination' whereby men at the time maintained dominance over women.

Evidence from the witch trial pamphlets, and in particular from sixteenth- and seventeenth-century literature, as discussed in Chapters 6, 7 and 8, suggests that the definition of the 'witch' relied on an eroticised construct of female behaviour, with women as potentially threatening and in need of control. Throughout most of the witch-hunt period, female sexuality was constructed as more active than male sexuality, in contrast to the twentieth century where it has tended to be male sexuality which has been construed as active (Jackson 1984a, 1984b). Yet in the witch-hunt period, as today, male and female sexuality as well as masculinity and femininity were perceived as both different and unequal, with men as superior. This eroticised gender ideology resulted, in the early modern period, in a particular double standard where accusing women of witchcraft seemed both reasonable and necessary – as did imprisonment or death. It was deemed part and parcel of female nature to be weak and sinful as well as sexually insatiable, women were themselves to blame for using witchcraft and also responsible for the consequences. *Women*, rather than men, were therefore likely to be labelled as witches and prone to witchcraft accusation. And women were to blame for their own victimisation, just as today it is women who 'ask' to be raped by supposedly presenting themselves as sexually enticing (see Chapter 4).

The eroticised notion of female inferiority outlined above was not mentioned explicitly in the trial pamphlets, except in that of 1645. But it does, none the less, provide a crucial backdrop to the accusations, and is reflected implicitly in the evidence against the accused. For instance, the focus in all the Essex trials on familiars is important, since these 'Devil's ambassadors' were deemed to be physically intimate with the 'witches'. There is also the mention, in the 1589 trial pamphlet, of Joan Prentice's familiar or spirit always appearing when she was getting ready for bed. In the, less representative, trial pamphlet of 1645 we even find that Elizabeth Clarke was accused of having sex with the Devil himself.

The witch-hunts constituted sexual violence against women, in the sense that the vast majority of those persecuted were women, and because it was only by constructing women as inferior to men in a *sexual* way that women became the primary targets of witch accusation. But unlike the case of rape, where an individual or group of men sexually violate a woman, the issue of the witch-hunts constituting *male* sexual violence is more complex: the legal apparatus, an essential ingredient of the persecutions, was entirely staffed by men (from the upper classes); and individuals such as Matthew Hopkins, who made witch-hunting their business, were also men. But more important, and underlying these examples, was the general male-dominated context of the witch-hunts (as discussed in Chapter 7). The belief that women were inferior and sinful was crucial, as was a social structure reflecting women's supposed inferiority, where women were supposed to be kept out of the important areas of societal power such as Church and state hierarchies. And especially important were the conflicts between men and women over economic participation, as illustrated by the attempts to curtail women's involvement in the more lucrative areas of the changing economy (see Chapter 7). The escalation into a witch-*hunt* was facilitated by the formalising of witchcraft accusation by the ruling class who were (in Europe at least) initially interested in controlling heresy rather than women specifically. But at this particular socio-historical juncture a number of elements were apparent at the same time, making the accusation of witchcraft both a possible and appropriate means of controlling women socially. At a general level, therefore, the witch-persecutions constituted sexual violence against women within a context of male supremacist social relations, rather than sexual violence by individual men against women.

That women's lives were profoundly controlled through the threat of witchcraft accusation is illustrated by the trial pamphlets. In the context of sixteenth- and seventeenth-century society any conversation, request for help, or movement about the village, could be construed as evidence of witch behaviour. Doing both good deeds as well as bad deeds left a woman open to the charge of witchcraft. Knowing a witch or being related to one was likely to label a woman as a witch herself. In short, it was very easy to be accused of witchcraft, and accusation might mean death. The fact that many women incriminated each other must also be seen in this light as an indication of the pressures they felt to avoid being accused of witchcraft, or to attempt to lessen the accusation against them. For this reason it is perhaps not surprising that women should incriminate each other. The pamphlets indicate that most of the women believed in witchcraft – that it could help them to attain a better life, or be used as a means of retribution. Moreover, women were also likely to believe, as members of a misogynist and superstitious society, that they themselves were more prone than men to be in league with the Devil, and might therefore accuse other women.

Alan MacFarlane has pointed to the predominance of women accusing other women in witch trials as evidence for his view that the witch-hunts did not involve 'hostility between the sexes' (1970: 55). If women accused each other, rather than men always accusing women, then, MacFarlane reckons, conflict was between women and not between the sexes. But his interpretation is much too simplistic. Just because women were 'bewitched' more often than men, and the deed carried out by other women, does not necessarily mean that an underlying structural antagonism between the sexes did not exist. As I have already indicated, the witch-hunts constituted male sexual violence against women precisely because of the structural inequality and conflict between men and women at the time.

In the case of rape and sexual harassment today, any woman could be the target of male violence, although some women may at times be more vulnerable. For instance, women living with male partners are more prone to domestic violence than women who do not live with men. And Albert De Salvo, the so-called 'Boston Strangler' who sexually murdered many women, saw elderly women as an easier target and used them to gain confidence before moving on to murder younger women also (Brownmiller 1976: 205). At the time of the witch-hunts we find an analogous picture. It was perhaps easier to accuse those women who were more vulnerable such as the old, widowed and poor, and those who stepped outside the socially-accepted stereotype, although the persecutions were based on a religious and inherently male supremacist ideology which saw *all women* as a threat and as potential 'witches'.

The witch-hunts are not a unique event to be filed under 'the historical unrepeatable past'. Rather, the persecutions may be seen as part of the ongoing attempt by men – acting as a group and with the support of some women – to ensure the continuance of male supremacy. The witch-hunts are particular to a specific historical period. Very significantly, they are a product of a society with a prevalent superstitious belief in evil and magic. But they also appear to have been a particular response to a possibly long-lived problem: a part of the dynamic process whereby men as a group actively attempted to maintain dominance over women, who were rarely passively compliant. With regard to this it is especially interesting that the accusation of witchcraft also appears to have been used among the peasantry in the centuries prior to (and after) the witch-hunts as a means of controlling women socially. In other words, the accusation of witchcraft against women appears to have been part of the ongoing dynamic of male domination over women, especially among the peasantry, and less so among the ruling class – who none the less held a similarly gendered view of witchcraft during the sixteenth and seventeenth centuries. Significantly, it was when a different gender construct became prevalent among the ruling classes – still eroticised but placing women in a more passive and domestic role – that the use of *formal* witchcraft accusation was superseded as the means of controlling women socially, and the witch-hunts eventually ceased, while informal accusation appears to have continued at a village level.

In conclusion, by using a revolutionary feminist framework it is possible to give an explanation of the witch-hunts, that situates the persecutions within the dynamic process of male domination in the sixteenth and seventeenth centuries, and also incorporates the many contextual features in evidence. Within this analysis the witch-hunts can be seen as one form of sexual violence against women, as experienced by women during the sixteenth and seventeenth centuries.[1] The witch-hunts were not entirely similar to the violence experienced by women today, and this is to be expected, because the witch-hunts occurred in a particular and different socio-historical context. What is important is that the general framework still applies.

The main implication of the theoretical framework presented here, for other feminist analyses and especially that of socialist and Marxist feminists (see Chapter 2), is that their focus of analysis is misplaced. The 'dual systems' theories of Hartmann (1979),

Eisenstein (1979) and to some extent Walby (1986), focus on the 'reproductive' sphere, and in particular the domestic family unit and the marriage relationship, as the most important arena of male dominance over women. What my framework suggests, however, is that in so doing, these perspectives do not uncover the fundamental male–female power relation, which is an eroticised or sexualised relation. The eroticised power relations between men and women have become institutionalised through the heterosexual family and marriage, but these institutions are merely examples of such relations. This, I would suggest, is why the socialist and Marxist feminist perspectives have great difficulty theorising the generality of male–female power relations within our society.

Most obviously, the framework I have used suggests that the male–female conflictual relations, which Cockburn (1983) and Walby (1986) have found to cut across capitalist relations, are inevitable in a male supremacist context and also directly affect capitalist social relations. By providing a more detailed understanding of the mechanism of such conflictual male–female relations, the revolutionary feminist framework moves beyond the restrictions of a purely economic analysis. Precisely because the mechanism of maintaining male dominance (through the eroticisation of male dominance and female inferiority) may be recognised at all levels of social relations, for example, as sexual harassment at work as well as domestic violence and other sexual violence within marriage and heterosexuality (MacKinnon 1979; Coveney *et al.* 1984a; Russell 1982, 1984), it overcomes the problems of Walby's separate 'modes of production', where economic considerations remain paramount.

Historical change is another important issue, especially explanation of the seeming longevity of male supremacy. I have argued that male supremacy as a sex–class system not only predates capitalism but played an integral and important part in shaping the capitalist economy (and presumably earlier economies also). What is particularly important is that the framework which I use also allows for changes in the social order. While the mechanisms involving the eroticisation of male power and sexual violence, by which male dominance is maintained and perpetuated, are generally apparent, the actual form that these take may vary over time. The material regarding the early modern witch-hunts provides an important example of this, with the witch-persecutions as an historically specific instance of sexual violence against women, different in certain respects from other instances of sexual violence both at the time and today. In other words, the mechanisms involved in the 'dynamics of domination' remain the same, but new forms result from the ongoing conflictual relations between men and women at many different levels and from the attempt by men to maintain power over women.

In this book I have focused my discussion on the ways male supremacy is maintained and perpetuated, and have argued that the pressures acting in the interests of male supremacy are complex, often hidden, and very strong. None the less, the notion of sex–class conflict also suggests that women are by no means passively compliant to the construct that is male supremacy. How and why male supremacy is maintained is, however, crucially important to understand precisely because this leads to a means of changing these unequal male–female power relations.

Notes

1 THE INTRODUCTION

1 Marx and Engels briefly mention this in *The German Ideology* (1968), and Engels takes it up in *The Family, Private Property and the State* (1968).

2 FROM MEN PARTIALLY TO MEN PRIMARILY RESPONSIBLE FOR WOMEN'S OPPRESSION

1 For discussion of the domestic labour debate see Hester 1988.
2 The term 'dual systems' originates from Iris Young (1980).
3 See Barrett (1984: Introduction) for an early overview, and Beechey (1986) for more recent material.
4 Cockburn is using a notion of 'sex and gender' here which is both interrelated and socially constructed. This is similar to my own preferred terminology; although Cockburn is referring specifically to the use of the term by Gayle Rubin (1975).
5 It should be noted that it is difficult to tell the actual extent of sexual violence, as women are often reluctant to report incidents. The apparent increase in the figures in recent years which Cockburn mentions may merely reflect greater numbers of recorded incidents (see London Rape Crisis Centre, undated; Hanmer and Saunders 1984). The area of sexual violence which does appear to have increased in recent years is the public availability of pornography (Walby 1990).
6 The recent equal pay legislation (Equal Pay Act 1975) has made the argument in favour of a 'family wage' for men more difficult, and has led to a contradiction between a family wage on the one hand and the notion of equal pay for both men and women on the other (Cockburn 1983: 183). It should be noted, however, that equal pay, despite the legislation, is not a reality.
7 Other strategies such as wage differentials may achieve a similar purpose (see Walby 1986).
8 Nowhere is her use of term 'structure' explained, though it is implied that it refers to recurring patterns of social behaviour and relations. It

becomes especially difficult to predict her intention when she also uses the terms 'structure' and 'institution' indiscriminately.

9 Acker suggests that the focus should be the problematic of 'gender', as 'the content of patriarchy is gender' (Acker 1989: 238). This is a point which I will discuss further in the following chapters.

10 I present an outline and detailed critique of *Patriarchy at Work* in Hester (1988). However, many of the points raised there have been superceded by Walby's more recent work on *Theorising Patriarchy* (1990).

11 It is interesting to note that a number of forces acted together to achieve the passage of the Factory Acts: the threatened male operatives, male philanthropists arguing for a strengthening of women's morality, and the landed interest in the Tory Party. As a result both women and manufacturers' interests were defeated (Walby 1986: 127).

12 This material is dealt with in some detail in *Patriarchy at Work* (1986), and referred to again without significant change in *Theorising Patriarchy* (1990).

13 See Walby (1990: 143). An interesting parallel to Walby's analysis can also be found in the work of Carrigan *et al.* (1987), who take a critical and socialist approach to the study of masculinity.

14 Hooks uses the term 'sexist' to denote discrimination and oppression of women by men.

15 See also Abercrombie *et al.* (1988: 67).

16 See Cameron (1985: 187). She also points out that the term 'discourse' is not very precise since its interpretation depends on the theoretical approach adopted.

17 See Stuart Hall's introduction to *Culture, Media, Language* (1980) for an overview of the post-war debate on 'ideology' and the place for discourse theory within this.

18 See Deborah Cameron (1985) for an overview of developments in linguistic theory.

19 Freud's work on 'penis-envy', which Mitchell uses, is rather muddled, and it is not always clear whether he is talking about this concept as an idea or as a biological reality (see also Barrett 1984: 55).

20 Cameron (1985) discusses the problem of determinism in post-structuralist and similar theories.

3   MEN AS PRIMARILY RESPONSIBLE FOR WOMEN'S OPPRESSION

1 For an example of consciousness-raising seen as merely confidence building see Ashton (1987).

2 Lynette Mitchell (1984) uses 'cultural' approach as a descriptive term.

3 First published 1970.

4 The way sexualised definitions have been used to place both black men and women in inferior categories to white men has also been discussed more recently elsewhere, for instance by Wallace (1979).

5 See, for instance, the journals *Trouble and Strife* and *The Revolutionary and Radical Feminist Newsletter*.

6 As related to Schutz (1972), Mead (1935), Blumer (1969), Goffman (1959), and Garfinkel (1967).

4   TOWARDS A REVOLUTIONARY FEMINIST APPROACH

1 In Chapters 4 and 5 I present the central theoretical approach within this book. My approach is rooted in the earlier feminist work of Kate Millett (1970), and closely related to the revolutionary feminist work referred to in Chapter 1, as well as the similar work of some American feminists (Coveney *et al.* 1984b; Jackson 1983, 1984a, 1984b, 1987; Jeffreys 1982, 1985a, 1990; MacKinnon 1982; Dworkin 1981).

2 See Jeffreys 1985a.

3 Feminists have, for example, identified the following 'types' of male violence: rape (Brownmiller 1976; Griffin 1971; Russell 1973, 1975), sexual abuse of children (Jeffreys 1982; Rush 1980), pornography (Dworkin 1981, Lederer 1982), domestic violence (Dobash and Dobash 1979; Homer et al. 1984), sexual harassment at work (MacKinnon 1979), and prostitution (Barry 1981; Jeffreys 1985b).

4 Russell used a woman-centred approach in her work to overcome the problem that official statistics grossly underestimate the numbers of incidences due to women's reluctance to report rape, and other sexual violence. See also the discussion by Betsy Stanko regarding the problem of documenting rape (Stanko 1985: ch.4).

5 This notion of non-consensual sex as rape applies to the United States as well. Note also that a man can rape another man, but legally in Britain this is seen as indecent assault – a lesser crime than rape.

6 The ethnomethodologists Simon and Gagnon have developed an analysis of social interactions involving 'scripts'. See Stevi Jackson (1978) for an application of this approach to the specific example of rape. Wise and Stanley (1987) have also developed a feminist analysis of male violence using this general approach.

7 See Lederer (1982) and Sellen and Young (1987) for overviews of the debate, especially with reference to America.

8 Campaigns by the publishers of pornography and their followers subsequently managed to overturn the legislation (Everywoman 1988).

9 Of particular importance is the recent work by Andrea Dworkin (1981) which presents one of the most comprehensive discussions of pornography. Closely related to Dworkin's work is also that of MacKinnon (1987a, 1989). The work of these American feminists is also similar to that presented by Lal Coveney *et al.* 1984b, and by the London revolutionary feminists in 'Pornography' (Katyachild *et al.* 1985: 13–18).

10 She is mainly using the definition of the United States Commission on Obscenity and Pornography.

11 See also de Beauvoir (1953), who is accredited with being the first feminist to analyse women as 'Other' from men.

5 A REVOLUTIONARY FEMINIST APPROACH

1 This can, for instance, be seen clearly in the case of Ellis's work, discussed later in this chapter.
2 This argument is expressed especially clearly by Steven Goldberg in his book *The Inevitability of Patriarchy* (1974).
3 See also Jane Egerton (1982) and Robin Ruth Linden *et al.* (1982) for further discussion of this problem.
4 Corinne Hutt's, *Males and Females* (1972) is an example of such a socio-biological stance. What is particularly interesting about this work is that Hutt specifically wrote the book in response to, and as a critique of, the contemporary Women's Liberation Movement, and the related reawakening of debate regarding sex differences.
5 For overview of these writings see Sayers (1982).
6 Ellis thought that divorce should be available when necessary, but that this should occur alongside a strengthening in the stability of marriage (see Jackson 1984a: 62).
7 See also Jeffreys for discussion of lesbianism in this context.
8 Kinsey wrote from the late 1930s to the 1950s. Masters and Johnson have been writing since the 1960s.
9 See also Jackson (1984b: 79–80).
10 Writing since the 1960s.
11 This is also the case amongst sexologists more generally (see Jackson 1987).
12 See Rowan (1987) for overview, and Pearson (1984) for discussion of different types of 'male sexual politics'.
13 See also Raynaud (1983).
14 The term 'political lesbian' originally came from the American radical feminist group, the Redstockings (1970).
15 See Kitzinger (1987) for a detailed discussion of lesbianism as a social construct.
16 See also Faderman (1981), Raymond (1986) and Jeffreys (1985a).

6 THE EARLY MODERN WITCH-HUNTS I

1 The theoretical framework presented in Chapter 4 has already demonstrated two important aspects regarding historical analysis. Firstly, Jeffreys (1985a) and Jackson (1984a, 1984b), for instance, have examined the reaction against the changes in male sexual practice being fought for by feminists at the turn of the century, and since, by Havelock Ellis and other sexologists. Secondly, the framework incorporates the (related) notion of conflict, or sex–class struggle, thus suggesting the inevitability of social change rather than stasis.
2 The term 'witch-craze' is used by Hugh Trevor-Roper (1969).
3 In a few countries, for instance, Finland, the number of men and

women accused were similar due to a different tradition and use of witchcraft.

4 She concludes that witches were hunted as *witches*, that is, as enemies of God and not as women.

5 Larner's emphasis on Christian political ideology leads her to consider amongst other questions why the witch-craze was less intense in England than in Europe or Scotland. She argues that this was partly due to the lower religious intensity in England, pointing out that the struggle for legitimacy by the Protestant state had already been won half a century before the witch-craze developed, under Henry VII. She also suggests that in England the legal procedure itself was not conducive to creating intense witch-hunting, partly because the notion of conspiracy did not exist in relation to witchcraft, and partly because the procedure was not centrally managed (as elsewhere) but dealt with by circuit judges.

6 See Barstow (1988) for an overview of the literature.

7 See also Hester (1988: Chapter 3).

8 Karlsen does not discuss the phrase 'violent struggle *against* women', nor does she link it explicitly with the feminist debate outlined in this book in Chapter 4, although there does seem to be some implicit reference to this – see page xii.

9 Faderman (1981), in one of the few books discussing lesbianism in early modern Europe, suggests that in seventeenth-century England 'lesbianism' (which she perceives as a non-sexual romantic friendship at this time) was not perceived as a threat, though Bray (1982), discussing male homosexuals in the period, argues that these men *were* perceived as a threat. More research needs to be done in this area before we can discuss these issues in greater detail. See also my discussion of the case of Elizabeth Bennett from the 1582 trial in Chapter 7.

10 See MacFarlane (1970: Chapter 3) for details of the workings of the Assizes, and Chapter 4 for the other courts. The other courts were considering instances of *maleficium* both prior to and during the witch-hunt period. Thomas (1971) considers this an important issue with regard to the English material, and European historians are also increasingly seeing this as an important area of work (see Gijswijt-Hofstra 1989).

11 There is a complete set of these in Notestein (1968: Appendix A).

12 See Merchant (1980) for review of primary literary sources.

13 First published in 1929.

14 Indictments were presentments from the Quarter Sessions and elsewhere which had been passed as a 'true bill' by a Grand Jury (See MacFarlane 1970: 23).

15 The Home Circuit consisted of the Assize Courts in the counties surrounding London – Essex, Hertford, Kent, Surrey and Sussex.

16 There is a direct similarity between the contents of the pamphlets and Church Court depositions. Both outline similar 'stories'. My thanks to Todd Gray for showing me the Church Court depositions from the South West which he has transcribed.

17 The period considered as most important for analysis of the witch-craze by MacFarlane (1970: 8).
18 There are two pamphlets for the 1645 trials, one written at the time about the Chelmsford trial and another written in 1700 about a 1645 trial in Worcester which appears to be based on the earlier pamphlet, but consists of seemingly false material and is considered irrelevant here (see MacFarlane 1970: 317).
19 MacFarlane points out that as a result of these exceptional features of the 1582 and 1645 trials, most descriptions of the Essex witch trials have unfortunately concentrated on this material (1970: 84–5).
20 The first witchcraft statute was enacted in 1542 and repealed within five years.
21 Montague Summers discusses the problem of documentation where it appears that the accused witch is burnt whereas in fact she was hanged (1971: 11–14). MacFarlane points out that there are no cases in existing English records of a woman burnt to death because of husband-murder.
22 Quotations from the leading contemporary manual for Justices of the Peace (Cockburn 1972: 16).
23 These figures are calculated from the Assize records compiled by James Cockburn – *Calender of Assize Records* (1978 & 1982 – Essex Indictments). It must also be noted that the term 'crime' did not exist during the sixteenth and seventeenth centuries in the sense of social deviance as it does now. In this earlier period crime generally was considered as 'sin', that is, in a religious sense (see Cockburn 1972).
24 A few more cases have been discovered since Ewen's work, but this does not significantly alter his view that the number of cases have generally been overestimated (see also MacFarlane 1970: 5).
25 Despite discussions about figures, Mies (1986) points out that no one has yet systematically assessed the numbers accused and executed for witchcraft.
26 There was another 'witchfinder' in the Home Counties during these years, in Kent.

7   THE EARLY MODERN WITCH-HUNTS II

1 These beliefs included nocturnal flights by women and cannibalism (see Cohn 1975: 209–11).
2 See also Thomas for discussion of beliefs in the Devil's powers during the sixteenth and seventeenth centuries (1971: 469–77).
3 An issue not identified by Cohn.
4 See Wrigley and Schofield (1981) for overview of population changes.
5 McLaren (1984), makes the point that the utilisation of mothers' milk was a vital, if not the most vital factor in determining pre-industrial population, due to the contraceptive effect of breastfeeding, although Amussen (1988) suggests that abortion also played an important part.
6 See also Watkins (1984) for discussion of spinsters.
7 He also points out that there is a problem regarding the economic

features attributed to this decline of equality by the contributors to the 'critical-pessimistic' tradition. Thus: 'while some authors attribute this loss principally to the development of capitalism, others attribute it to the spread of factory industry, and still others seem unaware of, or confused about, any distinction that might be made between the two' (Middleton 1985: 182).

8 Clark has been criticised by some feminists because she argues that women were more 'productive' in pre-industrial society. Also because of her ideological framework which is supportive of the family and women's primary role as mothers (see Chaytor and Lewis 1982).

9 As exemplified by the attitude of the Church Courts to fornication and illegitimacy (see Amussen 1988; Hair 1972).

10 There has been much debate in recent years about the typical household and family forms during the sixteenth and seventeenth centuries. The main features of this debate are outlined by Michael Anderson (1980). One of the most important conclusions which may be drawn is that the household during the sixteenth and seventeenth centuries tended to be based around the nuclear family, with the addition of servants and possibly apprentices in many households (Laslett 1977; Laslett and Wall 1972). Moreover, that there was perhaps a greater continuity in familial relations than authors such as Stone (1979) and Shorter (1975) allow (see Vann 1977; Tilly and Scott 1976; Ingram 1987; Chaytor 1980; Wrightson 1981).

11 Ingram (1987) provides extensive examples and interpretations of such cases from the Church Courts, and Hair (1972) lists many original indictments and outcomes.

12 Merchant (1980) documents how the cuckolding wife was a popular theme of literature and woodcuts.

13 For discussion of the popular controversy see Wright (1935), George (1973), Woodbridge (1986) and Kelly (1986). Some of the primary documents have been assembled by Shepherd (1985).

14 Woodbridge (1986) disagrees that such real events directly influenced the debate, seeing it instead as a primarily literary phenomenon. I find it difficult to agree, however, that contemporary events had no bearing on the debate.

15 Rachel Speght, for instance, wrote a scripture-based answer (see Shepherd 1985).

16 *Sowernam* to answer *Sweetnam*.

17 Faderman uses the rather inaccurate term 'transvestite' for women who cross-dressed for the purpose of taking on 'male' roles.

18 Interestingly, another consequence of his belief was his argument that male magicians should be punished because 'male magicians acted voluntarily in making pacts with the Devil and could therefore be punished' (Merchant 1980: 141).

19 Harvey's views concerning women (and men) may be gleaned from his work on reproduction, *On Animal Generation* (1651), which was widely discussed (see Frank 1979). Using Aristotle as his basis, Harvey argued that men had the main role in reproduction by providing the active male sperm which triggered fertilisation and endowed the

developing embryo with 'reason' while women merely contributed matter. *On Animal Generation* was mainly a study of animal reproduction, in deer and chickens, but Harvey suggested that these also applied to human reproduction. Concerning animal reproduction he thus suggested that:

> Among animals where the sexes are distinct, matters are so arranged that since the female alone is inadequate to engender an embryo and to nourish and protect the young a male is associated with her by nature, as the superior and more worthy progenitor, as the consort of her labour and the means of supplying her deficiencies.
> (in Merchant 1980: 158).

In this way women's passivity and men's active role was stressed.

20 The new 'scientific' and misogynist philosophy which was instrumental in bringing about the decline of the witch-hunts was also reflected in the work of influential contemporary philosophers such as Thomas Hobbes. He, for example, dismisses the belief in witchcraft in his book *Leviathan* (1651), written like Harvey's work towards the end of the main English witch-hunt period (see Coole 1988).

8   THE ACCUSED AND THE ACCUSATIONS AGAINST THEM

1 See Cockburn (1978) cases 1055, 1093, 273, 622, 1024; Ewen (1971) and MacFarlane (1970) cases 121, 131, 17, 50, 123.

2 It is also difficult to tell the marital status of the few men mentioned.

3 Adapted from MacFarlane (1970 Table 11: 150).

4 The pamphlet says she is four score years or thereabouts. But this seems excessive as she has small children and her mother appears to be still alive.

5 Most references in this section are from the reprint in Ewen (1971), except for the 'introduction' which refers to a reprint by the Philobiblon Society (1864). The original is without page numbers.

6 The judges, over the three-day trial, included Mr Justice Southcote and Mr Gerard, the Queen's Attorney.

7 Cockburn spells the surname of Agnes and Joan as Waterhowse.

8 I have taken advice from a number of archival experts and none could give another precise interpretation of the term 'waste his goodes'.

9 The introduction to the 1579 Essex pamphlet also refers to the use of prayer to 'shield thy self' against the Devil.

10 Reference throughout this section is to an original copy of the pamphlet, at the British Library, which does not have page numbers.

11 The justices for this trial were Justice Southcote, as in 1566, and Justice Gawdy (Ewen 1971: 103).

12 The indictable offences of Elizabeth Frauncis, Elleine Smithe and Margery Staunton are mentioned in the pamphlet; but not that of Alice Nokes, despite the fact that she was found guilty and hanged. Cockburn uses the names Helen Smythe, Margery Staunton and Alice Nokes.

13 See Cockburn (1978) case 669.
14 The judge in this instance was Brian Darcy, who may also have written the pamphlet of the trial, under the pseudonym W.W.
15 The names of the thirteen accused mentioned in the pamphlet are as follows:
Ursley Kempe
Ales Newman (Cockburn 1978: case 1300 – calls her Alice Newman)
Elizabeth Bennet
Ales Hunt (ibid.: case 1301 – calls her Alice Hunt)
Cysley Celles (ibid.: case 1302 – calls her Cicely Silles)
Ales Manfielde (ibid.: case 1302 – calls her Alice Manfield)
Margaret Grevell
Elizabeth Eustace (not mentioned in Assize records)
Annys Herd (ibid.: case 1312 – calls her Agnes Herd)
Joan Robynson (not mentioned in the Assize records)
Margery Sammon (not mentioned in the Assize records)
Annys Glascocke (ibid.: case 1304 – calls her Agnes Glascocke)
Joan Pechey (not mentioned in Assize records).
16 This does not include Ales Manfielde who is mentioned in the Assize records, but the outcome of her trial is not recorded.
17 Unfortunately without obvious page numbering.
18 See also Crompton (1981) who discusses lesbianism in the legal context.
19 It is interesting to note that the bread and beef was originally donated by Brian Darcy, the Judge.
20 References in this section are to an original copy of the pamphlet, held in the British Library.
21 There is another male suspect but his name is crossed out.
22 They are brought before Judge Anthony Mildemay, Esquire.
23 References are to an original copy of the pamphlet, held by the British Library.
24 References are to an original copy of the pamphlet. For general discussion of the trial and Matthew Hopkins, see MacFarlane (1970: Chapter 9) and Notestein (1968: Chapter 8).
25 The women were tried before the 'Right Honourable Robert Earle of Warwicke, and severall of his Majesties Justices of Peace' (H.F. 1645: front page).
26 It must be reiterated that we do not know how many women were informally accused of witchcraft.

9   THE CONCLUSION

1 Women at the time did, of course, experience other forms of male sexual violence such as rape (see Bashar 1983).

Bibliography

Abercrombie, N., Warde, A., Soothill, K., Urry, J. and Walby, S. (1988) *Contemporary British Society: A New Introduction to Sociology*, Cambridge, Polity.

Acker, J. (1989) 'The problem with patriarchy', *Sociology* 23, (2).

Al-Hibra, A. (1983) 'Reproduction, mothering and the origins of patriarchy' in J. Trebilcot (ed.) *Mothering: Essays in Feminist Theory*, New Jersey, Rowman and Allanheld.

Allen, S., Sanders, L. and Wallis, J. (eds) (1974) *Conditions of Illusion*, Leeds, Feminist Books.

Amir, M. (1971) *Patterns in Forcible Rape*, Chicago, University of Chicago Press.

Amos, V. and Parmar, P. (1984) 'Challenging imperial feminism', *Feminist Review* 17.

Amussen, S.D. (1988) *An Ordered Society: Gender and Class in Early Modern England*, Oxford, Blackwell.

Anderson, M. (1980) *Approaches to the History of the Western Family 1500–1914*, London, MacMillan.

Ankarloo, B. and Henningsen, G. (eds) (1990) *Early Modern European Witchcraft*, Oxford, Clarendon Press.

Anthias, F. and Yuval-Davis, N. (1983) 'Contextualising feminism – gender, ethnic and class divisions', *Feminist Review* 15.

Archer, J. (1978) 'Exploring sex differences' in Chetwynd, J. and Hartnett, O. (eds) *The Sex Role System*, London, Routledge & Kegan Paul.

Archer, J. and Lloyd, B. (eds) (1982) *Sex and Gender*, Harmondsworth, Penguin.

Arditti, R., Duelli Klein, R. and Minden, S. (eds) (1984) *Test-tube Women. What Future for Motherhood?*, London, Pandora Press.

Ashton, F. (1987) 'Feminism in the 80's: fact or fiction?', in Ashton, F., and Whitting G. (eds) *Feminist Theory and Political Policies*, Bristol, School for Advanced Urban Studies, University of Bristol.

Badinter, E.E. (1981) *The Myth of Motherhood: An Historical View of the Maternal Instinct*, London, Souvenir Press.

Barrett, M. (1984) *Women's Oppression Today*, London, Verso.

Barrett, M. and McIntosh, M. (1980) 'The family wage: some problems for socialists and feminists', *Capital and Class* 11.

Barron, R. and Norris, G.M. (1976) 'Sexual divisions and the dual labour market', in D.L. Barker and S. Allen (eds) *Dependence and Exploitation in Work and Marriage*, London, Longmans.

Barry, K. (1981) *Female Sexual Slavery*, New York, Avon Books.

Barstow, A.L. (1988) 'On studying witchcraft as women's history: a historiography of the European witch persecutions', *Journal of Feminist Studies in Religion* 4.

Bart, P. and O'Brien, P. (1985) *Stopping Rape*, Oxford, Pergamon Press.

Bashar, N. (1983) 'Rape in England between 1550 and 1700', in London Feminist History Group (eds) *The Sexual Dynamics of History: Men's Power, Women's Resistance*, London, Pluto Press.

de Beauvoir, S. (1953) *The Second Sex*, London, Jonathan Cape.

Beechey, V. (1977) 'Some notes on female wage labour in capitalist production', *Capital and Class* 3.

Beechey, V. (1986) 'Women and employment in contemporary Britain', in E. Whitelegg, (ed.) *Women in Britain Today*, London, Open University Press.

Beier, A.L. (1983) *The Problem of the Poor in Tudor and Early Stuart England*, London, Methuen.

Bellos, L. (1985) 'Advice to white collectives wishing to employ black workers', *Trouble and Strife* 5.

Benston, M. (1969) 'The political economy of women's liberation', *Monthly Review* 21, (4).

Birke, L. (1986) *Women, Feminism and Biology*, London, Harvester Press.

Bland, L. (1981) 'It's only human nature? Sociobiology and sex differences', *Schooling and Culture*, 10.

Blumer, H. (1969) *Symbolic Interactionism: Perspective and Method*, Englewood Cliffs, Prentice-Hall.

Bray, A. (1982) *Homosexuality in Renaissance England*, London, Gay Men's Press.

Braverman, H. (1974) *Labour and Monopoly Capital: the Degradation of Work*, New York, Monthly Review Press.

Bridenbaugh, C. (1968) *Vexed and Troubled Englishmen 1590–1642*, Oxford, Clarendon Press.

Bridenthal, R. and Koonz, C. (eds) (1977) *Becoming Visible, Women in European History*, Boston, Houghton Mifflin.

Brod, H. (1987a) 'The case for men's studies', in H. Brod (ed.) *The Making of Masculinities*, London, Allen & Unwin.

Brod, H. (ed.) (1987b) *The Making of Masculinities*, London, Allen & Unwin.

Brownmiller, S. (1976) *Against Our Will*, Harmondsworth, Penguin.

Brueghel, I. (1979) 'Women as a reserve army of labour: a note on recent British experience', *Feminist Review* 3.

Burke, P. (1990) 'The comparative approach to European witchcraft', in B. Ankarloo and G. Henningsen (eds) *Early Modern European Witchcraft*, Oxford, Clarendon Press.

Burstyn, V. (ed.) (1985) *Women Against Censorship*, Toronto, Douglas & McIntyre.

Callifia, P., Duggan, L., Ellis, K. and Hunter, N. (1986) (eds) *Caught Looking: Feminism, Pornography and Censorship*, New York, Caught Looking

Cameron, D. (1985) *Feminism and Linguistic Theory*, London, Macmillan.

Carrigan, T., Connell, B, and Lee, J. (1987) 'Towards a new sociology of masculinity' in H. Brod (ed.) *The Making of Masculinities*, London, Allen & Unwin.

Charles, L. and Duffin, L. (1985) (eds) *Women and Work in Pre-Industrial England*, London, Croom Helm.

Chaytor, M. (1980) 'Household and kinship: Ryton in the late sixteenth and early seventeenth centuries', *History Workshop* 10.

Chaytor, M. and Lewis, J. (1982) Introduction to Clark A. *The Working Life of Women in the Seventeenth Century*, London, Routledge & Kegan Paul.

Chester, G. (1979) 'I call myself a radical feminist', *Feminist Practice: Notes from the Tenth Year*, London, In Theory Press.

Chetwynd, J. and Hartnett, O. (eds) (1978) *The Sex Role System*, London, Routledge & Kegan Paul.

Clark, A. (1919/1982) *The Working Life of Women in the Seventeenth Century*, London, Routledge and Kegan Paul.

Clark, G. (1981) 'The beguines: a medieval women's community', in Quest (ed.) *Building Feminist Theory*, London, Longmans.

Clark, L. and Lewis, D. (1977) *Rape – The Price of Coercive Sexuality*, Toronto, The Women's Press.

Cockburn, C. (1983) *Brothers: Male Dominance and Technological Change*, London, Pluto Press.

Cockburn, J. (1972) 'Early modern Assize Records as historical evidence', *Journal of the Society of Archivists*, 5.

Cockburn, J. (1978) *Calendar of Assize Records: Essex Indictments, Elizabeth I*, London, HMSO.

Cockburn, J. (1982) *Calendar of Assize Records: Essex Indictments, James I*, London, HMSO.

Cohn, N. (1975) *Europe's Inner Demons*, London, Chatto, Heinemann.

Comfort, A. (1975) *The Joy of Sex: A Gourmet Guide to Lovemaking*, London, Quartet Books.

Coole, D.H. (1988) *Women in Political Theory*, Brighton, Harvester Press.

Corea, G. (1985a) *The Mother Machine*, London, Harper & Row.

Corea, G. (1985b) 'The reproductive brothel' in G. Corea *et al.*, *Man-Made Women*, London, Hutchinson.

Corea, G., Duelli Klein, R., Hanmer, J., Holmes, H.B., Hoskins, B., Kishwar, M., Raymond, J., Rowland, R. and Steinbacher, R. (1985) *Man-Made Women*, London, Hutchinson.

Coulson, M., Magas, B. and Wainwright, H. (1975) 'The housewife and her labour under capitalism', *New Left Review* 89.

Coveney, L., Kay, L. and Mahoney, P. (1984a) 'Theory into practice: sexual liberation or social control? (*Forum Magazine* 1968–81)', in L. Coveney *et al. The Sexuality Papers*, London, Hutchinson.

Coveney, L., Jackson, M., Jeffreys, S., Kay, L. and Mahony, P. (eds) (1984b)

Bibliography 217

The Sexuality Papers: Male Sexuality and the Social Control of Women, London, Hutchinson.
Coward, R. (1982) 'Sexual violence and sexuality', *Feminist Review* 11.
Coward, R. (1983) *Patriarchal Precedents*, London, Routledge & Kegan Paul.
Crawford, P. (1983) *Exploring Women's Past*, vol 6 nos 1/2, London, Allen & Unwin.
Crompton, L. (1981) 'The myth of lesbian impurity: capital laws from 1270 to 1791', *Journal of Homosexuality*.
Currie, E.P. (1973) 'The control of witchcraft in Renaissance Europe', *Law and Society Review* 3, (7).
Daly, M. (1979) *Gyn/Ecology*, London, The Women's Press.
Dekker, R. and Van de Pol, L.C. (1989) *The Tradition of Female Transvestism in Early Modern Europe*, Basingstoke, Macmillan.
Delphy, C. (1977) *The Main Enemy: A Materialist Analysis of Women's Oppression*, London, Women's Research and Resources Centre.
Delphy, C. (1980) 'A materialist feminism is possible', *Feminist Review* 4.
Derrida, J. (1987) 'Women in the beehive: a seminar with Jacques Derrida', in A. Jardine and P. Smith (eds) *Men in Feminism*, London, Methuen.
Dobash, R.E. and Dobash, R. (1979) *Violence Against Wives: A Case Against the Patriarchy*, London, Open Books.
Du Bois, B. (1983) 'Passionate scholarship: notes on values, knowing and method in feminist social science', in G. Bowles and R. Duelli Klein (eds) *Theories of Women's Studies*, London, Routledge & Kegan Paul.
Duchen, C. (1986) *Feminism in France*, London, Routledge & Kegan Paul.
Duelli Klein, R. (1983) 'How to do what we want to do', in G. Bowles and R. Duelli Klein (eds) *Theories of Women's Studies*, London, Routledge & Kegan Paul.
Duelli Klein, R. (1985) 'what's "new" about the "new" reproductive technologies?' in G. Corea *et al. Man-Made Women*, London, Hutchinson.
Dworkin, A. (1974) *Woman-Hating*, New York, E.P. Dutton.
Dworkin, A. (1981) *Pornography, Men Possessing Women*, London, The Women's Press.
Dworkin, A. (1983) *Right-Wing Women*, London, The Women's Press.
Dworkin, A. (1987) *Intercourse*, London, Secker & Warburg.
Eardley, T. (1985) 'Violence and sexuality', in A. Metcalf and M. Humphries (eds) *The Sexuality of Men*, London, Pluto Press.
Easlea, B. (1980) *Witch Hunting, Magic and the New Philosophy*, Brighton, Harvester.
East London Men's Centre (1978) 'I mean, you can have a male chauvinist fantasy', *Achilles Heel* 1.
Edwards, A. (1987) 'Male violence in feminist theory: an analysis of the changing conceptions of sex/gender violence and male dominance', in J. Hanmer and M. Maynard (eds) *Women, Violence and Social Control*, London, Macmillan.
Egerton, J. (1982) 'The goal of a feminist politics – the destruction of male supremacy or the pursuit of pleasure?', *Revolutionary and Radical Feminist Newsletter* 8.

Ehrenreich, B. and English, D. (1976) *Witches, Midwives and Nurses*, London, Writers and Readers.

Eichler, M. (1988) *Nonsexist Research Methods: a Practical Guide*, London, Allan & Unwin.

Eisenstein, Z. (1979) 'Developing a theory of capitalist patriarchy and socialist feminism', in Z.R. Eisenstein (ed.) *Capitalist Patriarchy and the Case for Socialist Feminism*, London, Monthly Review Press.

Eisenstein, Z. (1984) *Contemporary Feminist Thought*, London, Unwin.

Ellis, H. (1913) *Studies in the Psychology of Sex*, vols. 1–6, Philadelphia, F.A. Davis.

Engels, F. (1984/1968) *The Origin of the Family, Private Property and the State*, London, Pathfinder Press

English, D. Hollingbaugh, A. and Rubin, G. (1982) 'Talking sex: a conversation on sexuality and feminism', *Socialist Review* 11, (4).

Everywoman (1988) *Pornography and Sexual Violence: Evidence of the Links*, London, Everywoman.

Ewen, L.C. (1929/1971) *Witch Hunting and Witch Trials*, London, Frederick Miller.

Faderman, L. (1981) *Surpassing the Love of Men*, London, Junction Books.

Feminist Practice: Notes from the Tenth Year (1979) London, In Theory Press.

Feminist Anthology Collective (1981) *No Turning Back*, London, The Women's Press.

Feminist Review (1984) 17 [whole issue on Black Feminist Perspectives].

Feminist Review (1990) 'Perverse politics: lesbian issues', 34.

Firestone, S. (1979) *The Dialectic of Sex*, London, The Women's Press.

Flandrin, J. (1979) *Families in Former Times*, Cambridge, Cambridge University Press.

Foucault, M. (1979) *The History of Sexuality*, 1, London, Allen Lane.

Francombe, C. (1984) *Abortion Freedom*, London, Allen & Unwin.

Frank, R.G. Jr (1979) 'The image of Harvey', in J.J. Bylebyl (ed.) *William Harvey and His Age*, London, John Hopkins University Press.

Frankenburgh, R. and Martens, J. (1985) 'Racism: not a moral issue', *Trouble and Strife* 5.

Friedan, B. (1972) *The Feminine Mystique*, Harmondsworth, Penguin.

Friedman, S. and Sarah, E. (eds) (1982) *On the Problem of Men*, London, The Women's Press.

Gardiner, J. (1975) 'Women's Domestic Labour', *New Left Review* 89.

Garfinkel, H. (1967) *Studies in Ethnomethodology*, Englewood Cliffs, Prentice-Hall.

George, M. (1973) 'From goodwife to mistress: the transformation of the female in bourgeois culture', *Science and Society* xxxvii.

Gijswijt-Hofstra, M. (1989) 'Witchcraft in the Northern Netherlands', in Angerman *et al.* (eds) *Current Issues in Women's History*, London, Routledge.

Ginzburg, C. (1983) *The Night Battles: Witchcraft and Agrarian Cults in the Sixteenth and Seventeenth Centuries* (trans. by J. and A. Tedeschi) Baltimore, Baltimore University Press.

Gittins, D. (1985) *The Family in Question: Changing Households and Familiar Ideologies*, London, Macmillan.

Goffman, E. (1959) *The Presentation of Self in Everyday Life*, Harmonds-worth, Penguin.

Goldberg, S. (1974) *The Inevitability of Patriarchy*, London, Temple Smith.

Goode, W.J. (1964) *The Family*, Englewood Cliffs, Prentice-Hall.

Gothoskat, S. (1986) 'India: action against violence', *Trouble and Strife* 8.

Greenwood, V. and Young, J. (1976) *Abortion in Demand*, London, Pluto Press.

Griffin, S. (1971) 'Rape: the all-American crime', *Ramparts*, September.

Griffin, S. (1984) *Woman and Nature*, London, The Women's Press.

Hair, P.E.H. (ed.) (1972) *Before the Bawdy Court: Selections from Church Court and other Records Relating to the Correction of Moral Offences in England, Scotland and New England 1300–1800*, London, Elek.

Hall, S. (ed.) (1980) *Culture, Media, Language*, London, Hutchinson.

Hamblin, A. (1974) 'The suppressed power of female sexuality', in S. Allen *et al.* (eds) *Conditions of Illusion*, Leeds, Feminist Books.

Hamilton, R. (1978) *The Liberation of Women: A Study of Patriarchy and Capitalism*, London, Allen & Unwin.

Hanmer, J. (1978) 'Violence and the social control of women', in G. Littlejohn *et al.* (eds) *Power and the State*, London, Croom Helm.

Hanmer, J. and Allen, P. (1980) 'Reproductive engineering: the final solution?', in Brighton Women and Science Group (eds) *Alice Through the Microscope*, London, Virago.

Hanmer, J. and Maynard, M. (eds) (1987) *Women, Violence and Social Control*, London, Macmillan.

Hanmer, J. and Saunders, S. (1984) *Well-founded Fear*, London, Hutchinson.

Harding, S. (ed.) (1987) *Feminism and Methodology*, Indiana, Indiana University Press.

Harrison, J. (1973) 'The political economy of housework', in *Bulletin of the Conference of Socialist Economists*.

Hartman, M. and Banner, L.W. (1974) *Clio's Consciousness Raised*, New York, Harper & Row.

Hartmann, H. (1979) 'Capitalism, patriarchy and job segregation by sex', in Z.R. Eisenstein (ed.) *Capitalist Patriarchy and the case for Socialist Feminism*, London, Monthly Review Press.

Hartmann, H. (1981) 'The unhappy marriage of marxism and feminism', in L. Sargent (ed.) *Women and Revolution: The Unhappy Marriage of Marxism and Feminism*, London, Pluto Press.

Hearn, J. (1987) *The Gender of Oppression*, Brighton, Harvester Press.

Hearn, J. and Parkin, W. (1987) *Sex and Work*, Brighton, Harvester Press.

Heisch, A. (1980) 'Queen Elizabeth I and the persistence of patriarchy', *Feminist Review*, 4.

Henderson, R. (1979) 'Querying theory or what's in words', *Feminist Practice: Notes from the Tenth Year*, London, In Theory Press.

Hester, M. (1984) 'Anti-sexist men: a case of cloak-and-dagger chauvinism?', *Women's Studies International Forum* 7, (1).

Hester, M. (1988) *The Dynamics of Domination: Men as a Ruling Class and the Nature of Women's Subordination*, PhD thesis, University of Leeds.

Hester, M. (1990) 'The dynamics of male domination using the witchcraze in sixteenth and seventeenth century England as a case study', *Women's Studies International Forum* 13, (1/2).

Hester, M., Jackson, M., Mahoney, P. and Plaster, J. (1980) 'Gay lefty men' *Revolutionary and Radical Feminist Newsletter* 4.

Hill, C. (1964) *Society and Puritanism in Pre-Revolutionary England*, London, Secker & Warburg.

Hill, C. (1975) *The World Turned Upside Down*, Harmondsworth, Penguin.

Hilton, R.H. (1975) *The English Peasantry in the Later Middle Ages*, Oxford, Clarendon Press.

Hite, S. (1981) *The Hite Report on Male Sexuality*, London, MacDonald.

Hodson, P. (1984) *Men: An Investigation into the Emotional Male*, London, Ariel and BBC.

Hole, C. (1947) *Witchcraft in England*, London, Batsford.

Homer, M., Leonard, A. and Taylor, P. (1984) *Private Violence, Public Shame*, Middlesborough, Cleveland Refuge and Aid for Women and Children.

Hooks, B. (1982) *Ain't I a Woman?*, London, Pluto Press.

Hooks, B. (1985) *Feminist Theory from Margin to Center*, Boston, South End Press.

Hooks, B. (1989) *Talking Back: Thinking Feminist and Thinking Black*, London, Sheba.

Horobin, P. (1980) 'Response to the pornography article', *Anti-Sexist Men's Newsletter* 13.

Houlbrooke, R.A. (1984) *The English Family*, London, Longman.

Hughes, P. (1965) *Witchcraft*, Harmondsworth, Penguin.

Hunt, M. (1990) 'The de-eroticization of women's liberation: social purity and the revolutionary feminism of Sheila Jeffreys', *Feminist Review* 34.

Hutt, C. (1972) *Males and Females*, Harmondsworth, Penguin.

Ingram, M. (1987) *Church Courts, Sex and Marriage in England 1570–1640*, Cambridge, Cambridge University Press.

Jackson, M. (1983) 'Sexual liberation or social control', *Women's Studies International Forum* 6, (1).

Jackson, M. (1984a) 'Sexology and the universalization of male sexuality (from Ellis to Kinsey, and Masters and Johnson)', in L. Coveney *et al. The Sexuality Papers*, London, Hutchinson.

Jackson, M. (1984b) 'Sexology and the social construction of male sexuality (Havelock Ellis)', in L. Coveney *et al. The Sexuality Papers*, London, Hutchinson.

Jackson, M. (1987) '"Facts of Life" or the eroticization of women's oppression? Sexology and the social construction of heterosexuality', in P. Caplan (ed.) *The Cultural Construction of Sexuality*, London, Tavistock.

Jackson, S. (1978) 'The social context of rape: sexual scripts and motivation', *Women's Studies International Quarterly* 1.

Jardine, A. and Smith, P. (eds) (1987) *Men in Feminism*, London, Methuen.

Jeffreys, S. (1976) 'Male sexuality as social control' (unpublished paper).

Jeffreys, S. (1977) 'The need for revolutionary feminism', Paper to the 1977 National Women's Liberation Conference (unpublished paper).

Jeffreys, S. (1982) 'The sexual abuse of children in the home', in S.

Friedman and E. Sarah (eds) *On the Problem of Men*, London, The Women's Press.

Jeffreys, S. (1984) '"Free from all uninvited touch of man": women's campaigns around sexuality, 1880–1914' in L. Coveney *et al. The Sexuality Papers*, London, Hutchinson.

Jeffreys, S. (1985a) *The Spinster and Her Enemies*, London, Pandora.

Jeffreys, S. (1985b) 'Prostitution', in D. Rhodes and S. McNeill, (eds) *Women Against Violence Against Women*, London, Onlywomen Press.

Jeffreys, S. (1987) 'Butch and femme: now and then', *Gossip* 5.

Jeffreys, S. (1990) *Anticlimax*, London, The Women's Press.

Johnston, J. (1973) *Lesbian Nation: The Feminist Solution*, New York, Simon & Schuster.

Jones, J. (1981) 'Why I liked screwing? Or, is heterosexual enjoyment based on sexual violence', in Onlywomen (eds) *Love Your Enemy?*, London, Onlywomen Press.

Jordonova, L. (1981) 'Natural facts: a historical perspective on science and sexuality', in C.P. MacCormack and M. Strathern (eds) *Nature, Culture, Gender*, Cambridge, Cambridge University Press.

Kantor, H. (ed.) (1984) *Sweeping Statements*, London, The Women's Press.

Karlen, A. (1971) *Sexuality and Homosexuality*, New York, Norton.

Karlsen, C. (1987) *The Devil in the Shape of a Woman*, New York, Norton.

Katyachild, M., Jeffreys, S., McNeill, S., Winterlake, J. and one other woman (1985) 'Pornography', in D. Rhodes and S. McNeill (eds) *Women Against Violence Against Women*, London, Onlywomen Press.

Keickhefer, R. (1976) *European Witchtrials*, London, Routledge & Kegan Paul.

Kelly, J. (1986) *Women, History and Theory*, Chicago, University of Chicago Press.

Kelly, L. (1987) 'The continuum of sexual violence', in J. Hanmer and M. Maynard (eds) *Women, Violence and Social Control*, London, Macmillan.

Kelly, L. (1988) *Surviving Sexual Violence*, London, Pluto Press.

Kelso, R. (1978) *Doctrine for the Lady of the Renaissance*, Urbana, University of Illinois Press.

Keynes, G. (1966) *The Life of William Harvey*, Oxford, Clarendon Press.

Kinsey, A.C., Pomeroy, W.B. and Martin, C.E. (1948) *Sexual Behaviour in the Human Male*, Philadelphia, W.B. Saunders.

Kinsey, A.C., Pomeroy, W.B., Martin, C.E. and Gebhard, P.H. (1953) *Sexual Behaviour in the Human Female*, Philadelphia, W.B. Saunders.

Kishwar, M. and Vanita, R. (eds) (1984) *In Search of Answers*, London, Zed Books.

Kissling, E. and Kramarae, C. (1985) 'Stranger compliments: the interpretation of street remarks', *Language, Gender and Communication Conference*, Nebraska, University of Nebraska.

Kittredge, G.L. (1929/1956) *Witchcraft in Old and New England*, New York, Russell & Russell.

Kitzinger, C. (1987) *The Social Construction of Lesbianism*, London, Sage Publications.

Koedt, A. (1970) 'The myth of the vaginal orgasm', in Tanner, L.B. (ed.) *Voices from Women's Liberation* New York, Signet.

Larner, C. (1983) *The Enemies of God*, Oxford, Blackwell.

Larner, C. (1984) *Witchcraft and Religion*, Oxford, Blackwell.

Laslett, P. (1977) *Family Life and Illicit Love in Earlier Generations*, Cambridge, Cambridge University Press.

Laslett, P. and Wall, R. (1972) *Household and Family in Past Time*, Cambridge, Cambridge University Press.

Lea, H.C. (1906) *A History of the Inquisition of the Middle Ages*, I, New York, Harper & Bros.

Lederer, L. (ed.) (1982) *Take Back the Night: Women on Pornography*, New York, Bantam.

Leeds Revolutionary Feminist Group (1981) 'Political lesbianism: the case against heterosexuality', in Onlywomen (eds) *Love Your Enemy?*, London, Onlywomen Press.

Leonard, D. (1982) 'Male feminists and divided women', in S. Friedman and E. Sarah (eds) *On the Problem of Men*, London, The Women's Press.

Levack, B. (1987) *The Witch-hunt in Early Modern Europe*, London, Longmans.

Lewenhak, S. (1980) *Women and Work*, London, Fontana.

Lewis, J. (1981) 'Women lost and found: the impact of feminism on history', in D. Spender (ed.) *Men's Studies Modified*, Oxford, Pergamon Press.

Linden, R.R., Pagano, D.R., Russell, D. and Star, D.L. (eds) (1982) *Against Sadomasochism*, East Palo Alto, California, Frog in the Well.

Litewka, J. (1977) 'The socialised penis', in J. Snodgrass (ed.) *A Book of Readings for Men Against Sexism*, New York, Times Change Press.

London Rape Action Group (1985) 'Towards a revolutionary feminist analysis of rape', in D. Rhodes and S. McNeill (eds) *Women Against Violence Against Women*, London, Onlywomen Press.

London Rape Crisis Centre (1984) *The Reality for Women*, London, The Women's Press.

London Rape Crisis Centre (undated) *Strength in Numbers*, London, London Rape Crisis Centre.

Longino, H.E. (1982) 'Pornography, oppression and freedom: a closer look', in L. Lederer (ed.) *Take Back the Night: Women on Pornography*, New York, Bantam.

MacFarlane, A. (1970) *Witchcraft in Tudor and Stuart England, a Regional and Comparative Study*, London, Routledge & Kegan Paul.

MacIntyre, S. (1976) '"Who wants babies?" The social construction of instincts', in D.L. Barker and S. Allen (eds) *Sexual Division and Society: Process and Change*, London, Tavistock.

MacKinnon, C. (1979) *Sexual Harassment of Working Women*, New Haven, Connecticut, Yale University Press.

MacKinnon, C. (1982) 'Feminism, Marxism, method and the state: an agenda for theory', in N.O. Keohane, M.Z. Rosaldo and B.C. Gelpi (eds) *Feminist Theory: A Critique of Ideology*, Brighton, Harvester Press.

MacKinnon, C. (1987a) *Feminism Unmodified*, London, Harvard University Press.

MacKinnon, C. (1987b) 'Feminism, Marxism, method and the state: toward feminist jurisprudence', in S. Harding (ed.) *Feminism and Methodology*, Indiana, Indiana University Press.

MacKinnon, C. (1987c) 'Desire and Power', in MacKinnon, C. (1987a) *Feminism Unmodified*, London, Harvard University Press.

MacKinnon, C. (1989) *Toward a Feminist Theory of the State*, London, Harvard University Press.

McLaren, A. (1984) *Reproductive Rituals*, London, Methuen.

McNeill, S. (1985) 'Rape, sexuality and crimes of violence', in D. Rhodes and S. McNeill (eds) *Women Against Violence Against Women*, London, Onlywomen Press.

Mahony, P. (1985) *Schools for the Boys? Co-education Re-assessed*, London, Hutchinson.

Mair, L. (1969) *Witchcraft*, London, Weidenfeld & Nicolson.

Malinowski, B. (1954) *Magic, Science and Religion and Other Essays*, New York, Doubleday.

Marks, E. and de Courtivron, I. (eds) (1981) *New French Feminism*, Brighton, Harvester Press.

Marwick, M. (ed.) (1982) *Witchcraft and Sorcery*, Harmondsworth, Penguin.

Marx, K. and Engels, F. (1968) *The German Ideology*, Ryazarskaya, S. (ed.), Moscow, Progress.

Masters, W. and Johnson, V. (1966) *Human Sexual Response*, Boston, Little Brown & Co.

Maycock, A. (1926) *The Inquisition from its Establishment to the Great Schism: An Introductory Study*, London, Constable & Co.

Mead, M. (1935) *Sex and Temperament in Three Primitive Societies*, London, Routledge & Kegan Paul.

Medea, A. and Thompson, K. (1974) *Against Rape*, New York, Farrar, Straus & Givouy.

Merchant, C. (1980) *The Death of Nature: Women, Ecology and the Scientific Revolution*, London, Harper & Row.

Metcalf, A. (1985) 'Introduction' in A. Metcalf and M. Humphries *The Sexuality of Men*, London, Pluto Press.

Metcalf, A. and Humphries, M. (eds) (1985) *The Sexuality of Men*, London, Pluto Press.

Middleton, C. (1979) 'The sexual division of labour in feudal England', *New Left Review*, 113–14.

Middleton, C. (1981) 'Peasants, patriarch and the feudal mode of production in England', *Sociological Review* 29, (1).

Middleton, C. (1985) 'Women's labour and the transition to pre-industrial capitalism', in L. Charles and L. Duffin (eds) *Women and Work in Pre-Industrial England*, London, Croom Helm.

Miller, P.Y. and Fowlkes, M.R. (1980) 'Social and behavioural constructions of female sexuality' in *Signs: Journal of Women in Culture and Society*, 5, 4.

Millett, K. (1970) *Sexual Politics*, London, Hart-Davis.

Mitchell, J. (1971) *Women's Estate*, Harmondsworth, Penguin.

Mitchell, J. (1975) *Psychoanalysis and Feminism*, Harmondsworth, Penguin.

Mitchell, L. (1984) 'Against cultural separation', *Trouble and Strife* 4.

Monter, E.W. (1976) *Witchcraft in France and Switzerland*, Cornell, Cornell University Press.

Monter, E.W. (1977) 'The pedestal and the stake: courtly love and witchcraft', in R. Bridenthal and C. Koonz (eds) *Becoming Visible, Women in European History*, London, Houghton Mifflin.

Morgan, R. (ed.) (1970) *Sisterhood is Powerful*, New York, Vintage Random House.

Morgan, R. (1982) 'Theory and practice: pornography and rape', in L. Lederer (ed.) *Take Back the Night: Women on Pornography*, New York, Bantam.

Morris, T. (1976) *Deviance and Control: The Secular Heresy*, London, Hutchinson.

Moye, A. (1985) 'Pornography', in A. Metcalf and M. Humphries (eds) *The Sexuality of Men*, London, Pluto Press.

Muchembled, R. (1979) *La Sorcière au Village (XVIe au XVIIe siècle)*, Paris, Gallimard.

Muchembled, R. (1990) 'Satanic myths and cultural reality', in B. Ankarloo and G. Henningsen (eds) *Early Modern European Witchcraft*, Oxford, Clarendon Press.

Murray, M. (1921/1962) *The Witch-Cult in Western Europe*, Oxford, Clarendon Press.

National Women's Aid Federation (1976) *Battered Women Need Refuges*, London, National Women's Aid Federation.

New York Radical Lesbians (1970) 'New York Radical Lesbians', in R. Morgan (ed.) *Sisterhood is Powerful*, New York, Vintage Random House.

Notestein, W. (1911/1968) *The History of Witchcraft in England from 1558 to 1728*, New York, Thomas Y. Crowell.

Nye, A. (1988) *Feminist Theory and the Philosophies of Man*, London, Croom Helm.

Oakley, A. (1972) *Sex, Gender and Society*, London, Temple-Smith.

Oakley, A. (1974) 'Cultural influences on female sexuality', in S. Allen *et al.* (eds) *Conditions of Illusion*, Leeds, Feminist Books.

Oakley, A. (1985) *The Captured Womb: History of the Medical Care of Pregnant Women*, Oxford, Blackwell.

O'Brien, M. (1981) *The Politics of Reproduction*, London, Routledge & Kegan Paul.

O'Faolain, J. and Martines, L. (1979) *Not in God's Image*, London, Virago.

Oxford English Dictionary (1975) Oxford, Oxford University Press.

Pahl, J. (1980) 'Patterns of money management within marriage', *Journal of Social Policy* 9, (3).

Pahl, J. (1985) (ed.) *Private Violence and Public Policy*, London, Routledge & Kegan Paul.

Parmar, P. (1986) 'Can black and white women work together?', *Spare Rib* 168.

Pearson, C. (1984) 'Male sexual politics and men's gender practice', *Women's Studies International Forum* 7, (1).

Pennington, D. and Thomas, K. (1978) *Puritans and Revolutionaries*, Oxford, Oxford University Press.

Phillips, A. and Taylor, B. (1980) 'Sex and skill: notes towards a feminist economics', *Feminist Review* 6.

Pinchbeck, I. (1977) *Women Workers and the Industrial Revolution 1750–1850*, London, Cass.

Pomeroy, W.B. (1972) *Dr. Kinsey and the Institute for Sex Research*, New York, Harper & Row.

Prior, M. (ed.) (1985) *Women In English Society 1500–1800*, London, Methuen.

Radford, J. (1987) 'Policing male violence – policing women', in J. Hanmer and M. Maynard (eds) *Women, Violence and Social Control*, London, Macmillan.

Radford, L. (1987) 'Legalising woman abuse', in J. Hanmer and M. Maynard (eds) *Women, Violence and Social Control*, London, Macmillan.

Raymond, J. (1986) *A Passion for Friends*, Boston, Beacon Press.

Raynaud, E. (1983) *Holy Virility: The Social Construction of Masculinity*, London, Pluto Press.

Redstockings (1970) 'Redstocking manifesto', in R. Morgan (ed.) *Sisterhood is Powerful*, New York, Vintage Random House.

Reynell, S. (1980) 'Pornography', *Anti-Sexist Men's Newsletter* 12.

Rhodes, D. and McNeill, S. (eds) (1985) *Women Against Violence Against Women*, London, Onlywomen Press.

Rich, A. (1977) *Of Woman Born – Motherhood as Experience and Institution*, London, Virago.

Rich, A. (1980) 'Compulsory heterosexuality and lesbian existence', *Signs: Journal of Women in Culture and Society* 5, (4).

Roberts, M. (1985) '"Words they are women, and deeds they are men": Images of work and gender in early modern England', in L. Charles and L. Duffin (eds) *Women and Work in Pre-Industrial England*, London, Croom Helm.

Robbins, R.H. (1959) *The Encyclopaedia of Witchcraft and Demonology*, London, Peter Nevill.

Robinson, P. (1976) *The Modernization of Sex*, New York, Harper & Row.

Rose, H. and Hanmer, J. (1976) 'Women's liberation: reproduction and the technological fix', in H. Rose and S. Rose (eds) *The Political Economy of Science*, London, Macmillan.

Rowan, J. (1987) *The Horned God*, London, Routledge & Kegan Paul.

Rowbotham, S. (1972) 'The beginnings of women's liberation in Britain' in M. Wandor (ed.) *The Body Politic*, London, Stage I.

Rowbotham, S. (1974) *Hidden from History*, London, Pluto Press.

Rowbotham, S. (1982) 'The trouble with patriarchy', in M. Evans (ed.) *The Woman Question*, London, Fontana.

Rowbotham, S., Segal, L. and Wainwright, H. (1980) *Beyond the Fragments*, London, Pluto Press.

Rowland, R. (1984) 'Reproductive technologies: the final solution to the woman question?', in R. Arditti *et al.* (eds) *Test-Tube Women. What Future for Motherhood?*, London, Pandora Press.

Rubin, G. (1975) 'The traffic in women: notes on the "political economy" of sex', in R.R. Reiter *Toward an Anthropology of Women*, London, Monthly Review Press.

Rush, F. (1980) *The Best-Kept Secret, The Sexual Abuse of Children*, New York, Prentice-Hall.

Russell, D. (1973) *The Politics of Rape*, New York, Macmillan.

Russell, D. (1975) *Rape: The Victim's Perspective*, New York, Macmillan.

Russell, D. (1982) *Rape in Marriage*, New York, Macmillan.

Russell, D. (1984) *Sexual Exploitation; Rape, Child Sexual Abuse and Workplace Harassment*, Beverly Hills, Sage.

Russell, J. (1972) *Witchcraft in the Middle Ages*, New York, Cornell University Press.

Sargent, L. (ed.) (1981) *Women and Revolution: The Unhappy Marriage of Marxism and Feminism*, London, Pluto Press.

Saville, J. (1969) 'Primitive accumulation and early industrialization in Britain', *Socialist Register*.

Sayers, J. (1982) *Biological Politics*, London, Tavistock.

Scarre, G. (1987) *Witchcraft and Magic in Sixteenth and Seventeenth Century Europe*, London, Macmillan.

Schucking, L.L. (1969) *The Puritan Family*, London, Routledge & Kegan Paul.

Schutz, A. (1972) *The Phenomenology of the Social World*, London, Heinemann.

Scott, H. (1984) *Working Your Way to the Bottom: The Feminization of Poverty*, London, Pandora Press.

Scully, D. (1990) *Understanding Sexual Violence*, Boston, Unwin Hyman.

Seccombe, W. (1974) 'The housewife and her labour under capitalism', *New Left Review* 83.

Segal, L. (1987) *Is the Future Female?*, London, Virago.

Sellen, B-C. and Young, P.A. (1987) *Feminists, Pornography and the Law*, Hemdon, Conn., The Library Professional Publications.

Sharpe, S. (1976) *Just Like a Girl: How Girls Learn to be Women*, Harmondsworth, Penguin.

Shepherd, S. (1985) *The Women's Sharp Revenge*, London, Fourth Estate.

Shiers, J. (1988) 'One step to heaven?', in B. Cant and S. Hemmings (eds) *Radical Records: Thirty Years of Lesbian and Gay History*, London, Routledge & Kegan Paul.

Shorter, E. (1975) *The Making of the Modern Family*, New York, Basic Books.

Smart, C. (1984) *The Ties that Bind: Law, Marriage and the Reproduction of Patriarchal Relations*, London, Routledge & Kegan Paul.

Smith, D.E. (1987) 'Women's perspective as a radical critique of sociology', in S. Harding (ed.) *Feminism and Methodology*, Indiana, Indiana University Press.

Smith, P (1978) 'Domestic labour and Marx's theory of value', in A. Kuhn and A.M. Wolpe (eds) *Feminism and Materialism: Women and Modes of Production*, London, Routledge & Kegan Paul.

Snodgrass, J. (ed.) (1977) *A Book of Readings for Men Against Sexism*, New York, Times Change Press.

Spender, D. (1980) *Man-Made Language*, London, Routledge & Kegan Paul.

Spender, D. (1982) *Women of Ideas and What Men Have Done to Them from Aphra Behn to Adrienne Rich*, London, Routledge & Kegan Paul.

Spender, L. (1983) *Intruders on the Rights of Men*, London, Routledge & Kegan Paul.

Spufford, M. (1974) *Contrasting Communities. English Villagers in the Sixteenth and Seventeenth Centuries*, Cambridge, Cambridge University Press.

Stanko, E. (1985) *Intimate Intrusions: Women's Experience of Male Violence*, London, Routledge & Kegan Paul.

Stanley, L. (1982) 'Male needs: the problem and problem of working with gay men', in S. Friedman and E. Sarah (eds) *On the Problem of Men*, London, The Women's Press.

Stanley, L. and Wise, S. (1983) *Breaking Out: Feminist Consciousness and Feminist Research*, London, Routledge & Kegan Paul.

Stenton, D.M. (1957) *The English Woman in History*, London, Allen & Unwin.

Stoltenberg, J. (1977) 'Refusing to be a man', in J. Snodgrass (ed.) *A Book of Readings for Men Against Sexism*, New York, Times Change Press.

Stoltenberg, J. (1982) 'Sadomasochism: eroticized violence, eroticized powerlessness', in R.R. Linden *et al. Against Sadomasochism*, East Palo Alto, California, Frog in the Well.

Stone, L. (1979) *The Family, Sex and Marriage*, Harmondsworth, Penguin.

Sullerot, E. (1979) *Women on Love – Eight Centuries of Feminine Writing*, London, Doubleday.

Summers, The Reverend Montague (1971) 'Introduction to 1928 edition', of H. Kramer and J. Sprenger *Malleus Maleficarum*, New York, Dover Publications.

Tanner, L.B. (1970) *Voices from Women's Liberation*, New York, Signet.

Tedeschi, J. (1990) 'Inquisitorial Law and the Witch', in B. Ankarloo and G. Henningsen (eds) *Early Modern European Witchcraft*, Oxford, Clarendon Press.

Thomas, K. (1971) *Religion and the Decline of Magic*, London, Weidenfeld & Nicolson.

Tilly, L.A. and Scott, H. (1976) 'Women's work and European fertility patterns', *Journal of Interdisciplinary History* VI.

Tolson, A. (1977) *The Limits of Masculinity*, London, Tavistock.

Trevor-Roper, H. (1969) *The European Witchcraze of the 16th and 17th Centuries*, Harmondsworth, Penguin.

Trivers, R.L. (1972) 'Parental investment and sexual selection', in B. Campbell (ed.) *Sexual Selection and the Descent of Man 1871–1971*, Chicago, Aldine.

Vance, C.S. (1984) *Pleasure and Danger – Exploring Female Sexuality*, London, Routledge & Kegan Paul.

Vann, R.T. (1977) 'Toward a new lifestyle: women in pre-industrial capitalism', in R. Bridenthal and C. Koonz (eds) *Becoming Visible: Women in European History*, London, Houghton Mifflin.

Walby, S. (1986) *Patriarchy at Work*, Cambridge, Polity.

Walby, S. (1990) *Theorising Patriarchy*, Oxford, Blackwell.

Walker, A. (1982) 'Coming apart' in L. Lederer (ed.) *Take Back the Night: Women on Pornography*, New York, Bantam.

Wall, R. (1981) 'Women alone in English society', *Annales de Demographie Historique*.

Wallace, M. (1979) *Black Macho and the Myth of the Superwoman*, London, John Calder.

Ward, E. (1984) *Father–Daughter Rape*, London, The Women's Press.

Watkins, S.C. (1984) 'Spinsters', *Journal of Family History*, winter.

Webster, C. (1979) 'William Harvey and the crisis of medicine in Jacobean England', in J. Bylebyl (ed.) *William Harvey and his Age*, London, John Hopkins University Press.

Weedon, C. (1987) *Feminist Practice and Poststructuralist Theory*, London, Blackwell.

Weeks, J. (1981) *Sex, Politics and Society, the Regulation of Sexuality since 1800*, London, Longmans.

Weeks, J. (1982) *Gay News* 243.

Whiting, P. (1972) 'Female sexuality: its political implications', in M. Wandor (ed.) *The Body Politic*, London, Stage 1.

Wilson, E. (1983) *What is to be Done about Violence against Woman?*, Harmondsworth, Penguin.

Wilson, E.O. (1978) *On Human Nature*, Cambridge, Harvard University Press.

Wise, S. and Stanley, L. (1987) *Georgie Porgie*, London, Pandora Press.

Wolfgang, M. (1979) 'Women's war on porn', *Time*, August 27.

Wood, J. (1981) 'Dear Onlywomen Press', in Onlywomen (eds) *Love your Enemy?*, London, Onlywomen Press.

Woodbridge, L. (1986) *Women and the English Renaissance*, Urbana, University of Illinois.

Wright, L.B. (1935) *Middle Class Culture in Elizabethan England*, Chapel Hill, University of North Caroline Press.

Wrightson, K. (1981) 'Household and kinship in sixteenth century England', *History Workshop Journal* 12.

Wrigley, E.A. and Schofield, R.S. (1981) *The Population History of England 1541–1871. A Reconstruction*, London, Edward Arnold.

Young, I. (1980) 'Socialist feminism and the limits of dual systems theory', *Socialist Review* 10.

Young, I. (1981) 'Beyond the unhappy marriage: a critique of the dual systems theory', in L. Sargent (ed.) *Women and Revolution: The Unhappy Marriage of Marxism and Feminism*, London, Pluto Press.

Zaretsky, E. (1976) *Capitalism, the Family and Personal Life*, London, Pluto Press.

Zilboorg, G. (1935) *The Medical Man and the Witch During the Renaissance*, Baltimore, Baltimore University Press.

PRIMARY SOURCES CONSULTED

Witch trial pamphlets from Essex

(original copy or microfilm copy of original are available for all the pamphlets at the British Library, London)

The Examination and Confession of Certain Wytches at Chensforde in the Countie of Essex before the Queens maiesties Judges, the xxvi daye of July Anno 1566, London, 1566.
(largely reprinted in Ewen L.C. 1929/1971, *Witch Hunting and Witch Trials,* and by the Philobiblon Society, *Miscellanies,* vol. viii)

A Detection of damnable driftes, practized by three witches arraigned at Chelmisford in Essex, at the late Assizes there holden, whiche were executed in Aprill, 1579, London, 1579.

A True and Just Recorde of the Information, Examination and confession of all the Witches, taken at S. Oses in the countie of Essex: whereof some were executed, and other some entreated according to the determination of lawe, by W.W., London, 1582.
(there are two copies, one of which has a list of the accused attached)

The Apprehension and Confession of three notorious Witches, Arraigned and by Justice condemned and executed at Chelmesforde, in the Countye of Essex, the 5. day of Iylue, last past. 1589, London, 1589.

A True and Exact Relation of the Several Informations, Examinations and Confessions of the late Witches, arraigned and executed in the County of Essex, by H.F., London 1645.

OTHER PRIMARY SOURCES

Burton, R. (1621) *Anatomy of Melancholy,* London.
    (republished New York, Dutton, 1932)
Gifford, G. (1593) *A Dialogue Concerning Witches and Witchcrafts,* London.
    (reprinted in Percy Society (eds) *Early English Poetry, Ballads and Popular Literature of the Middle Ages,* III, Percy Society, 1906)
Harvey, W. (1651) *On Animal Generation,* London.
    (reprinted in Maynard, R. (ed.) *Great Books of the Western World,* London, Hutchinson)
Hobbes, J. (1651) *Leviathan* (reprinted in Scheider, H.W. (ed.) *Leviathan,* parts I and II, New York, Bobbs Merrill, 1958).
Hopkins, M. (1647) *The Discovery of Witches,* London.
    (copy in British Library)
James, I. (1597) *Daemonology* (reprint New York, Barnes & Noble, 1966).
Kramer, H. and Sprenger, J. (1496) *Malleus Maleficarum,* Nurenburg.
    (republished New York, Dover Publications, 1971)
Norris, J. (1620) *Haec and Hic; or, the feminine gender more worthy than the masculine,* London.
    (copy in Fawcett Library)
Scot, R. (1584) *The Discoverie of Witchcraft,* London.
    (copy in British Library)
Sowrenam E. (1617) *Ester hath hang'd Haman: or an Answere to a lewd Pamphlet,*

entitled 'The Arraignment of Women', With the arraignment of lewd, idle, froward, and unconstant men, and husbands, London, Nicholas Bourne.
(copy of facsimile reprint in Fawcett Library)

Sprint J. (1709) The Bride-Woman's Counsellor: being a sermon preached at a wedding, May the eleventh 1699, at Sherbourn, London, H. Hills.
(copy in British Library)

Swetnam, J. (1615) The Arraignment of Lewde, Idle, Froward and unconstant Women: or the vanitie of them, choose you whether. With a Commendacion of wise, vertuous, and honest Women, Pleasant for married Men, profitable for young Men, and hurtfull to none. London, Edward Aude.
(copy of facsimile reprint in Fawcett Library)

Tattle-well, M. and Hit-him-home, I. (1640) The Women's Sharpe Revenge: or An answer to Sir Seldom Sober that writ those railing Pamphlets called the Juniper and Crabtree lectures, etc, London.
(reprinted in Shepherd, S. (ed.) The Women's Sharp Revenge, London, Fourth Estate, 1985)

Taylor, J. (1639) Divers Crabtree Lecture and A Juniper Lecture, Extracts in S. Shepherd (1985) The Women's Sharp Revenge, London, Fourth Estate.

Vaughan, R. (1542) Dyalogue defensyue for women, agaynst malyeyous detractors, stc 246001.

Name index

Subject index